The King's Coroner: Being a Complete Collection of the Statutes Relating to the Office Together with a Short History of the Same, Volume 1

Great Britain, Richard Henslowe Wellington

Nabu Public Domain Reprints:

You are holding a reproduction of an original work published before 1923 that is in the public domain in the United States of America, and possibly other countries. You may freely copy and distribute this work as no entity (individual or corporate) has a copyright on the body of the work. This book may contain prior copyright references, and library stamps (as most of these works were scanned from library copies). These have been scanned and retained as part of the historical artifact.

This book may have occasional imperfections such as missing or blurred pages, poor pictures, errant marks, etc. that were either part of the original artifact, or were introduced by the scanning process. We believe this work is culturally important, and despite the imperfections, have elected to bring it back into print as part of our continuing commitment to the preservation of printed works worldwide. We appreciate your understanding of the imperfections in the preservation process, and hope you enjoy this valuable book.

CORONER'S SEAL OF THE 14TH CENTURY.
(ENLARGED 3 DIAMETERS.)

For description see page 20.

JERVIS CORONER

THE STATUTES

OF THE SAME

LONDON

THE
KING'S CORONER

BEING

A COMPLETE COLLECTION

OF

THE STATUTES

RELATING TO THE OFFICE

TOGETHER WITH

A SHORT HISTORY OF THE SAME

BY

R. HENSLOWE WELLINGTON

*Of the Middle Temple, and South Eastern Circuit, Barrister-at-Law,
Deputy Coroner for the City and Liberty of Westminster,
and South Western Division of the County of London;*

*Member of the Royal College of Surgeons of England, and Licentiate
of the Royal College of Physicians of London.*

LONDON
WILLIAM CLOWES & SONS, LIMITED
7, FLEET STREET
1905

PREFACE.

Upon being appointed one of the deputy-coroners for the County of London, and for the City and Liberty of Westminster, I sought for such further knowledge as would enable me to fulfil the duties of my office with credit to myself and satisfaction to those to whose liberality and kindness I am indebted for my appointments. In the course of this pursuit, and for my own use, I made a complete collection of all the statutes relating to the office of coroner from the earliest times down to the present day, remembering that to understand the present state of affairs in any matter a knowledge of the past is necessary. I look forward, I trust in the near future, to seeing yet one more statute added to the list, for the present legislation needs much reformation.

I have allowed myself to be persuaded to publish this collection, together with a short history of the office, with all its deficiencies. Perhaps the little merit it may possess is that of being the only publication of the kind.

I am indebted to Dr. G. F. Warner, Keeper of the Seals at the British Museum, for this opportunity of presenting the frontispiece to my readers: also to the authorities at the Record Office for their courteous assistance in my researches.

R. HENSLOWE WELLINGTON.

2, Essex Court, Temple.
October 2nd, 1904.

CHRONOLOGICAL LIST OF THE RULERS OF ENGLAND.

William I.	1066–1087	Henry VIII.	1509–1547
,, II.	1087–1100	Edward VI.	1547–1553
Henry I.	1100–1135	Mary I.	1553–1558
Stephen.	1135–1154	Elizabeth	1558–1603
Henry II.	1154–1189	James I.	1603–1625
Richard I.	1189–1199	Charles I.	1625–1649
John.	1199–1216	Commonwealth	1649–1659
Henry III.	1216–1272	Charles II.	1660–1685
Edward I.	1272–1307	James II.	1685–1688
,, II.	1307–1327	William III. (and Mary)	1689–1694 / 1702
,, III.	1327–1377	Anne	1702–1714
Richard II.	1377–1399	George I.	1714–1727
Henry IV.	1399–1413	,, II.	1727–1760
,, V.	1413–1422	,, III.	1760–1820
,, VI.	1422–1461	,, IV.	1820–1830
Edward IV.	1461–1483	William IV.	1830–1837
,, V.	1483–1483	Victoria.	1837–1901
Richard III.	1483–1485	Edward VII.	1901–
Henry VII.	1485–1509		

THE KING'S CORONER.

PART I.

AN HISTORICAL OUTLINE OF THE OFFICE.

The Coroner is so named from *a coronâ*, because he is an officer of the Crown who *kept* some of the "pleas of the Crown" (2 Inst. 30; 4 Inst. 271; 1 Bl. Com. 346). At different times he has had various names; in the reign of Henry II. (1154–89) that of *Serviens regis* (Umfrex, Lex Cor. xx.) and *Coronarius* (Wilkins, Leg. Ang. Sax. 337). In the time of Richard I. (1189–99) he was termed *Custos placitorum coronæ* (Wilkins, Leg. Ang. Sax. 346), being a *keeper* of the pleas of the Crown, as distinguished from that of *holding* (tenere) them. He did not "hear and determine," but *kept* records of all that went on in the county and that in any way concerned the administration of criminal justice, and more particularly did he guard the revenues which went to the king if such justice was duly carried into effect. In all the statutes he is spoken of as *Coronator* or Coroner, with the exception of 3 Hen. VII. c. 2 (A.D. 1487), and 34 Hen. VIII. c. 26 (A.D. 1542–43), where the term *Crowner* is used, though this last has generally been regarded as a vulgarism.

The office of Coroner obtains in England, Wales, and Ireland; whilst in Scotland the corresponding duties are carried out by the Procurator Fiscal.

The origin of the office is lost in the mists of antiquity

(Justice Dodderidge, 3 Bulst. 176). Some authorities state that it existed at the time of King Alfred (871–910), for it is said that he put to death a judge who refused a prisoner the right to traverse and was sentenced to death on the Coroner's record (Bac. on Gov. 66; 6 Vin. Abridg. 242). The office is mentioned in 'The Charter of Privileges granted by King Athelstan (925–40) to St. John of Beverley in the year of our Lord 925.' The charter (Dug. Monast. 171), written in eighty lines of rhyme, contains the following:—

> "If man be founden slain i drunkend,
> Sterved on Saint John rike, his aghen men
> Withouten swike his aghen bailiffs make ye fight,
> Nan oyer coroner have ye might
> Swa mikel freedom give i ye,
> Swa hert may think or eghe fee."

Prof. C. Gross, of Harvard University, states that this charter is not reliable, but he does not show what has led him to this conclusion.

In the Mirror of Justices,' chap. iii. we read "of the original Constitutions" that "For the good estate of his realm King Alfred caused his Counts (or Earls) to assemble and that Coroners were ordained in every county, etc." Unfortunately this work is an enigmatical treatise said to have been made before the Conquest (Plowden, Com. 8), but it could not have been written before the time of Edward I. (1272–1307). Sir F. Palgrave speaks of it as an apocrypha of law and says that we are compelled to reject it as evidence concerning the early jurisprudence of Anglo-Saxon England (Palgrave, 'English Commonwealth,' vol. ii. p. cxiv). Other authorities, *e.g.* Bigelow, Gneist, Maitland, Reeves, Stephens, and Stubbs, fix the date of the origin of the office at the time of the Articles of Eyre, September, 1194. Art. XX.: "Preterea inquolibet comitatu eligantur tres milites et unus clericus custodes placitorum coronæ" (Furthermore three knights and one cleric shall be elected by each county keepers of the pleadings of the Crown). But we have at least one authenticated case, which goes to prove their existence previous to these Articles, re-

AN HISTORICAL OUTLINE OF THE OFFICE.

corded in Rotuli Curiæ Regis (ed. Palgrave), i. 50, 51, when in November, 1194, Geoffry Fitz-Peter and William de Stuttville, itinerant judges in Lincolnshire, reported before the judges at Westminster that Hugh de Severbi had accused one Alured de Glentham as principal and Jordan as accessory of killing his brother. Hugh stated that after the crime the accused were placed in the custody of the bailiffs of Sheriff Gerard de Camville of Lincolnshire. The Coroners (milites custodientes placita coronæ) were called to Westminster, and stated that at the first county court after the murder Hugh de Severbi accused the two men: the Sheriff confirms the testimony of the Coroners. Now the point to determine is when the crime and the county court took place; also when the case was laid before the itinerant justices. Gerard de Camville, the Sheriff, was in office from 1189-94. In March, 1194, he was deposed from office by Richard I. and a month later charged with treason;[1] the accusation in the presence of the coroners must therefore have been made before March 31st, 1194, and therefore before September, 1194, the month that the Articles of Eyre were issued. This, surely, is proof of the existence of the Coroner before the Articles of Eyre. It is probable, though not certain, that the accusation was made in 1189 or 1190, for in the reign of Richard I. both Fitz-Peter and William de Stuttville acted as itinerant justices (Foss. Judges, i. 335), and they may have tried the case of *Hugh de Severbi* v. *Alured de Glentham and Jordan* in the eyre of that year. It is evident, then, that Chapter XX. of the Articles of Eyre is merely a declaratory Act referring to an institution which was already in existence (Prof. C. Gross, Political Science Quarterly, vol. vii. p. 660).

The Coroner himself is an elected magistrate. He holds the next rank in the county to the Sheriff, and is, indeed, in many cases substituted for the latter. It is greatly to be regretted that the true character and dignity[2]

Authority and duty.

---

[1] Hoveden III. 241-43.
[2] Chaucer (1340?-1400) in one of his Prologues to the Canterbury Tales entitled 'The Frankelein,' who was a freeholder distinguished from the common freeholder by the extent of his

of this office are not better understood, and with the great advancement of municipalities at the present day the office has many opportunities of vast usefulness to the community.

Coroners are conservators of the king's peace at common law. They are the principal conservators or justices of the peace within the county, and take precedence of all those justices who are, as it is termed, in the commission of the peace.[1] The latter are of far more modern origin, and owe their existence and powers to Statute only (A.D. 1327).[2] And a justice of the peace who is elected Coroner for a county or division does not thereby become disqualified from acting as a justice for such county or division (*Davies* v. *Pembrokeshire* (Justices), 7 Q.B.D. 513).

"Not only have Coroners the power to attach 'manslayers' by their warrants after inquisition, whereby they are found guilty, but they may make out warrants for apprehending those persons that are not, or cannot be, presented before them, or those that were present and not guilty; Lay also of burglars and robbers, and yet they cannot take an inquisition touching them; this appears evidently by the statutes of 3 Edw. I. c. 9 and 4 Edw. I. *De officio coronatoris*. And with this agrees the common usage at this day (A.D. 1736) for the coroners to take 'manslayers' before their inquisition be taken, for many

---

possessions and by his eligibility to the dignitaries of Sheriff, Knight of the Shire, etc., says:—

"At Sessions there was he [the Frankelein] Lord and Sire,
Full often times he was Knight of the Shire.
An anlas * and a gipfire † all of silk
Hung at his girdil, white as morrowe ‡ milk.
A Shereve had he been, and a Corouner
Was no wher such a worthy Vavassour." §

[1] The Coroner, in addition, becomes a justice of the peace by virtue of his office (Dalt. p. 2; Com. Dig. Justices of Peace (A. 4)).

[2] 1 Edw. III. c. 16: "For the better keeping and maintenance of the peace, the King will that in every county good men and lawful, which be no maintainers of evils, or barretors in the county, shall be assigned to keep the peace."

---

* Dagger. † A pouch or purse. ‡ Morning. § A sub-vassal next in dignity to a baron.

times the inquest is long in their inquiry, and the offender may escape, if he stay till the inquisition delivered up. But at this day the greatest part of the business of this nature is dispatched by the justices of the peace" (Hales, P. C. ii. p. 107).

The inquiry, or "inquest," as it is commonly called, is held by the free men of the neighbourhood *before* the coroner and not *by* him. The composition of the jury, in the thirteenth and fourteenth centuries, varied somewhat in different localities and at different times. Most commonly it consisted, wholly or in part, of a representation from "four neighbouring townships" (*villatæ*), namely, that in which the body was found, or in which the death took place, and the three nearest vills. The most common form mentioned in our rolls is that in which the verdict is found by twelve men, together with four neighbouring townships or tithings, the twelve men probably representing the whole hundred. The four vills and the twelve men seem often to be regarded as two distinct bodies; their verdicts could be given separately.

The Coroner is elected for life and during good behaviour, but he may be removed, either by being made a sheriff, or chosen as verderor,[1] which offices are inconsistent with that of Coroner, or by the King's writ *De coronatore exonerando*, for any reasonable cause assigned in the writ. <small>Duration of the office.</small>

It was laid down in 1 Queen Elizabeth (A.D. 1558) by "Resolutions at Serjeants' Inn by all the Justices, Chief Baron, Attorney- and Solicitor-General, upon the Statute of the 1st Edw. VI. c. 7 for discontinuance by the demise of the king: that all patents of the Judges of the one Bench and the other, the Barons of the Exchequer, Sheriffs, Escheators, and Commissioners of Oyer and Terminer, Gaol Delivery, and Justices of the Peace, are <small>Demise of the Crown.</small>

---

[1] Verderor, *Vindarius*, is a judicial officer of the King's Forest . . . sworn to maintain and keep the assizes of the Forest, and to view receive and enrol the attachments and presentments of all manner of trespasses of Vert and Venison in the Forest, *Manwood*. (Cowel: Vf, Termes de la Ley: 3 Bl. Com. 71.)

law. The former, at its latest stage, divided it between the finder and the owner of the land on which it was found, except where it was found on public or imperial property, when one half went to the fisc. If a man found treasure on his own land, he had the right to the whole. The rights of the Crown, modified by those of the feudal lord, gradually became more extensive in the feudal law of Europe, so much so as to become, in the words of Grotius, "jus commune et quasi gentium." In more recent times there has been a return, at any rate in the case of France, to the division made by the Roman law. In England the common law, which at one time apparently conferred treasure-trove, wherever found, upon the finder, now gives it all to the king, in accordance with the maxim "quod nullius est fit domini regis." This is always provided that the owner cannot be known or discovered. If he can be, he and not the king is entitled to it. A right to treasure-trove may be granted by the Crown as a franchise.

The finding of deposited treasure was much more frequent, and the treasures themselves more considerable, in the infancy of our constitution than at present. It is the duty of one finding it to make it known to the Coroner, and the punishment of such as concealed from the king the finding of hidden treasure was formerly no less than death (Glanv. l.l. ch. 2; Craig, l. 16, 40; 3 Inst. 133). Concealment of treasure-trove is still a misdemeanour at common law,[1] and there can be no larceny of it until it has been found by the Coroner to be the property of the Crown.

Royal fishes and wrecks. Coroners also inquired of royal fishes, as sturgeons, whales and the like, and of wrecks (Staund. P.C. 51; Bract. 120). Their duties in this respect were defined by Britton as follows: "It also belongs to their office to inquire of the wrecks of the sea, of sturgeons and of whales, when they shall have notice thereof, and to attach and let to main prize the finders, and those who eloign and secrete them, and to enrol and record their names, and to secure the findings to our use" (1 Britton, c. 2, s. 18).

---

[1] R. v. Thomas (1868), Le. and Ca. 313.

And by the statute *De officio Coronatoris*, it was enacted: "Concerning wreck of the sea, wheresoever it be found, if any lay hands on it he shall be attached by sufficient pledges, and the price of the wreck shall be valued, and delivered to the towns." But now, by the Coroners Act, 1887, "A Coroner shall not take pleas of the Crown nor hold inquests of royal fish nor of wreck," etc.

Royal fish were the whale and the sturgeon, which when either thrown ashore, or caught near the coast, were the property of the king, on account, as it is said in the books, of their superior excellence.[1] Indeed, our ancestors seem to have entertained a very high notion of the importance of this right, it being the prerogative of the Kings of Denmark and of the Dukes of Normandy; and from one of these it was probably derived to our princes.[2] It is expressly claimed and allowed in the *De Prærogativâ Regis*,[3] and the most ancient treatises of the law now extant make mention of it, though they seem to have made a distinction between the whale and the sturgeon, the head only of the whale belonging to the king, while the tail belonged to the queen. But the whole of the sturgeon belonged to the king (Stephen's Com. vol. ii. p. 532).

Shipwrecks are also declared by the *De Prærogativâ Regis*[4] to be the king's property, and were so, long before, at the common law. Wreck, by the ancient common law, was where any ship was lost at sea, and the goods or cargo were thrown upon the land (*Sir Henry Constable's Case*, 1599 (5 Rep. 106), in which case the goods so

---

[1] Plowd. 315. It is said, in the *Case of Swans* (1592), 7 Rep. 16 a, that a swan is, in like manner, a royal fowl; and that all swans, which have no other known owner, do belong to the king by his prerogative.

[2] Stiern. *De jure Sueonum*, i. 2, ch. 8; *Gr. Coustum*, ch. 17.

[3] The *Prærogativa Regis* is "an *apocryphal* statute which may represent the earlier practice of Edward I." (Pollock and Maitland, *Hist. of Eng. Law*, i. p. 886).

[4] Of the king's prerogative, 17 Edw. II.: "Also the King shall have Wreck of the Sea throughout the Realm, Whales and (great) Sturgeons taken in the sea or elsewhere within the Realm, except in certain places privileged by the King."

wrecked were adjudged to belong to the king, for it was held by the loss of the ship all property was gone out of the original owner (Dr. and St. d. 2, ch. 51). But it was ordained by Henry I. that, if any person escaped alive out of the ship, it should be no wreck (Spelm. Cod. *apud* Wilkins, 305); and afterwards Henry II., by his charter, 26th May, 1174 (1 Rymer, *Fœd.* i. 36), declared that, if on the coast of either England, Poictou, Oleron, or Gascony, any ship should be distressed, and either man or beast [1] should escape or be found therein alive, the goods should remain to the owners, if they claimed them within three months, but otherwise should be esteemed a wreck, and should belong to the king or other lord of the franchise. And the law, as laid down by Bracton in the reign of Henry III., was to this effect: that if only a dog, for instance, escaped, by which the owner might be discovered, nay, if any certain mark were set on the goods by which they might be known again, it was held to be no wreck (Bract. l. 3, ch. 3. s. 5).

In appeals of felony.

Before the Stat. 59 Geo. III. c. 46, which completely abrogated this mode of prosecution, Coroners were empowered, by the Stat. 4 Edw. I., to receive an appeal of felony or maihem in the county court, "upon the plaintiff's finding sufficient pledges to the sheriff for the prosecution of the suit" (2 Hawk. P. C. ch. 9, s. 39).

Sanctuary.

Anciently, it was the duty of Coroners to take the confession and abjurations of felons, and also the confession of a felon by an approver.[2] The duty with respect to confession is now become obsolete, and that relating to abjuration is repealed by the Stat. 21 Jac. I. c. 28, which

---

[1] *Vide* 8 Edw. I. c. 4.

[2] An approver was an accomplice in treason or felony, who, on arraignment, confessed the fact before plea pleaded, took an oath to reveal all treasons and felons he knew, and appealed or accused others, in order to obtain pardon (3 Co. Inst. 129; 3 Russell on *Crimes*, 6th ed. 642; Hawk. P. C. bk. ii. c. 24). No person could be an approver who was attainted or incapable of taking an oath or unable to wage battle (see Pollock and Maitland, *Hist. of Eng. Law*, 681). Approvement has long fallen into disuse (2 Hale, P. C. 226), but the term "approver" is still used in Ireland of accomplices who turn king's evidence.

AN HISTORICAL OUTLINE OF THE OFFICE. 11

enacted, "That no sanctuary or privilege of sanctuary shall be allowed in any case."

One of the commonest results of the attempt to catch a criminal was his flight to sanctuary, and his abjuration of the realm. This picturesque episode of mediæval justice has been so admirably described by other hands that we shall say little about it.[1] Every consecrated church was a sanctuary. If a malefactor took refuge therein he could not be extracted; but it was the duty of the four neighbouring vills to beset the holy place, prevent his escape and send for a Coroner. The Coroner came and parleyed with the refugee, who had his choice between submitting to trial and abjuring the realm. If he chose the latter course, he hurried, dressed in pilgrim's guise, to the port that was assigned to him, and left England, being bound by his oath never to return. His lands escheated; his chattels were forfeited and if he came back his fate was that of an outlaw. If he would neither submit to trial nor abjure the realm, then the contention of the civil power was that, at all events after he had enjoyed the right of asylum for forty days, he was to be starved into submission; but the clergy resented this interference with the peace of Holy Church. However, large numbers of our felons were induced to relieve England of their presence, and were shipped off at Dover to France or Flanders[2] (*History of English Law*, Maitland and Pollock). A definite number of days to get to port was always fixed by the Coroner, and if the felon did not reach it in the allotted time, he was liable to be murdered on the road.

---

[1] Réville. L'Abjuratio regni, Revue historique, vol. 50, p. 1 (1892).

[2] For the right of asylum under the continental folk-laws, see Brunner, D R G, ii. 610; for A-S law, see Schmid, Gesetze, p. 584. M. Réville holds that the law of abjuration is developed from ancient English elements (Probably introduced into England after the conversion of the Saxons to Christianity.—Pike), and passes from England to Normandy. It must have taken its permanent shape late in the twelfth century. Some leading passages are Leg. Edw. Conf. c. 5; Bracton, fol. 135 b; Britton, i. 63; Fleta, p. 45; Mat. Par. Chron. Maj. vi. 357. For early cases, see Select Pleas of the Crown, pl. 48, 49, 89, etc.

The time allowed for travelling from Yorkshire to Dover is mentioned in a passage which is in other respects illustrative of the whole subject, and is to be found in the 'Placita Corone,' 22 Edw. III. county of York. A jury presents that one William of Coventry took sanctuary in the church of Thweng, and remained there from Sunday the 9th to Friday the 21st of December (1349), when he confessed various robberies before the Coroner, and abjured the realm. "Et dati sunt ei novem dies usque portum de Dovor ad transfretandum mare."

The immunity extended formerly not only to churches and churchyards, but also to various other places in England, such as Westminster, Wells, Norwich, York, etc.;[1] and it was even claimed for certain localities on the ground of their having been ancient palaces of the Crown, examples of which were the districts of Whitefriars, the Savoy and the Mint in London.[2] Immunity was claimed in these places both from criminal and civil process.[3] The towns were in fact cities of permanent refuge for persons who should according to ancient usage have abjured the realm, after having fled in the ordinary way to a church. There was a governor in each of those privileged places, and he had to muster every day[4] his men, who were not to exceed twenty[5] in each town, and who had to wear a

[1] *Vide* stat. 32 Hen. VIII. c. 12, p. 72.

[2] In London and its neighbourhood, sanctuary districts abounded. To a fugitive in the extreme east a convenient retreat was offered by the Minories; to one in Fleet Street by Salisbury Court, Whitefriars, Ram Alley and Mitre Court; to one in Holborn by Fuller's Rents; to one in Gray's Inn Lane by Baldwin's Gardens; to one in Southwark by Montague Close, Deadman's Place, the Clink and the Mint. Southwark was notorious for its sanctuaries in the fourteenth century, and that of the Mint existed down to 1722. For the abolition of these, *vide* 32 Hen. VIII. c. 12.

[3] To some extent, a man's own house is of the nature of a sanctuary, in so far as he cannot be served with civil process there unless he himself admit the person serving the process. But when a crime has been committed, a private house may be broken open to get at the criminal.

[4] "Sanctuary-men shall be daily mustered; and not appearing for three days shall lose their privilege" (32 Hen. VIII. c. 12, s. 6).

[5] 32 Hen. VIII. c. 12, s. 8.

AN HISTORICAL OUTLINE OF THE OFFICE. 13

badge whenever they appeared out of doors. But when these regulations were made, the protection of sanctuary was taken away from persons guilty of murder, rape, burglary, highway robbery, and arson, and their accessories —in other words, from all the greatest offenders.[1] The privilege of sanctuary was closely connected with the privilege known as "benefit of clergy," and the violation of the former was punished by Othobon with excommunication, and, if satisfaction were not made within a limited time, with deprivation (Othon. Athon. p. 101).

The ancient custom of assigning a port and forcing the sanctuary-man into exile seems to have been extinct in the sixteenth century. Banishment became one of the methods by which England was relieved of her rogues and vagabonds; but this was at most only an extension of the old law according to which persons who had taken sanctuary might abjure the realm.

The crime which we call rape had in the very old days been hardly severed from that which we should call abduction; if it had wronged the woman it had wronged her kinsmen also, and they would have felt themselves seriously wronged even if she had given her consent, and had, as we should say, eloped.[2]

In appeals of Rape.

Appeals of rape were often brought in the thirteenth century; but they were often quashed, abandoned or compromised. The judges seem to have thought that if the woman was satisfied public justice might be satisfied. She could prosecute her ravisher and use "words of felony"; but if she made no appeal and the man was arraigned at the king's suit, then imprisonment and fine were a sufficient punishment.[3] In 1275 the first Statute of Westminster gave the woman forty days for her appeal and fixed the punishment of an indicted ravisher two years' imprisonment to be followed by ransom at the king's pleasure.[4]

---

[1] A history of crime in England (2 vols.), by L. Owen Pike.

[2] Brunner, D R G, ii. 665.

[3] Northumberland Assize Rolls (A.D. 1256), p. 92, the ravisher is fined one mark; p. 94, a similar fine; (A.D. 1279), p. 329, a fine of four marks.

[4] *Hist of Eng. Law*, Maitland and Pollock.

Deodands.

It is not only the duty of the Coroner to ascertain the *cause* of the death (Keilw. 67 b.; 1 Hale, P.C. 422; 2 Id. 62; 2 Hawk. P.C. c. 9, s. 28), but also to inquire of the circumstances attending it; and if, in the result of that inquiry, the death were found to be attributable to any instrument, or " beast animate," that instrument or animal was, by the common law, forfeited as a deodand [1] in order to raise the greater abhorrence of homicide. As in the instance of murder the life of the murderer is forfeited, so in that species of homicide *per infortunium*, *i.e.* by misadventure[2] or casual death not punishable as a crime, any instrument "inanimate or beast animate" which occasioned the death was forfeited as a deodand; and much learning has been employed in considering in what case and to what extent such forfeiture attached.

The sanctity of human life is the principle on which deodands rest; it was believed dangerous and impolitic to allow death to be inflicted, whatever might be the means, without displaying some token of the State's displeasure. The seizure of the obnoxious instrument, whether an inanimate object or an animate creature unendowed with reason, naturally suggested itself as a means of increasing that instinctive awe which man feels at taking the life of his fellow man. The very cause of death seemed to be accursed and excommunicated, as it were, from society; it was declared unworthy of further use, and its services to men were for ever prohibited. So apparent was the advantage of this proceeding, that it was adopted into the codes of the most eminent nations of antiquity. The Jews, in accordance with the divine law, " *Your blood of your lives will I require; at the hand of every beast will I*

---

[1] Deodand—something "given to God," a "res deo data." Lord Coke, 3 Inst. c. 9, has these words: "Deodands when any moveable thing inanimate or beast animate, do move to, or cause the untimely death of any reasonable creature by *mischance* in any county of the realm (and not upon the sea, or upon any salt water), *without the will, offence, or fault of himself, or of any person.*"

[2] Per infortunium—by misadventure. When a person doing a lawful act, without any intention of hurt, by accident kills another: as, for example, a man is at work with a hatchet, the head flies off by accident and kills a bystander. Harris's Criminal Law.

AN HISTORICAL OUTLINE OF THE OFFICE. 15

require it, and at the hand of man" (Gen. ix. 5), never suffered the lives of their people to be taken away without requiring some expiation. Hence we find it declared (in the Mosaic law) that an ox, which had "gored a man" (that he die) should be stoned (and his flesh shall not be eaten. (Ex. xxi. 28)), and the man who killed another "unawares," or "ignorantly," was to flee to the cities of refuge (Numbers xxxv. and Deut. xix.).

Among the Greeks, homicide by misfortune was atoned for by voluntary banishment for a year (Plato de Leg. L. 9), and in Athens, whatever was the cause of a man's death by falling upon him was exterminated or cast out of the dominions of the republic[1] (*Vide* Æschin. cont. Ctesiph. and Pott. Archæol. Gr. 3, 178). In Rome, casual homicide was excused by the indulgence of the Emperor (Cod. 9, 16, 5), and, by the *Lex Aquilia*, a forfeiture prevailed in the nature of a deodand.

The composition exacted for casual slaying among the ancient Germans was little inferior to that required for voluntary homicide (Stiernhook, 1, 3, c. 4). By the laws of the Ripuarians, when a man was killed by a piece of wood, or any instrument made by man, the instrument itself was deemed culpable, and the relations seized it to their own use; and, if a beast caused the death of man, the beast itself was forfeited as a part of the requisite composition (Leg. Rip. Tit. 46. Edit. Lindembrock).

From these nations the law of deodands seems to have been imported into this country,[2] and there exist two hypotheses as to the motives which led to its establishment among our ancestors. The first, and most common, is that these penalties arose from religious institutions (*e.g.* purgatory), and were intended for the purchase of masses in favour of the soul thus suddenly sent to its account (without the sacrament of extreme unction). The

---

[1] Compare also the rule of the Twelve Tables, by which an animal which had inflicted mischief might be surrendered in lieu of compensation.

[2] Deodands are mentioned in the laws of Alfred (Leg. Alf. 18), and *vide* an instance given by Reeve (*Hist. of Eng. Law*, vol. i. p. 17), under the Saxon Government.

second, and more probable supposition, treats this donation for the sake of the soul as the *subsequent application*, not the origin, of deodands. They are regarded as fines to the Crown for the loss of a subject, as the *pretium sanguinis* (the price of blood), and as having had a *civil* origin,[1] and seem to have been at first devoted by the Crown to works of charity, and afterwards to have been given to the church [2] for the sake of the deceased. About the time of the Reformation they were resumed by the sovereign, and either retained as a portion of his casual revenues, or granted to subjects.

Deodands class themselves under two heads, viz.:—

1. *Moventia*, or those which were moving to the death of a human being.
2. *Quiescentia*, or those which caused death while at rest.

1. It was laid down as a rule that, wherever that which is the occasion of a man's death is in *motion* at the time, not only that part which immediately wounds him but all things which move together with it and help to make the wound more dangerous are forfeited also (Hawk. P. C. c. 27). This is expressed in pithy terms by the well-known dictum of Montagu, C.J., in Dyer, 77, b: "Omnia quæ movent ad mortem, deodanda sunt";

2. Where the thing causing death was not in motion, that part only which was the *immediate* cause of death was forfeited; as where a man climbing on the wheel of a cart, while it was at rest, fell and died from the fall, only the wheel was forfeited (Hale, P. C. 422, cites 8 E. 2 Cor. 407).

Lord Hale, when writing upon deodands (1 P. C. 419), observes, the inquisition should inquire of the goods that

---

[1] In support of this view, *vide* Foster (Crown Law, 278, etc.) and Bacon's Abridgment, by Dodd, tit. "Deodands."

[2] The opinion appears to be apocryphal of those who think the clergy, from the notion of purgatory, first introduced this kind of forfeiture or penalty; though from ancient times, by means of a clerical power, they might have acquired the disposition of it, in *pios usus* amongst the poor, and thence not improperly called *fœdum clericale*. *Vide* Umfreville.

AN HISTORICAL OUTLINE OF THE OFFICE. 17

occasioned the death, etc. "And this is the reason," he continues, "that *in every indictment of murder, manslaughter*, etc., the indictment finding he was killed with a sword, staff, etc., ought to find also the price, viz. 5 solidorum, because the King is entitled to it," and again (2 P. C. 185), speaking of indictments: "It should be set down the price of the sword or other weapon, or else say *nullius valoris*, for the weapon is a deodand forfeited to the King."

Unless the party wounded died of his wound within a year and a day after its infliction nothing could be forfeited and nothing could be a deodand, or be seized as such, until it be found by the inquest to have caused death (Hawk. P. C. c. 27). After the inquest had found the deodand, the sheriff[1] was, it was said, answerable for the value,[2] and could levy the same on the ville or township where the accident happened (Hawk. P. C. c. 26), and it then became a part of the revenue of the Crown, or the property of a lord of the franchise.

Among the Romans, and with many of the northern nations, the relatives of the deceased were allowed to participate in the deodand; in England, the king, or the party to whom it was granted, formerly devoted it to works of charity, but in the last days of deodands, it merely swelled the property of those who could easily dispense with the addition.

For some centuries deodands scarcely exceeded the amount of a few shillings,[3] but in 1840 they rapidly

---

[1] The mode of paying the deodand, etc., into the exchequer was regulated by the stat. 3 & 4 Will. IV. c. 99, s. 29, etc., and the provisions of this Act extended to Ireland by 5 & 6 Will. IV. c. 55.

[2] 3 Inst. 57; *R.* v. *Brownlow* (1839), 11 A. & E. 119; *R.* v. *Polwart* (1841), 1 Q. B. 818; and Umfreville, in his *Lex Coronatoria*, say it was valued by the jury. *Vide* also Coroners' Rolls, p. 21, of the present work.

[3] These forfeitures became so extremely unpopular that "juries very frequently took upon themselves to mitigate them, by finding only some trifling thing to have been the occasion of the death; and although such finding of the jury may have been hardly warrantable by law, the court in general refused to interfere" (Blackstone).

C

ascended to £500, £800, and at length £2000. This last penalty was inflicted on the London and Birmingham Railway Company, which was opened in 1838, in connection with a verdict of wilful murder[1] and *felo de se* against the engineer. Much discussion arose upon this proceeding, particularly on the question of the deodand, as it was said that such a forfeiture could be incurred in cases of *casual*[2] death alone, not where a verdict of criminal homicide had been returned, and therefore that the inquest had overstepped their mark (Monthly Law Mag. vol. x. 1841, p. 15). But deodands are now abolished by the statute 9 & 10 Vict. c. 62 (*q.v.*) p. 169. The date of this statute (1846) may suggest the great inconvenience which the law, if it had remained in operation, would have caused, as is clearly seen in the above case, to railway and other enterprise in which loss of life is a frequent occurrence.

Such, then, were the duties of the Coroner in bygone days. They are now limited, in accordance with the Coroners Act, 1887, s. 3, to an inquiry upon "the dead body of a person lying within his jurisdiction" as to how, when, where, and by what means the deceased came by his (or her) death in such cases where "there is reasonable cause to suspect that such person has died either a violent or an unnatural death, or has died a sudden death of which the cause is unknown, or that such person has died in prison, or in such place or under such circumstances as to require an inquest in pursuance of any Act," and upon treasure trove.

Coroners' Rolls. Their number and arrangement. The Coroners' Rolls have been preserved in the Public Record Office among the Assize Rolls of the King's Bench

[1] Deodand was found in a case of *manslaughter* for the first time on view of the body of Richard Mason in 1840 and quashed by Lord Denman, C.J., in Trinity Term, 1841. *Vide Queen v. Polwart*, 1 Q. B. 818.

[2] Deodands are treated in the same manner in connection with death by misadventure, *i.e.* casual death, in Coke, 3 Inst. c. 9; in Fleta, book 1, c. 25, s. 9; in Bac. Abridg. tit. Deodand, Discourse 2, ch. 1, s. 5; in Foster's Crown Law, p. 265; in 1 East's P. C. 386; in Hawkins's P. C. b. 1, c. 26; in Staundforde's P. C. 20 a; and in Foxley's Case, 5 Rep, 110 b.

(Crown Side). There are 260 rolls, arranged according to counties, containing in all about 2140 membranes.[1] The following Table shows their chronological distribution :—

49-56 Henry III.: Rolls 1, 2, 46. (Bedfordshire.)
Edward I.: Rolls 3-5, 106, 107, 128, 208, 254-6.
Edward II.: Rolls 6, 47, 94A, 106-10.
Henry IV. and Henry V.: Rolls 60-63, 101, 145, 147-51, 162, 166-70, 253.
4 Henry VI.: Roll 158.
Edward III. and Richard II.: those not mentioned above, and Rolls 47, 60, 61, 145, 147, 162, 166.

These records are not the original "rotuli coronatorum," but merely transcripts and in some cases abstracts of the originals. Though mere abstracts and transcripts, they are doubtless contemporary or almost contemporary with the originals. They contain little or no direct testimony regarding their origin and object. We know that the Coroners' Rolls seem to be abstracts made by order of the king's justices for the use of the Crown. The attention paid to the property of felons in the body of the cases and in the marginal notes indicates that the rolls were made especially for the use of the royal treasury. Britton (i. 133) says that "at the eyre estreats of amercements and of the fines and chattels of felons were made and sent to the exchequer." Some of the so-called Coroners' Rolls are simply rolls of estreats; for example, Roll 47, "Extractæ catallorum felonum," and Roll 172, "Inquisitio de bonis utlagatorum" (Charles Gross).

Not the originals.

The Coroners' Rolls or Inquisitions were anciently returned to the Crown Office, and filed along with the Indictments and Informations; but the practice of returning them to that Court has been for many years discontinued, and many have been consequently either lost after a few years or now remain in the hands of private individuals having no right to them, no knowledge of their contents, and no wish even to preserve them. Modern Coroners' Inquisitions are retained at the respec-

[1] A printed list of these rolls will be found in 'Lists and Indexes' (Public Record Office), No. IV. Rolls Series, 1894, pp. 197-208.

tive Coroners' Offices, but it would, perhaps, be wiser if they were collected at some central county office where much knowledge could be abstracted from them by some competent officer.

Inquisitions on which proceedings have subsequently taken place, as where the jurors have found verdicts of murder and manslaughter, may be "searched for" at the office of the Clerk of Assize, or Clerk of the Court, where the further investigation occurred.

Coroners' Rolls or Inquisitions in the reigns of Edward I., II., III., Richard II., and Henry IV., will be found at the Chapter House, and matters concerning Coroners are entered on the Close Rolls, at the Tower: whilst Inquisitions taken on view of the bodies of Prisoners who have died in the King's Bench Prisons, from the year 1771, are at the Crown Office, and Returns of Writs for electing Coroners will be found at the Petty Bag Office in Rolls Yard, Chancery Lane.

Seal of Office, etc.

The frontispiece to this work represents the seal[1] of the Coroner of the King's Household during the fourteenth century, but how or for what purpose it was used is quite unknown; neither does it appear ever to have been affixed to inquisitions or documents of any kind. When the Justices in Eyre came into the counties to hold the Eyre, the Coroners, who were almost indispensable and whose presence was enforced under severe penalties,[2] were called upon to present their Rolls or Inquisitions, in use since the last circuit, to the justices, who sealed them with their (the justices) own seals—probably to prevent altera-

---

[1] Proof. Red 1¼ in. A shield of arms: field diapered lozengy —a wheel, ensigned with coronet; on left, a staff or verge of coroner's office and wavy sprig of foliage.

S. CORONAT.' HOSPIC.' DNI.' REGIS.

within two beaded borders. (Presented to the British Museum by the late William Maskett, Esq., in 1867.)

[2] "As to the coroners who did not come, the sheriff was ordered to go to their houses and turn out their wives and children, and to take their lands into the King's hands until they should come" (Year Books, 30–31 Edw. I. 75–77; *cf. ibid.* pp. lvi. lvii.).

tions in the records during the proceedings of the Court[1] and returned them without examining them.

At the Record Office there is a number of inquisitions (A.D. 1748–1767) upon which the Coroners and the juries have affixed seals, using red wax; many of the jurymen appear to have used the same seal, probably that of a fellow-juryman, and in some instances the Coroner has also used the same; whilst a few of the Borough Coroners used the Corporation seal. It has been held that "an inquisition, to which is affixed a printed stamp opposite the signatures of the Coroner and jurymen respectively, and concluding with the usual averment that it was given under their hands and seals, is sufficient" (*Reg.* v. *Skeats and Biles*, 7 L. T. 433 (1846).

The following are a few select cases from the Norfolk Rolls :—

MARSHLAND[2] (NORFOLK).

Roll of Hugh Birdey, the King's Coroner of the liberty of the Bishop of Ely in the parts of Marshland.

Four townships, to wit, Tilney, Terrington, Walsoken, and Walpole, present that John of Nettleham, who was thirty years of age, was found slain in the fens of Marshland on Monday[3] next after the Nativity of St. John the Baptist, in the thirty-fifth year of King Edward the Third.

Inquest was taken before the said coroner at Terrington on the following Thursday by (twelve sworn men) and by the said four townships (sworn). They say on their oath that on Monday next after the feast of St. John the Baptist in the thirty-fifth year of King Edward the Third, Peter Wrenn assaulted John of Nettleham with a drawn

[1] Britton, i. 28; Year Books, 80–81 Edw. I. pp. lvi. lvii. (Liber Cust. 295, 296); Rogers, Documents, 188; Plac. quo War. 25, 809; *cf.* Fleta, i. chap. 18.

[2] The present hundred of Freebridge-Marshland in Norfolk, the peninsula between King's Lynn and Cambridgeshire. Some of the manors in Marshland belonged to the Bishop of Ely, and for these there was evidently a separate coroner. *Vide* Blomefield, *Norfolk*, ix. 90, 101, 128, 134.

[3] June 28, 1861.

knife at Tilney, to wit, in the fens of Marshland, and feloniously killed him by striking him with the said knife on the left arm, of which wound he died forthwith. The knife[1] was worth twopence, for which the township of Tilney will account.

The townships of Terrington, Walpole, Walsoken, and Walton with Emneth present that (Walter Caley) was found slain at Walsoken about the hour of none on Sunday[2] next before the feast of St. Gregory the Pope in the thirty-sixth year of King Edward the Third.

Inquest was taken on the following Monday at Walsoken by (twelve sworn men) and by the said four townships (sworn). They say on their oath that on Saturday next before the feast of St. Gregory the Pope in the thirty-sixth year of King Edward the Third at Walsoken, John Odey of Emneth, with a knife called a broach, assaulted Walter, Bartholomew Caley's son, who was forty years of age, and feloniously killed him by striking him on the left side of the belly near the navel; and he suffered from this wound until the hour of none on the following Sunday, when he died, after having the rites of the Church. And they say that John Odey fled forthwith, and he had chattels worth half a mark, for which the township of West Walton with Emneth will account. The knife[1] was worth four pence, for which the said township with the hamlet (Emneth) will account. It was ordered that he be arrested, etc.

The townships of Terrington, Walpole, Walsoken, and West Walton with the hamlet of Emneth present that Robert, son of Adam of Emneth, who was forty years of age, was found slain at Emneth about the hour of vespers on Monday[3] next before the feast of

---

[1] A *deodand* is only where the death happens by misadventure; the instrument of death could indeed be forfeited to the king in cases of felony; but that is not an instance of deodand properly speaking (Sir W. W. Follett in *Queen* v. *Polwart*, 1840). See Deodands, p. 14.

[2] 3 P.M. March 6, 1362. None, the ninth hour after sunrise at the Equinoxes.

[3] July 18, 1362.

St. Margaret in the thirty-sixth year of King Edward the Third.

Inquest was taken at Emneth on Tuesday[1] next after the feast of St. Margaret in the said year by (twelve sworn men) and by the said four townships (sworn). They say on their oath that on Monday next before the feast of St. Margaret in the thirty-sixth year of King Edward the Third, at Emneth, a certain William Grantpee of Hertfordshire assaulted Robert, son of Adam of Emneth, with a drawn knife, and feloniously killed him by striking him with the said knife to the heart; and thereof he died on the same day about sunset, after receiving the rites of the Church. And no other person is suspected of the said death. William had no chattels, etc.; the knife[2] is worth a half-penny, for which the township of West Walton with Emneth will account. And the said William was arrested immediately after committing the act and was sent and delivered to the prison of the Bishop of Ely at Dereham, etc.

The townships of Walsoken, West Walton with Emneth, Walpole, and Terrington present that (John Thurkle) was found slain about the hour of vespers on Thursday the feast of the Apostles Peter and Paul[3] in the thirty-sixth year of King Edward the Third.

Inquest was taken at Terrington before William Alexander, the King's Coroner in the County of Norfolk, and before the said Hugh, the King's Coroner of the liberty of the Bishop of Ely in the parts of Marshland, on Thursday[4] next before the feast of the Translation of St. Thomas the Archbishop, in the thirty-sixth year of King Edward the Third, by (twelve sworn men) and by the said four townships (sworn). They say on their oath that on Thursday the feast of the Apostles Peter and Paul in the aforesaid year, John Thurkle of Walsoken, who was thirty years of age, was killed at Walsoken by foreign

---

[1] July 26, 1362.   [2] *Vide* footnote 1, p. 22.
[3] June 29 is the date of that feast, but in 1362 it was on Wednesday, not Thursday.
[4] June 30, 1362.

archers of Cambridgeshire, whose names are utterly unknown (to the jurors); they discharged at him iron arrows from their bows, and one of (the archers) struck him with a discharged arrow on the right side of the belly, of which wound he died forthwith. The arrow[1] was worth one penny, for which the township of Walsoken will account.

The Different Kinds of Coroners and their Jurisdictions.

Coroners are of three kinds, viz:—

  i. Virtute officii.
  ii. Virtute cartæ sive commissionis.
  iii. Virtute electionis, *e.g.* County and Borough Coroners.

I. The Coroners *virtute officii* are:—

  (a) The Lord Chief Justice of the King's Bench, who, by virtue of his office is the chief or supreme Coroner of *England* (4 Co. Rep. 57 b. in case de comminaltie de Sadlers).
  (b) The Puisne Judges of the King's Bench are sovereign Coroners (4 Inst. 73).

The jurisdiction of these Coroners (a and b) extends over the whole realm, and may, if they think proper, be exercised within the Verge, and in all other exempt jurisdictions and liberties (4 Rep. 47). But they have no power to delegate their authority, which can be exercised in person only.

II. The Coroners by charter or commission or privilege were ordinarily made by grant or commission without election; such are the Coroners of particular lords of liberties and franchises[2] who by charter have power to create their own Coroners or to be Coroners themselves. (Hales, P. C. vol. ii. p. 53.)

The acts of Coroners by charter or commission must

---

[1] *Vide* footnote 1, p. 22.
[2] For definition of "franchise" and "franchise coroner," see Coroners Act, 1887, s. 42.

be confined within the particular precincts over which they are appointed, and cannot in any case be extended beyond it. Where the lord of a franchise, or the head or chief of a corporation, personally discharges this office, whatever be the case with respect to his other duties, yet if he take an inquisition *super visum corporis*, he must entitle himself "Coroner" upon the record, for otherwise the inquisition will be erroneous, and *coram non judice*, *i.e.* in the presence of a person not a judge; for except as Coroner he has no authority, even though both offices be vested in the same person. (Bro. Ab. "Nosme," 50; 22 Ed. IV, 12). And depositions taken on an inquisition before a mayor *quâ* Coroner are not admissible, unless by the proceedings he appear to have acted as Coroner (1 C. Cass. 306).

The extent of the jurisdiction, in particular liberties, depends *upon the grants* applicable to each.

Thus the Lord Mayor of *London* is by charter Coroner of London (2 Hale P. C. 53), *vide* p. 33.

The Bishop of Ely has power to make Coroners in the Isle of Ely by charter of Hen. VII.

Queen Catharine had the hundred of Colridge granted to her by the king (35 Hen. VIII.) with power to nominate Coroners (9 Co. Rep. 29 b. Ameredith's case).

The Cinque Ports have their own Coroners.

The Dean and Chapter of Westminster have their Coroner, who, by their appointment, is Coroner for the City and liberties of Westminster.

In the Stannaries in Cornwall the Wardens are Coroners.

The Master of the Crown Office, or Clerk of the Crown, is Coroner of the King's Bench, and has jurisdiction over matters arising within the prison of that court. He holds his office by letters patent under the Great Seal.

In addition to which there are many exclusive jurisdictions and corporations for which Coroners are appointed.

But the two great precincts or jurisdictions over which, by the King's grants, Coroners may be appointed, are the Verge and the Admiralty.

The Verge, and the precincts of the palace. The *The Verge.*

Coroner of the King's house, usually called the Coroner of the Verge, who it seems at common law was appointed by the King's letters patent, but by 33 Hen. VIII. c. 12, the granting thereof is settled in perpetuity in the Lord Steward, or Lord Great Master of the King's house for the time being.

At common law the Coroner of the Verge had an exempt jurisdiction within the Verge, which comprehends a circuit of twelve miles round the residence of the King's Courts (13 R. II. c. 3), and had power to do all things belonging to his office, exclusive of the Coroner of the county (4 Rep. 46 b.; Brit. c. 1, s. 6 (Edition by Nichols); 2 Hale, P. C. 54; 2 Inst. 550). The consequence of this jurisdiction, the King's Court being movable, was that, if a person had been killed within the Verge of the Court, and the King had removed his Court before an inquisition had been taken by the Coroner of the King's household, there was no Coroner who had any jurisdiction of the fact. The Coroner of the County could not interfere, for he had no authority in matters arising within the Verge of the Court, neither had the Coroner of the King's household, for his jurisdiction ceased when the place where the death occurred was, by the removal of the Court, no longer within the Verge of the Court. It is evident that a jurisdiction so exclusive must necessarily have been attended with inconveniences, and must in many cases have frustrated the due course of justice, by the delay in the punishment, and frequently by the escape of offenders. This seems to be confirmed by the recital of the statute *Articuli super Cartas* (28 Ed. I. c. 3), that "many felonies committed within the Verge had been unpunished, because the Coroners of the County had not been authorized to inquire of felonies done within the Verge, but the Coroner of the King's house, which never continued in one place; by reason whereof there can be no trial made in due manner, nor the felons put in *exigent*, nor outlawed nor anything prosecuted in the circuit, the which had been to the great damage of the King, and nothing to the preservation of the peace."

To remedy this, it is ordained by the same statute

"that from thenceforth, in cases of the death of man, whereof the Coroner's office is to make view and inquest, it shall be commanded to the Coroner of the county, that he, with the Coroner of the King's house, shall do as belongeth to his office, and enrol it." By this statute (the whole of which is repealed by Coroners Act, 1887), the Coroner of the county had to join with the Coroner of the Verge; but, without the assistance of the latter officer the Coroner of the county could not act within the Verge (*Hamlin's Case*, 1610, K. B.; see 2 Leon. 160; 4 Rep. 45 b). So neither could the Coroner of the Verge act in such cases, unless he be associated with the Coroner of the county; and this had to appear upon the inquisition, or otherwise it would be erroneous and void (2 Inst. 550). But if the same person be Coroner both of the county and of the Verge, an inquisition taken by him in both characters would be good, if upon the face of the inquisition both characters are stated, because the mischief expressed in the statute was remedied as well when both offices were in the same, as when they were filled by different persons (2 Hale, P. C. 55; 3 Inst. 134). And even though the Court remove, the Coroner who holds both offices could proceed upon the inquisition as Coroner of the county (4 Co. Rep. 45 and 46 b; *Wrote* v. *Wigges*).

The *precincts* of the palace differ from the Verge, and are defined by statute 33 Hen. VIII. c. 12, s. 24, to be "within the edifice, courts, places, gardens, orchards, privy-walk, tilt-yards, wood-yards, tennis-plays, cock-fights, bowling-alleys, near adjoining to any of the houses above rehearsed, and being part of the same, or within two hundred feet of the standard of any outward gate or gates of any of the houses above rehearsed, commonly used for passage out or from any of the houses above rehearsed." *The precincts of the palace.*

If a murder or manslaughter be committed within the *precincts* of the King's palace, the inquest must be taken by the Coroner of the King's household alone. The same statute, sect. 3, enacts, "that all inquisitions upon the view of persons slain within any of the King's palaces or houses, or other house or houses, at such time as his Majesty shall happen to be there demurrant or abiding in his royal person, shall be taken by the Coroner for the time being for the King's household, without the adjoining or assisting of another Coroner of any shire within this realm, by the oath of twelve or more of the yeomen officers of the King's household, returned by the two clerks controllers, the clerks of the check and the clerks marshals, or one of them, for the time being, of the said household, to whom the said Coroner of the said household shall direct his precept."

By the Coroners Act 1887 (50 & 51 Vict. c. 71, sch. 3), repealing 28 Ed. I. c. 3, the jurisdiction of the Verge is entirely abolished and becomes absorbed in that of the county, giving the county Coroner absolute jurisdiction; whilst the precincts of the palace remain as before, for which see the Coroners Act, 1887, sect. 29.

The Admiralty.

The Admiralty, concerning which the President of the Admiralty Division of the High Court is made Coroner by letters patent, so also the Lord High Admiral,[1] now the First Lord of the Admiralty, is likewise appointed by patent, and by the same authority has power to appoint Coroners within his jurisdiction, who are usually the Judge Marshal of the Admiralty and, *pro hâc vice*, his deputy.

This jurisdiction was anciently, at common law, confined to matters arising upon the high sea, *super altum mare*, but by 15 Rich. II. c. 3, the Coroners of the Admiralty have now jurisdiction concurrently with the Coroners of the county "of the death of a man, and of maihem, done in great ships being and hovering in the main stream of great rivers only, beneath the bridges of the same rivers nigh to the sea, and in no other place of the same rivers the Admiral shall have cognizance." The jurisdiction of the Admiralty extends to matters arising upon the open sea between the high and low water-mark when the tide is in; but when the tide is out the authority of the county Coroner obtains in such places;

[1] The office of Lord High Admiral first put into commission in 1682.

so there is *divisum imperium* at different times (3 Inst. 113; 5 Rep. 107).

By the common law, the Coroner of the county had jurisdiction in matters arising on the arms of the sea, *infra corpus comitatûs*, exclusive of the Coroner of the Admiralty (2 Hale, P. C. 15, 54); according to some authorities, in all cases whose one shore might have been seen from the other (Owen, 122; Moor. 892, 2 Hale, P. C. 54; Saund. P. C. 51; Hale, Sum. 151, 8 E. 2 Cor. 399); but, by others, only where a man standing upon the one side might see what was done on the other (F. Cor. 399; 4 Inst. 140; 2 Roll. Abr. 169). Upon such places, the Coroner of the Admiralty had originally no jurisdiction. That was first conferred by the statute 15 Rich. II. c. 3, as quoted above.

But even this is not exclusive of the county Coroner, who has a concurrent jurisdiction with the Coroner of the Admiralty, and may still take an inquisition in great rivers of the death of man and maihem, to which alone the statute applies (2 Hale, P. C. 15, 16, 54; 8 E. 2 Cor. 399). It extends only to rivers that are arms of the sea, that flow and reflow, and bear great ships; and does not apply to deaths which happen in small vessels, but to great ships only (*vide* the same authorities). The body of A. was taken up drowned at St. Katherine's, on the river Thames, below the bridge: the Coroner of the Admiralty having taken an inquisition upon a view of the body, which was found to have been drowned by accident, the Coroner of the county afterwards demanded the body, that he might take an inquisition, which the Coroner of the Admiralty refused to permit, and had the body buried. This was complained of as an abuse, the Admiralty having no jurisdiction unless the death happened in a great ship; and an attachment was granted against the Coroner of the Admiralty (cited Umf. Lex. Cor. 93).

Portsmouth Harbour has been decided to be *infra corpus comitatûs*; and the Court of King's Bench granted an information against the captain of a ship lying there for obstructing the Coroner of that place, who attempted to enter the ship for the purpose of taking a view of a body lying dead there, no inquisition having previously been taken by the Coroner of the Admiralty (2 Str. 1097; Andrews, 231).

Where the jurisdiction of the county or borough and of the Admiralty is concurrent, the Coroner who first proceeds to take the inquisition ousts the authority of the other (Sir John Jervis).

Section 3 of the Coroners Act, 1887 (50 & 51 Vict. c. 71), enacts that "where a Coroner is informed that the dead body of a person is lying within his jurisdiction under such circumstances as to require an inquest, the Coroner, whether the cause of death arose within his jurisdiction or not, shall inquire touching the death of such person as aforesaid"; but section 7, sub-s. 1 of the same statute enacts that "the Coroner *only* within whose jurisdiction the body of a person is lying shall hold the inquest, and *where a body is found dead in the sea or any creek, river, or navigable canal within the flowing of the sea*, where there is no deputy Coroner for the jurisdiction of the Admiralty of England, the inquest shall be held *only* by the Coroner having jurisdiction in the place where the body is *first* brought to land." How, then, are these two sections 3 and 7 to be reconciled? Whilst section 3 is the rule, section 7 is the exception, and the body, if removed from the jurisdiction whence it was "first brought to land," must be brought back to within that jurisdiction, and the inquest held before the Coroner of that jurisdiction (*Queen* v. *Hinde*, 13 L. J. N. S. Magis. Cases, p. 150; 5 Q. B. 944).

III. The Coroners *virtute electionis* are:—

    (*a*) County Coroners and
    (*b*) Borough Coroners.

(*a*) During the thirteenth and fourteenth centuries there were four Coroners in each county[1] who did duty over the county generally, irrespective of districts. Each was assisted by a "clericus," or deputy, who occasionally

---
[1] Pl. of Gl. 97; Rot. Claus. i. 402, 622, 648 (*cf. ibid.* 463, 506, ii. 91, 105, 119, 126); Bracton, ii. 430; Salt. Soc. iv. 78, 208, 215, v. 121, vi. pt. i. 256, xii. 170.

AN HISTORICAL OUTLINE OF THE OFFICE. 31

held inquests.[1] Coroners of certain hundreds, ridings, or rapes, are, however, sometimes mentioned.

Coroners of the county were chosen by all the freeholders in the county court, *i.e.* "with the assent of the whole county," by virtue of the King's writ *De Coronatore eligendo*, as, by the policy of our ancient laws, the sheriff and conservators of the peace and all other officers were chosen who were concerned in matters which affected the liberty of the subject (1 Bl. Com. 347).

The newly-appointed Coroner took his oath of office, "ad custodienda ea quae pertinent ad Coronam" (*to the preserving of those matters which relate to the office of Coroner*) in the county court before the Sheriff, who afterwards sent his name to the King.

The mode of proceeding by the Sheriff, upon the receipt of the writ *De Coronatore eligendo*, was clearly laid down under 7 & 8 Vict. c. 92 (*q.v.*), and the candidates for office had to undergo all the expenses and anxieties inseparable from a contested election; all this, together with the duties of the Sheriff, are now avoided, and by the Local Government Act, 1888 (51 & 52 Vict. c. 41, s. 5) the responsibility of electing the county Coroner rests with the County Council of the respective counties (*vide* the statute, p. 258). The original writ *De Coronatore eligendo* is still issued by the Lord Chancellor, but to the County Council instead of to the Sheriff.

The main qualifications for the office during the thirteenth century were knighthood and residence in the county. At common law, confirmed by statute (1 Edw. II. c. 1, *De Militibus*), every man of full age and possessing a knight's fee, which at the time of the Statute amounted to £20, arising out of land, or (according to Cay, as from the Cotton MS.) £40, which latter sum appears from 16 Car. s. 20, rendering knighthood no longer compulsory, to be the correct one, was compellable to take upon himself the degree

<small>Qualification. 13th century.</small>

---

[1] The "clericus" referred to in the articles of Eyre, 1194 (Sel. Charters, 260), was probably an ecclesiastic who acted as clerk or scribe. Deputies or "clerici" are often mentioned under Henry III. and his successors: Bracton, ii. 588; Britton, i. 54; Fleta, fol. 20.

of knighthood, *pour faire service al roy, et al realme in course de justice*; from which prerogative arose a principal source of the revenue of the Crown. In consequence of this usage, all, or the greater part of the public officers, under the degree of Barons, were *Milites*; from which class of persons, by the statute of 3 Edw. I.[1] c. 10 the Coroners for counties were chosen " of the most wise and discreet knights which know, will, and may best attend upon such offices, &c." But as the sheriffs, who enquired of such as were of age and sufficiency to take the degree of knighthood, were empowered also to receive for the use of the Crown pecuniary commutations or aids from those who were desirous of purchasing their redemption or respite from that service,[2] this so far decreased the number of persons compellable to assume the degree of knighthood that at length there was a deficiency of knights to fill the public offices. This probably was the reason why the Statute of Westminster, above referred to, fell into disuse and gave rise to the statute 28 Edw. III. c. 6,[3] which enacted that Coroners shall be elected of "the most meet and lawful people that shall be found in the said counties to execute the said office."[4] Thus the necessary knighthood qualification of the thirteenth century ceased to be so in the fourteenth. And now in the twentieth, all that is necessary is that he "shall be a fit person having land in fee sufficient in the same county whereof he may answer to all manner of people" (*vide* Coroners Act, 1887, s. 12).

Borough Coroners.—Anciently, boroughs had their own Coroners by a special grant from the King. They were elected by the civic community, or whole body of burgesses, and were usually sworn into office in the shire court by the sheriff or itinerant justices; nowadays they are appointed much in the same manner by the councils of quarter sessions

---

[1] Rot. Claus. i. 419; Cal. of Close Rolls (1307-13), 287, 372; Rot. Parl. ii. 260.
[2] Seld. Tit. Hon. 1; Britton, 88 (ed. by Nichols); Bracton, 117; Fleta, i. c. 20, s. 94.
[3] Repealed by the Coroners Act, 1887.
[4] Sir John Jervis.
[5] Gross. Gild Merchant, ii. 116, 117.

boroughs having the power of appointment. By the Local Government Act, 1888, boroughs are divided into three kinds, viz :—

(1) County boroughs; those with a population of 50,000 and upwards on June 1, 1881 (s. 31); these form administrative counties of themselves.

(2) Larger quarter sessions boroughs; those with a population of 10,000 at the census of 1881; they form part of the county, but retain the power of appointing their own Coroners under the Municipal Corporations Act, 1882.

(3) Smaller quarter sessions boroughs; those with a population of less than 10,000 at the census of 1881 (s. 38). Concerning Coroners they are merged in the county.

Boroughs without quarter sessions did not come within the Municipal Corporations Act, 1882; concerning Coroners then they remain, as before, part of the county.

During the thirteenth and fourteenth centuries, the citizens of London did not have the right to elect their Coroner. The functions of that office were exercised by the chamberlain and the sheriffs; with them the aldermen of the various wards co-operated.[1] The statement made by some writers that the offices of mayor, chamberlain, and Coroner were held by the same person,[2] is not tenable. "Et nota," says a record of 14 Edw. II., "quod Botellarius domini regis et Camerarius domini regis et Coronator idem sunt"[3] (*and note that the Butler of the Lord King and the Chamberlain of the Lord King and the Coroner are the same*). The mayor and the chamberlain were usually distinct persons,[4] but the chamberlain

City of London Coroner.

---

[1] Liber Albus, 52, 96; Liber de Antiq. Legibus, 51.

[2] Riley, Memorials, 8; Loftie, London, 29; *cf.* Pulling, Laws of London, 19, 128.

[3] Liber Cust. 296.

[4] The same person was, however, both mayor and chamberlain in 4–6 Edw. I. (Riley, Memorials, 8–17; Liber Cust. 289, 291); and John de Wengrave was both Mayor and Coroner, or "sub-coronator," in 10–11 Edw. II. (Liber Cust. 245–46). These are merely exceptions to the general rule.

D

was *ex officio* Coroner, at all events, in the reigns of Edw I. and Edw. II.—and both these offices were held by the King's butler; the duties of Coroner were usually performed by his deputy or by two deputies, who were called "sub-coronatores." In the year 51 Edw. III. and again in 1 Rich. II. the commons and community of London complain to the King that they suffer many mischiefs because the Coroner is not subject to the civic authorities "n'est pas justisable par maire, aldermans, ne par autres ministres d'icels" (*is not liable to be tried by the mayor, aldermen, or any other of their officers*), and they pray that they may be allowed to elect a Coroner of themselves, and to remove him when they please, as various cities and towns are wont to do. The King responded that he would not depart from his ancient right.[1] But in 1478 the mayor and community were granted the right to have a Coroner of their own, distinct from the chief butler's Coroner.[2]

[1] Rot. Parl. ii. 867, iii. 19.
[2] Hist. Charters of London, 92.

PART II.

THE STATUTES.

9 HENRY III. c. 17.

THE GREAT CHARTER, A.D. 1225.

No Sheriff, Constable, Escheator, Coroner, nor any other of our Bailiffs, shall hold Pleas of our Crown.   *Holding Pleas of the Crown.*

NOTE.—This statute is the first which contains the word "Coroner" in any printed edition of Statutes, and reappears as 25 Edw. I. c. 17 (A.D. 1297).

---

43 HENRY III. c. 24.

PROVISIONS MADE BY THE KING AND HIS COUNCIL, A.D. 1259.

Attendance of those of twelve years old on inquests.

The Justices in Eyre from henceforth shall not amerce the Township in their Circuit, because all that are twelve years old do not appear before the Sheriffs and Coroners upon Inquests for the death of man, or other things pertaining to the Crown; so that from those Townships there come enough for the making of such inquests fully. [Repealed by Stat. Law Rev. Act, 1863 (26 & 27 Vict. c. 125).]

52 HENRY III. c. 24.

THE STATUTE OF MARLBOROUGH, A.D. 1267.

Concerning the attendance of those of twelve years old on inquests.

The Justices in Eyre from henceforth shall not amerce Townships in their Circuits, because all being twelve years old came not afore the Sheriffs and Coroners, to make Inquiry of Robberies, Burnings of Houses or other things pertaining to the Crown; so that there come sufficient out of those Towns, by whom such Inquests may be made full: except Inquests for the Death of Man, whereat all being twelve years of age, ought to appear unless they have reasonable cause of absence. [Repealed as to England by Stat. Law Rev. Act, 1863 (26 & 27 Vict. c. 125), as to Ireland by Stat. Law (Ireland) Rev. Act, 1872.]

---

3 EDWARD I. c. 4.

THE STATUTES OF WESTMINSTER, A.D. 1275.

What shall be adjudged Wreck of the Sea, and what not.

Concerning Wrecks of the Sea, it is agreed that where a Man, a Dog, or a Cat escapes quick[1] out of the Ship, that such Ship nor Barge, nor anything within them, shall be adjudged Wreck: but the goods shall be saved and kept by View of the Sheriff, Coroner, or the King's Bailiff, and delivered in the hands of such as are of the Town were the Goods were found; so that if any sue for those goods, and after prove that they were his[2] or in his keeping, within a year and a day, they shall be restored to him without delay; and if not, they shall remain to the King, and be seised by the Sheriffs, Coroners and Bailiffs, and shall be delivered to them of

---

[1] *I.e.* alive.   [2] Or his Lord's.—MS. Tr. 1.

the Town,[1] which shall answer before the Justices of the Wreck belonging to the King. And where Wreck belongeth to another than to the King, he shall have it in like manner. And he that otherwise doth, and thereof be attainted, shall be awarded to Prison and make fine at the King's Will, and shall yield damages also, and if a Bailiff do it, and it be disallowed by the Lord, and the Lord will not pretend any Title thereunto[2] the Bailiff shall answer, if he have whereof; and if he have not whereof, the Lord shall deliver his Bailiff's Body to the King. [Repealed as to England by Stat. Law Rev. Act, 1863 (26 & 27 Vict. c. 125), as to Ireland by Stat. Law Rev. Act, 1872.]

---

3 EDWARD I. c. 9.

THE STATUTES OF WESTMINSTER, A.D. 1275.

Pursuit of felons, and punishment for neglect or corruption in Officers.

And forasmuch as the Peace of this Realm hath been evil observed[3] heretofore for lack of quick and fresh Suit making after felons in due manner, and namely because of Franchises, where felons are received; it is provided, that all generally be ready and apparelled, at the Commandment and Summons of Sheriffs, and at the Cry of the Country, to sue[4] and arrest felons, when any need is, as well within Franchise as without and they that will not so do, and thereof be attainted, shall make a grievous Fine to the King. And if default be found in the Lord of the Franchise, the King shall take the same Franchise to himself, and if default be in the Bailiff, he shall have one year's imprisonment and after shall make a grievous fine; and if he have not whereof, he shall have imprison-

---

[1] The translations previous to Pulton read, "shall be delivered to the Bailiffs of the Town."

[2] Will not discharge him thereof. *Old Printed Copies.* Nabbe nougt therof idrawe to himsulf.—MS. Tr. 1.

[3] "Weakly kept."   [4] Pursue.

ment of two years. And if the Sheriff, Coroner, or any other Bailiff within such Franchise, or without, for Reward, or for Prayer, [or for fear [1]], or for any manner of Affinity, conceal, consent, or procure to conceal, the felonies done in their Liberties, or otherwise will not attach nor arrest such felons there, as they may, or otherwise will not do their Office, for favour borne to such Misdoers, and be attainted thereof, they shall have one year's imprisonment, and after make a grievous fine [at the King's Pleasure, if they have wherewith [2]]; and if they have not whereof, they shall have imprisonment of three years. [Repealed in part by Sheriffs Act, 1887 (50 & 51 Vict. c. 55 s. 39); remainder repealed by Coroners Act, 1887 (50 & 51 Vict. c. 71 s. 45 and Sch.).]

---

3 EDWARD I. c. 10.

THE STATUTES OF WESTMINSTER, A.D. 1275.

Who shall be chosen Coroners.—Their duties.

And forasmuch as mean persons, and undiscreet, now of late are commonly chosen to the office of Coroners, where it is requisite that persons honest, lawful, and wise should occupy such offices: It is provided, that through all Shires sufficient men shall be chosen to be Coroners, of the most wise and discreet Knights, which know, will, and may best attend upon such Offices, and which lawfully shall attach and present Pleas of the Crown: and that Sheriffs shall have Counter-Rolls with the Coroners, as well of Appeals, as of Inquests, of attachments, or of other things which to that office belong; and that no Coroner demand nor take any thing of any man to do his Office, upon pain of great forfeiture to the King. [Repealed by Coroner's Act, 1887 (50 & 51 Vict. c. 71, sec. 45, 3rd Sch.).]

[1] The words in brackets are not in the original, nor in transcations previous to Pulton.

[2] The words in brackets are not in translations previous to Pulton.

4 EDWARD I.

A.D. 1275-76.

Officiū Coronatoris or *De Officio Coronatoris.*
The office of the Coroner.

A Coroner of our Lord the King ought to inquire of these things.

i. If he be certified by the King's Bailiffs, or other honest men of the country: First he shall go to the places where any be slain, or suddenly dead, or wounded, or where houses are broken, or where treasure is said to be found, and shall forthwith command four of the next Towns, or five or six to appear before him in such a place.

ii. And when they are come thither: The Coroner, upon the oath of them shall inquire in this manner, that is to wit,

If they know where the person was slain, whether it were in any house, field, bed, tavern, or company, and who were there: Likewise it is to be inquired, who were culpable either of the Act, or of the force, and who were present, either men or women, and of what age soever they be, if they can speak or have any discretion.

iii. And how many soever be found culpable by Inquisition in any of the manners aforesaid, they shall be taken and delivered to the Sheriff and shall be committed to the Gaol.

iv. And such as be found and be not culpable, shall be attached until the coming of the Justices, and their name shall be written in the Coroner's Rolls.

v. If it fortune any such man be slain, which is found in the fields, or in the woods, first it is to be inquired, whether he were slain in the same place or not;

vi. And if he were brought and laid there, they shall do so much as they can to follow their steps that brought the body thither, whether he were brought upon a horse or in a cart.

vii. It shall be inquired also if the dead person were known, or else a stranger, and where he lay the night before.

viii. And if any be found culpable of the murder the Coroner shall immediately go into his house, and shall inquire what goods he hath, and what corn he hath in his Graunge; and if he be a freemen they shall inquire how much land he hath and what it is worth yearly; and further what corn he hath upon the ground.

ix. And when they have thus inquired upon everything, they shall cause all the land, corn, and goods to be valued, in like manner as if they should be sold incontinently, and thereupon they shall be delivered to the whole Township which shall be answerable before the Justices for all.[1]

x. And likewise of his freehold, how much it is worth yearly over and above the Service due to the Lords of the Fee; and the land shall remain in the King's Hands until the Lords of the Fee have made Fine for it.

xi. And immediately upon these things being inquired, the Bodies of such persons being dead or slain shall be buried.

In like manner it is to be inquired of them that be drowned, or suddenly dead: and after, such bodies are to be seen whether they were so drowned or slain or strangled by the sign of a cord tied straight about their necks, or about any of their members or upon any other hurt found upon their bodies, whereupon they shall proceed in the form aforesaid.

(2) And if they were not slain, then ought the

---

[1] For the same.

Coroner to attach the finders and all others in the company.

(3) A Coroner also ought to inquire of Treasure that is found who were the finders and likewise who is suspected thereof; and that may be well perceived where one liveth riotously haunting tavern and hath done so of long time; hereupon he may be attached for this suspicion by four or six or more pledges if he may be found.

(4) Further, if any be appealed of Rape, he must be attached, if the appeal be Fresh, and they must see apparent sign of truth by effusion of blood, or an open cry made.

(5) And such shall be attached by four or six pledges if they may be found:

(6) If the appeal were without cry, or without any manifest sign or token two pledges shall be sufficient.

(7) Upon Appeal of wounds and such like, especially if the wounds be mortal, the parties appealed shall be taken immediately and kept until it be known perfectly, whether he that is hurt shall recover or not;

(8) And if he die, the defendant shall be kept; and if he recover health, they shall be attached by four or six pledges, after as the wound is great or small.

(9) If it be for a maim, he shall find no less than four pledges; if it be for a small wound (*without a maim*) two pledges shall suffice.

(10) Also all wounds ought to be viewed, the length, breadth and deepness, and with what weapons, and in what part of the body the wound or hurt is; and how many be culpable, and how many wounds there be, who gave the wound.

(11) All which things must be enrolled in the Roll of the Coroners.

(12) Moreover if any be appealed of any act done, as principal, they that be appealed of the force

shall be attached also and surely kept in ward until the principals be attainted or delivered.

(13) Concerning horses, boats, carts (*mills*) etc., whereby any are slain, that properly are called deodands,[1] they shall be valued and delivered into the Towns, as before is said.

(14) Concerning wreck of the Sea, wheresoever it be found, if any lay hands on it, he shall be attached by sufficient pledges, and the price of the wreck shall be valued and delivered to the Towns.

(15) If any be suspected of the Death of any man being in danger of life he shall be taken and imprisoned as before is said;

(16) In like manner Huy shall be levied for all murders, burglaries and for men slain, or in peril to be slain,[2] as otherwhere is used in England, and all shall follow the Huy and Steps,[3] as near as can be; and he that doth not, and is convict thereupon, shall be attached to be afore the Justices of the Gaol, &c. [Repealed by Coroners Act, 1887 (50 & 51 Vict. c. 71, s. 45, 3rd Sch.).]

---

12 EDWARD I. c. 2.

THE STATUTES OF WALES, A.D. 1284.

Regulations of the jurisdiction and its divisions into Counties, etc. Sheriffs and other officers appointed.

We have provided and by our command ordained, that the Justice of Snowden shall have the custody and government of the peace of us the King in Snowden, and our lands in Wales adjoining; and shall administer Justice to all persons whatsoever, according to original writs of us the King and also the laws and customs underwritten.

---

[1] So in all translations—query "fines." See Spelm. and Du Cange in Bannum: Bannus.
[2] Homicides and burglaries.
[3] Hue and cry.

We likewise will and ordain that there be Sheriffs, Coroners, and Bailiffs of Commotes in Snowden, and our land of those parts. A Sheriff of Anglesea under whom shall be the whole land of Anglesea with its Cantreds, Metes and Bounds. A Sheriff of Caernarvan under whom shall be the Cantred of Arvan, the Cantred of Asthlencoyth, the Commote of Creethin, the Cantred of Thleen and the Commote of Yvionith. A Sheriff of Merioneth, under whom shall be the Cantred of Merioneth, the Commote of Ardovey, and the Commote of Penthlin, and the Commote of Deyrinoin with their Metes and Bounds. A Sheriff of Flint, under whom shall be the Cantred of Englefeud, the land of Maillor Sexeneyth and the Land of Hope, and the land adjoining to our Castle and Town of Rothelan unto the town of Chester, shall from henceforth be obedient under us to our Justices of Chester and shall answer for the issues of the same Commote at our Exchequer of Chester. There shall be Coroners in the same Counties, to be chosen by the King's Writ, the tenor whereof is to be found among the original Writs of the Chancery. There shall likewise be Bailiffs of Commotes, who shall faithfully do and discharge their Offices, and diligently attend thereto, according to what shall be given them in charge by the Justice and Sheriffs A Sheriff of Carmarthen with its Cantreds and Commotes and antient Metes and Bounds. A Sheriff of Cardigan and Llampeter with its Cantreds and Commotes and Metes and Bounds. There shall be Coroners in these Counties, and Bailiffs of Commotes as before. [Repealed by Stat. Law Rev. Act, 1887 (50 & 51 Vict. c. 59 Sch.).]

---

12 EDWARD I. c. 8.

THE STATUTES OF WALES, A.D. 1284.

Of the office of Sheriff in Wales; and the Manner of holding Courts.

The Sheriff ought to execute his office in this form, to wit: When any one shall have complained to him of an

Trespass done to him against the peace of our Lord the King, or of the taking and wrongful detaining of Cattle, or of an unjust taking, or of debt, or any other contract not fulfilled and the like, either by Writ or without Writ, first let him take pledges of prosecuting his claim, or the party's oath if he be a poor man, and afterwards make execution as is more declared, in this manner, the Defendants in each case shall be summoned to be at the next County Court, to answer unto the plaintiffs; at which court, after summons made and proof thereof, if they come not, they shall be summoned again by Award of the Court, to be at another Court next ensuing, to answer as before; at which, if they come not, after summons repeated and proof thereof, they shall be summoned by Award of the Court a third time, to be at the next third County Court to answer as before; at which court, if they come not, then the plaintiffs by Judgment of the Court, as well in Pleas by Writ as Plaints without Writ, shall recover their demands together with damages or amends, as well in moveables as immoveables, according as the Actions require. And for such defaults a penalty shall be incurred to our Lord the King according to the Law and Custom of Wales. And when the parties shall have appeared to plead, each shall be received without Fine to relate the truth of his case; and according to the plaints, answers, and allegations on either side, shall be the proceeding to Judgment for the plaintiff or defendant by the award of the County Court, and the punishment shall be according to the quality and quantity of the offence. And it is to be known that the County Court ought to be holden in this manner, to wit, from Month to Month, in such place as our Lord the King shall ordain; and this upon Monday in one County, upon Tuesday in another, upon Wednesday in a third county, and upon Thursday in a fourth, and not upon any other days. And the Sheriff shall proceed thus in the holding of his County Court:—

First he shall hear and receive before himself and the Coroner and the Suitors of the County, the Presentments of Felonies and of Casualties that shall have happened between two Counties, touching the death of a man in this manner; that the four Townships next to the place where the fact of Manslaughter or Mis-adventure shall have happened, shall come to the next County Court, together with him that found the dead man, and the Welshery, that is, the kindred of the Person slain, and there shall present the fact of felony, the case of mis-adventure, and the manner of either: Declaring thus, that on such a day, at such a place, it fell out that such an one, known or unknown, was found slain feloniously, or drowned, or otherwise dead by mis-adventure, and such an one found him, who is present, etc. and that presentment shall be forthwith inrolled, as well in the Coroner's Roll as in the Sheriff's. And if there should be present man or woman that would sue by appeal, there shall be pledges to prosecute taken forthwith, and the appeal shall be sued in that County Court. So that if the appellees should appear, they shall straight be taken, and detained in the prison of our Lord the King until the coming of Justice, and be safely kept; and if they should not appear, then upon the prosecution of the appellor they shall be exacted from one County Court to another; and if they come not at the fourth Court, or be not taken to pledge, they shall be outlawed and women shall be waived. And if they should not appear at the first County Court where they shall be exacted, their lands and chattels shall be forthwith taken and seised in the hands of our Lord the King, and shall be delivered into Ward to the Townships, as hereunder. In the same manner shall the proceeding be in an appeal of Wounding, Mayhem, Rape, Arson, and Robbery, against the Appellees if they should not appear. And if they should appear, and find sufficient pledges, six at the least, or more, to abide Judgment at the coming of the Justice, they shall straight be replevied. And it is to be known, that the proceeding to Outlawry is not to have place against Appellees of Force, Command, Direction, or Receit, until some one be convicted of the fact. [Repealed by Stat. Law Rev. Act, 1887 (50 & 51 Vict. c. 59 Sch.).]

12 EDWARD I. c. 5.

THE STATUTES OF WALES, A.D. 1284.

De officio Coronatoris.

Of the office of Coroner; that is to say, of the Pleas of the Crown in Wales.

<small>Election of the Coroner.</small> It is provided, that in every Commote in Wales there shall be one Coroner at the least who shall be chosen in the full County Court, by the Writ of our Lord the King, according to the form among other Royal Writs in the following Roll contained; and he shall there make oath before the Sheriff, that he will be faithful to our Lord the King, and that he will faithfully do and execute all things belonging to the office of Coroner. And his office shall be this.

<small>His Office; In cases of Homicide; and dangerous Wounding.</small> That when he shall be required by any one to come to view a man dead by Felony, or Drowned, or in any other manner dead by Misadventure; and also to view a man grievously wounded, so that his life be despaired of, that he shall forthwith require the Sheriff or Bailiff of the Commote to cause to come before him at a certain day, and place, all persons of twelve years of age and upwards of that Town wherein the casualty shall have happened, and of the four Townships next adjoining; and by their oaths he shall faithfully, cautiously, and secretly and diligently make inquiry of the Felony, the Felons and their Chattels; likewise of the fact and manner thereof, that is to say, who hath been guilty of the fact, who of force, and what manner of force, who of command or direction, and who of Receit after the fact; and of the chattels of those who shall be found guilty thereof by the Inquest. He shall likewise make Inquiry who first found the body and his name shall be enrolled, and he shall be attached by pledges, whose names shall be enrolled, to come to the next County Court, and also before the Justice in his Circuit. <small>Inrollment of proceedings in such cases.</small> And, the Inquisition being made, he shall forthwith cause the same to be inrolled distinctly and openly, together with the names of those who shall have

been found guilty, and their Chattels; and he shall secretly deliver to the Sheriff, if he be present, or to the Bailiff of the Commote, their names in writing; giving in charge on the behalf of our Lord the King, that straight their bodies be taken and safely kept in the prison of our Lord the King until they stand upon their acquittal in the Court of our Lord the King. And he shall cause their Chattels to be faithfully appraised and shall set down in his Roll as well the particular chattels, as the value thereof; and shall cause the said chattels by the view of the Sheriff or Bailiff, and of the other liege Subjects of our Lord the King who shall be there present, to be delivered to every of the Townships wherein the said chattels shall severally be found; that they may duly answer for the same upon the coming of the Justice of our Lord the King. The Coroner, when he shall make inquisition concerning the dead, shall inquire of the Welshery, that is to say, the kindred of the dead man. And if any one on the part of the father, and another on the part of the mother shall appear, and say that they are of his kindred, and the same be testified by liege subjects of the King, he shall straight cause their names to be inrolled in this Roll. But if none of the kindred should appear, it shall likewise be inrolled in his Roll that none doth appear; that the Justice at his coming may the more clearly proceed in what is yet to be done thereupon. The Coroner shall also diligently make inquiry of the happening of the accident, and the manner thereof; and according to what he shall find upon the Inquest, shall cause the same to be distinctly inrolled. He shall likewise inquire who found the body, and cause his name to be inrolled as above.

Moreover when a Thief, or Manslayer, or other Malefactor shall fly to the Church, the Coroner, as soon as he shall be certified thereof, shall direct the Bailiff of our Lord the King for that Commote to cause to come before him at a certain day the good and lawful men of the neighbourhood; and in their presence, after recognition made of the Felony, shall cause the abjuration to be made in this manner:— *Sanctuary.*

Abjuring the Realm.

That the Felon shall be brought out unto the Church Door, and a Sea Port shall be assigned to him by the Coroner, and then he shall abjure the realm; and, according as the port assigned shall be far or near, the term shall be set for his going out of the Realm aforesaid: So that in Journeying towards that Port, bearing in his hand a Cross, he shall not in any manner turn out of the King's highway, that is to say, neither upon the right hand, nor upon the left, but shall always hold to the same until he shall depart the Realm. [Repealed in part by 6 Geo. 4, c. 50, s. 62 (as to summoning persons of twelve years). Repealed by Stat. Law Rev. Act, 1887 (50 & 51 Vict. c. 59, sch.). Also repealed by Coroners Act, 1887 (50 & 51 Vict. c. 71, s. 45, sch. 3).]

---

12 EDWARD I. c. 6, s. 9.

THE STATUTES OF WALES, A.D. 1284.

The form of the Writ for choosing a Coroner.

The King to the Sheriff, Greeting; We command you, that in your full County Court, and by the assent of the same County, you cause a Coroner to be chosen; who having taken the oath, as the custom is, shall hereafter do and observe those things that belong to the office of Coroner in the aforesaid County. And that you cause to be chosen, one who hath best knowledge and ability to execute that office; and that you make known unto us his Name, Dated, etc. And if he should be sick, or should die, or for any other cause be unable to execute his office, then let another Writ be made changing what ought to be changed. [Repealed by Stat. Law Rev. Act, 1887 (50 & 51 Vict. c. 59 sch.); also repealed by Coroners Act, 1887 (50 & 51 Vict. c. 71, s. 45, sch. 3)].

12 EDWARD I. c. 7, s. 5.

The Statutes of Wales, A.D. 1284.

Of Pleas, some are to be determined by the Assize, some by Juries.

The deforciant[1] may allege many other things against the Assize; to wit, that the Ancestor of whose death, etc. committed Felony, for which he was hanged, outlawed or as a public thief escaping, and not obedient to the Law, beheaded; or that he abjured Wales, upon confession of the Felony before the Coroner. *(Other defences of the Deforciant.)*

The deforciant may also object Bastardy to the demandant; and thereupon the Bishop of the place shall be directed to make inquiry of the truth of the fact; and thereof to certify the Chief Justice of Wales; and according to what the Bishop shall have certified, they shall proceed to Judgment, without taking the Assize. And if the Bishop return that he is a Bastard, he shall be estopped from making the demand; and if he return that he is legitimate the Justice shall cause the Deforciant to come by summons, and if it be necessary, by Re-Summons; reserving to the King as hath been often said the Amercement for default. After the Re-Summons, whether he come or not, the demandant shall recover his demand by the Bishop's testimony, whose testimony shall not be gainsayed; and he shall remain in the King's mercy. Many other things he may allege which is hard to enumerate; as that the ancestor on whose death the Assize is arraigned was a villain, and held the land in Villenage; or that he held it at Will, or for term of life, or years: In which cases the Assize of Mortdancester lieth not. And the above assizes of Novel Disseisin or Mortdancester ought not to be taken but in their proper Counties, lest the Country should be overcharged with trouble and expence; but the Assizes shall be taken by the Justice twice, thrice or four times in the year. [Repealed by Stat. Law Rev. Act, 1887 (50 & 51 Vict. c. 59, Sch.).]

[1] The deforciant is one who keeps out of possession the rightful owner of an estate.

12 EDWARD I. c. 8. ss. 1 AND 3 (PARTS RELATING TO THE CORONER).

S. 1. It hath been treated in Writs and Assizes and of the proceeding therein. It behoveth now to speak of Pleas that are to be determined by Inquests or by Juries.

* * * * *

S. 3. And by the verdict of the Inquest shall the Plea be determined; because pleas of land in those parts are not to be determined by battle, nor by the Grand Assize. So if he (the deforciant) should accept the Ancestor or any one in the descent committed felony, whereby the action lieth not for him; in which case, if he, to whom this is opposed denieth it, the matter ought rather to be determined by the Record of the Justice, or of the Inquest of the country of the hanging and beheading, and also by the Record of the Coroner of the Outlawry and Abjuration. In like manner, on the demand of a tenement that ought to revert after a term past, or by the condition of the gift, upon the Affirmation of the one party and the denial of the other, they shall descend to the Inquest of the country, and according to their verdict shall the Judgment be. [Repealed by Stat. Law Rev. Act, 1887 (50 & 51 Vict. c. 59, Sch.).]

Record of Coroner of outlawry and abjuration to determine Pleas.

---

14 EDWARD I. STAT. 1.

THE STATUTES OF EXETER, A.D. 1285–86.

No date is assigned to this Act in the authorised version of the Statutes. *Vide* vol. i. p. 210.[1]

This is the form ordained by the King and his Council, whereby the Inquirers ought to take the Inquests against

---

[1] In the printed copies this Statute is ascribed to 14 Edw. I. It is printed as two instruments, the first entitled, "Statutum Exonie de Inquisitione facienda super Coronatores," and the second, "Articuli super precedens Statutum Exonie." No translation either of the Statute or articles has been printed in any copy of the Statutes at large; but in Rastall's English Collection is contained an incorrect and imperfect translation of the Statute

THE STATUTES. 51

a Coroner, how he hath borne himself in his office. It is **Proceedings of Enquirers in summoning Bailiffs of Hundreds, etc.** provided and ordained, that the Enquirers shall command the Sheriff of the place, that he do cause to come at a certain day, and at a certain place, which shall be assigned him by the aforesaid Enquirers, all the Bailiffs within the Wapentakes, Hundreds and Franchises, that are and have been Bailiffs or Beadles, if they be living, during the time when P. de C. was the Coroner of our Lord the King in that County; that is to say, all that are and have been Bailiffs or Beadles within the Precincts of Bailiwick belonging to that Coroner, or without, if need be. And that they do also cause to come before them the Coroner, concerning whom they take the Inquest, with all his Rolls of the whole time of his being Coroner of our Lord the King and all his clerks who are living. And the Enquirers **Sealing up the Coroner's Rolls.** shall forthwith safely seal, with their seals, all the Rolls of the aforesaid Coroner, and re-deliver them to the Coroner, that he may have them ready when the Justices in Eyre shall come to sit in that County, or that the King shall otherwise ordain in the matter. And if the Coroner be dead, after the same manner shall it be done to his heir, for his father's time; so that neither the Coroner nor his heir, nor their clerks may forge the Rolls against the coming of the Justices, nor otherwise do any thing, in what may respect the Crown, to the prejudice of the King and damage of the people, and in hindrance of any man's Right as they have heretofore done.

And, afterwards the Enquirers before named shall **Oaths and Charge of Bailiffs.** cause all the aforesaid Bailiffs to swear, that they will well and faithfully do that which they shall give them in charge on the King's behalf, and keep the King's counsel. And then when they shall have made the oath, every bailiff of a Wapentake, Hundred, and Franchise shall be severally charged to bring before the Enquirers aforesaid, at a day, in a place certain, that shall be given him by

---

only. The Statute and the Articles were printed by Cay from MS. *Cott. Claudius*, D. II. (fo. 228 b and 256 b, as separate Articles). In MS. Harl. 395, fo. 65 b, the Statute and the Articles form one instrument, as in the text, with the title, " Statuta edita apud Exoniam."

E 2

them, the names of all the Towns, Half-Towns, and Hamlets within his Wapentake, Hundred, and Franchise, written in a Roll, and at the same day and place shall deliver them to the aforesaid enquirers: And afterwards the Enquirers shall charge the aforesaid Bailiffs to cause to come before them at a certain day and place which they shall appoint, from each town eight men, from an half-town six men, and from an Hamlet four, of the best and most lawful men except the Lords of such Towns, Half-Towns, and Hamlets aforesaid, by whom the aforesaid Enquirers shall take the grand Inquest of twelve, of each Wapentake, Hundred, and Franchise, and town answering by twelve, if there be any in the Precinct aforesaid; and every one of the aforesaid eight, six, and four men shall have a seal. And if the aforesaid Towns, Half-Towns and Hamlets be deficient, so that they have not so many freemen, there shall be added some from the best and most discreet and lawful bondsmen, and each shall have a Seal. And then the Enquirers shall choose out of the eight, six; and out of the six, four; and out of the four two; of the best and most lawful, at their discretion; and shall then charge them on the King's behalf with the following oath:—

Forming the Grand Inquest.

Here this you A. and B. enquirers assigned by our Lord the King, that I will truth say, and nothing conceal, nor suffer to be concealed nor suppress before you, for promise or gift for Terrour or doubt, nor for affinity or alliance, nor for love or hatred, nor by others abetting or procuring: nor for any other matter will I be let from saying or presenting to you the truth of what you shall direct and give me in charge upon this Inquest for the King: So help me God and the Saints according to my knowledge of that which I have for Inquiry, or may in any manner obtain. Amen.

Oath of the Grand Inquest.

This oath, every town, half-town and Hamlet shall make severally; and the afore-named Enquirers shall charge the twelve with the same oath; after this the Enquirers shall deliver to the sworn men of each Town, Half-Town and Hamlet, of each Wapentake, Hundred, and Franchise, within the precinct aforesaid, and without if

Charge and presentment of the Grand Inquest.

need be, the articles under written; and shall enjoin them on the King's behalf, the freemen upon pain of disherison and the bondmen of perpetual imprisonment, if they aught conceal or suppress for any cause or for any person, that what shall come to their knowledge by any manner or means of Inquiry, they shall deliver and present to the Enquirers before named, and to the Dozen of their Wapentake, Hundred and Franchise under their Seals, in the form which the Enquirers shall direct them; each Town, Half-Town and Hamlet by itself. And their presentment ought to be by way of Cyrograph and both parts sealed under their Seals, with their Seals pendant; and one part, they shall deliver to the Enquirers, and the other part, they shall retain to themselves, and shall give them forth to the Twelve when they shall be sworn, at such time as the enquirers shall direct them, so that the twelve may be the better certified of their presentment of the same verdict before the aforesaid enquirers, when they shall take their Inquest.

First. Inquest is to be taken of every Town, Half-Town and Hamlet, and they are to be enjoined on the King's behalf, and upon their oath, that they do lawfully present without any concealment, all the accidents and abjurations, appeals of men taken within the Mainour, Murders and Felonies done, by whom, and when, in Land, Wood, Marsh, Water, within Towns or without, and everywhere within the Marches of Hundreds, of every Town, Half-Town, and Hamlet for the whole time of the Coroner aforesaid, or of him who by virtue of the office of Coroner, ought to intermeddle. And whether the Coroner in his proper person went thither to do his duty, or sent another in his stead to do that which belonged to him to do. And if he did so, how many times, and for how many accidents, And who it was that went in his stead. And if the Coroner went thither willingly, without making delay or Excuse, by his best endeavour or not. Or if he demanded any thing, or his clerk took any thing for his hasting to do his office, or if he wilfully stayed back for the sake of gain, after he had knowledge of the accident upon being sent for; how and what thing, and how much, and by whose

<small>The Articles of the Inquest.</small>

<small>Attendance of the Coroner.</small>

<small>Extortion by him.</small>

hand, and how often they did so. And if the goods of felons, as well by their friends as by others, have been heretofore duly appraised before the Coroner, and delivered to the town to be kept, as they ought to be, upon good inquest, or not appraised, and entered in his Roll. And if the Coroner hath taken ought of any man for making a false inquest, by procurement to suppress any man's right; or to appraise the goods at less than their value, in prejudice of the Crown, and to the loss of our Lord the King or any other; or if he caused the matters entered in his Roll to be inrolled falsely, or otherwise than had been found by lawful Inquest and presented to him; how and what, and how much and how often, and in what matter he took it for such falsifying, and by whose hand, whether the Coroner or his clerk. Or if he or his clerk have taken any of the goods to themselves, after they have been appraised, and caused them to be entered in his Rolls at a less price than they were appraised at by the Inquest, in order to discharge himself in part at the coming of the Justices, and falsely to charge the town; how and what thing. Or if any appeal of Rape, or the like matter belonging to his office, be caused to be falsely inrolled, or suffered to be suppressed by himself or another, or to be withdrawn from out of the Rolls after being inrolled: or would not readily receive the Plaint of a plaintiff by reason of poverty, or for hatred, in prejudice of the King and the Crown, and to the damage of the plaintiff, and the hindrance of Justice; or if on such Plaint, for promise, gift, affinity, fear, or favour of the adverse party, he caused the same to be suppressed or withdrawn as aforesaid; or took any thing for that cause; what, and how much, and by whose hand. And if he took any thing of the Towns where he made his abjurations and views; what, and how much, and by whose hand: and in what manner; or if he, or any on his behalf took and carried away any of the goods of any dead person upon whose body he made the view, how and what and how often, and if he made or caused to be made all the attachments belonging to his office in due manner or not. Or if he caused any man to be attached wrongfully for another, in

Suppressing of Appeals, Plaints, etc., by him.

another's name, in order to oppress him and obtain something from him, and maliciously caused it to be entered in his Rolls to the suppression of right, and falsely to grieve any one; by whose procurement and for what matter. Or if he executed his office at his own Costs, without taking anything of others, according to statutes or not. Or if at any County Court he hath concealed or suppressed, or procured to be suppressed any matter, to the grievance of the appellor or appellee, or any others to the prejudice of the King or the party, for fear, doubt, affinity, favour, gift, or promise, by any man's procurement. And if he hath, the manner how, by whom and wherefore, and for what bribe, for what cause, and how often, and in what case. And if all the attachments belonging to his office, he prosecuted and caused to be prosecuted faithfully and readily, as he ought to do for the King, and for the plaintiff, or not. And if the goods and chattels of persons flying from the towns of their abode, upon suspicion of Robberies, Murders, and Receits of Felons, found within the precinct of his bailiwick after their flight, he caused to be attached, and the same to be faithfully entered in his Rolls upon lawful Inquest; and to be delivered to the Towns where they were found, to be kept until the Eyre of the Justices as he ought to do; and if to others, to whom, and by what warrant, and for what thing; or if he hath taken away or suffered to be taken away, or embezzled or destroyed any appeal or any other sort of plaint unto him made; or by himself or by the procurement of any others withdrawn from his Rolls by the plaintiff or the other party, for any man abetting or other cause. And if he took any thing for such falsifying and suppression; what and how much, for what cause, and in what manner, and how often. Or if any Treasure were found in the time of the Coroner aforesaid, under ground or above, in what place and the manner of it, and how much and what treasure, and in whose hands remaining, and by whose delivery. And after this manner ought the Enquirers to go from Wapentake to Wapentake, Hundred, Franchise, and Towns answering by twelve, if there be such with the precinct or bailiwick belonging to the afore-

Extortion against the Statute.

Other neglects of duty.

Embezzling Records of Plaints, etc.

Treasure-trove.

The said articles shall be enquired of in every Wapentake, Hundred, etc.

said Coroner; and to deliver to the Jurors aforesaid of the aforesaid Towns, Half-Towns, and Hamlets, all the aforementioned articles of enquiry in writing, for them to take counsel secretly, and make Inquiry of the matters aforesaid. And a day shall be given them on the fourth day after they shall have received the articles, to give in their presentment, to the aforesaid enquirers, in certain places with their Seals pendant to their presentment. And if they need to have a longer day for their better information, it shall be given and granted them by the Enquirers. And as soon as the Enquirers shall have received all the presentments of the Towns, Half-Towns and Hamlets, they shall then cause to come before them, the twelve out of each Wapentake, Hundred, Franchise and Town, answering by twelve; and according to the points of the Articles before-mentioned; and in any other manner as the Enquirers shall deem best to ordain and provide, shall they be charged, and if it happen that the Enquirers find *Attaint of the inquest for falsehood, etc.* any wilful falsifying, hindrance, or concealment made by the twelve in their Inquests, they shall then always take against the twelve, twenty-four, all of whom shall be of the most lawful men of the County; and by the same oath before-mentioned, and by the articles in the same manner, shall they be charged. And if it happen that the twelve should be attainted by the twenty-four, they shall be attached; each man separately by good mainprise to have their bodies at whatsoever time the King shall direct and *Attaint of the Coroner.* if the Coroner or his clerk or other false procurer, in prejudice of the Crown be attainted, he shall be attached by good mainprise as aforesaid. And when the twelve give in their verdict to the aforesaid enquirers, they shall *Returns of presentments to the enquirers, and by them to the king, etc.* likewise make return to them of all presentments that have been delivered to them by the aforesaid Towns, Half-Towns, and Hamlets; and when the enquirers shall have taken the Inquests after this manner they shall seal those verdicts of the Twelve, and twenty-four, the which they shall hold the most true, under their seals, and send them unto the King by one of the Enquirers, and the King himself shall order right thereupon, and strict and secure punishment against the Coroner and his clerk, and all others who shall be attainted of having any thing done suppressed, or concealed, in prejudice of the Crown, or of having procured the same, whereby the King or any other hath suffered loss. [Repealed by Stat. Law Rev. Act, 1863 (26 & 27 Vict. c. 125, sch.).]

---

25 EDWARD I. c. 17.
THE GREAT CHARTER OF THE LIBERTIES OF ENGLAND CONFIRMED, A.D. 1297.

No Sheriff, Constable, [Escheator] Coroner, nor any other our Bailiffs shall hold Pleas of our Crown. [Repealed by Stat. Law Rev. Act, 1892. Concerning Sheriffs or Officer of a Sheriff, see Sheriffs Act, 1887 (50 & 51 Vict. c. 55, 3rd Sch.)]. *The Pleas of the Crown.*

---

28 EDWARD I. c. 3, s. 2.
ARTICLES UPON THE CHARTERS, A.D. 1300.

And forasmuch as heretofore many felonies committed within the verge have been unpunished, because the Coroners of the county have not been authorised to enquire of such manner of felonies done within the verge, but the Coroner of the King's House, which never continueth in one place, by reason whereof there can be no trial made in due manner, nor the felons put in exigent, nor outlawed, nor anything (thereof) presented in the Circuit, the which hath been to the great damage of the King, and nothing to the good preservation of his peace; it is ordained, that from henceforth in cases of the death of men, whereof the Coroner's Office is to make view and Enquest, it shall be commanded to the Coroner of the County, that he, with the Coroner of the (King's) House, shall do as belongeth to his office and inroll it. And that thing that cannot be determined before the Steward where[1] the felons cannot be attached[2] or for other *That Coroners shall inquire of the death of a man slain within the Verge.*

[1] Because.   [2] There.

like cause, shall be remitted to the Common Law, so that Exigents, Outlawries and Presentments, shall be made thereupon in Eyre by the Coroner of the country, as well as of other felonies done out of the Verge. Nevertheless, they, shall not omit by reason hereof to make attachments freshly upon the felonies done. [Repealed by the Coroners Act, 1887 (50 & 51 Vict. c. 71 s. 45 & 3rd Sch.)].

---

5 EDWARD II. c. 27.

THE NEW ORDINANCES,[1] A.D. 1311.

Of performing the office of Coroner within the Verge.

And forasmuch as heretofore many felonies done within the verge have been unpunished, because that the Coroners of the Country have not been authorised to enquire of such manner of felonies done within the verge, but the Coroner of the King's Household, by reason whereof there hath been no trial made in due manner nor the felons put in Exigent, nor outlawed, nor anything of such felony presented in Eyre which is to the great damage of the King, and the less secure maintenance of his peace: We do ordain, that from henceforth in case of homicide, whereof the Coroner's office is to make view and Inquest, it shall be commanded to the Coroner of the Country or of the Franchises where the dead persons shall be found, that he, together with the Coroner of the Household do execute the office which thereunto pertaineth, and shall enter it in his Roll: and of that which cannot be determined before the Steward, because that the felons cannot be attached or found, or for any other reason, the process shall remain at the Common Law, so that the Exigents, and the outlawries and the presentments made

---

[1] The text of these Ordinances (of which the above is one) is given from an exemplification of them under the Great Seal of King Edward II., preserved in the British Museum among the Cotton Charters.

In the Tower of London is preserved, among the Parliament Rolls, a Roll containing these Ordinances.

A Roll marked K. 11, containing these Ordinances, is in the Treasury of Canterbury Cathedral.

thereof be shewed in Eyre by the Coroner of the Country, as well as of other felonies done out of the verge; Nevertheless they shall not omit, by reason hereof, to make attachments freshly upon the felonies done: if they can be found [Repealed by 15 Edw. 2 (16 Edw. 2 Ruff. Ed.) (Revocation of the New Ordinances) 1322].

14 EDWARD III. STAT. 1, c. 8.
A.D. 1340.

Item. Whereas sometime there were no more but two Escheators in England, that is to say, one Escheator on this side Trent, and another beyond, whereby the King and the people were worse served than in the time when there were divers Escheators, and of less estate: It is assented and accorded, that from henceforth there shall be as many Escheators assigned, as were in the time when the King that now it did take the Governance of this Realm upon him; and that the same Escheators be chosen by the Chancellor, Treasurer and the Chief Baron of the Exchequer, taking to them the Chief Justices of the one Bench and the other, if they be present, in manner as is afore said of Sheriffs; and that no Escheator tarry in his office above a year; and that no Coroner be chosen unless he have land in Fee sufficient in the same County, whereof he may answer to all manner of people [Repealed by Coroners Act 1887 (50 & 51 Vict. c. 71, s. 45, & Sch. 3)]. *Coroners: their sufficiency*

28 EDWARD III.[1] c. 6.
A.D. 1354.

Item. It is ordained and accorded. That all Coroners of the Counties shall be chosen in the full Counties, by the Commons of the Counties. *Coroners shall be chosen by*

[1] In the old printed copies this is intituled "Statutum apud Westmonasterium de libertatibus Londoniarum," and in MS. Harl. 4999, "The Statute of Westminster of the Liberties of London."

the Commons of the same Counties of the most meet and most lawful people that shall be found in the said Counties to execute the said office: Saved always to the King and other lords which ought to make such Coroners, their Seigniories and Franchises [Repealed by Coroners Act, 1887 (50 & 51 Vict. c. 71, s. 45 & Sch. 3)].

---

34 EDWARD III. c. 4.
A.D. 1360–61.

Panels of inquests shall be of the neighbourhood.

Item. Because that the Sheriffs and other Ministers often do array their Panels in all manner of Inquests of people procured, and most far off from[1] the Counties which have no knowledge of the deed whereof the Inquest shall be taken: It is accorded, that such Panels shall be made of the next people, which shall not be suspect nor procured: and that the Sheriffs, Coroners, and other ministers which do against the same shall be punished before the Justices that take the said Inquest according to the quantity of their trespass, as well against the King as against the party, for the quantity of the damage which he hath suffered in such manner [Repealed as to England by 6 Geo. 4, c. 50 s, 62, and as to Ireland by 3 & 4 Will. IV. c. 91 s. 50].

---

2 HENRY V. STAT. 1, c. 8.
A.D. 1414.
Sects. 3, 4 and 5.

"On default of Justices, &c. in executing recited statute, Commissions shall be awarded to inquire of Riot and of such default."

* * * * *

Sect. 3. The Jury shall be returned by the Coroners if the Sheriff is in default.

And that the said commissioners presently shall return into the Chancery the Inquests and Matters before them in this behalf taken and found: And, moreover, that the Coroners of the same County for the time

[1] of.

THE STATUTES. 61

being in which County such Riot, Assembly, or Rout shall be made, shall make the Panel upon the said Commission returnable, for the time that the Sheriff so supposed in default shall continue in his office; which Coroners shall return no persons, but only such which have lands, Tenements, or Rents to the value of xl. (£10) by the year at least; And also that the same Coroners shall return upon every of the said persons empanelled at the first day when Issues be to be lost xx. s. (20s.) at the least, and at the second day xl. s. (40s.) at the least, and at the third day c. s. (100s.) at the least, and at every day after the double at the least; which issues so returned by cause of non-appearance of such persons empanelled shall be adjudged as forfeit to the King, and leviable to his use: and if default be found in the said Coroners, touching the return of such persons to be empanelled, or touching the returns of such Issues, as afore is said, that every of them shall forfeit to the King's use Forty Pounds: And if it happen that the said Sheriff so reputed in default, be discharged of his office at the time that such commission shall be awarded out of the Chancery, that then the new Sheriff of the same County, his successor mediate or immediate for the time being and not the Coroners of the Same County, shall make the panel upon this Commission returnable in manner and form, as the said Coroners should do in time when the Sheriff so reputed in default continued in his office, and that the same new Sheriff shall incur like Pain of Forty Pounds to the King, if any default in him be found touching the return of other persons by him empanelled, which have not Lands, Tenements, or Rents to the value of Ten Pounds by year, or for returning such issues as the said Coroners be above charged to return, as the said Coroners are to lose to the King in this behalf. [This statute is still extant.]

62 THE KING'S CORONER.

15 HENRY VI. c. 5.
A.D. 1436–37.
Sects. 2, 5, 7, 8 and 9.

"*Qualification of persons to be empanelled on juries in Attaint.*"

That no Sheriff, Bailiff of franchise, nor Coroner in actions or writs of Attaint of Plea of land, of the yearly value of xl. s. (40s.) or more, nor action of attaint of deeds concerning lands or tenements of like value, or more, nor of plea personal whereof the judgment of recovery shall extend to the sum of Forty Pounds, or more, shall return or empanel in any inquisition nor inquest, any persons but such as be inhabiting within his bailiwick, which have estate to their own use, or they to whose Use other persons have Estate, of Fee-Simple Fee-Tail, or Freehold, in lands and tenements, of the yearly value of xxli. or more in his bailiwick out of ancient Demesne the Five Ports, and the tenure of gavelkind; nor shall return in the King's Court less issues in the same actions of Attaint than xl. s. (40s.) at the first Writ of distress and c s. (£5) at the second writ of distress, and the double at every other writ of distress against the persons impanelled and returned to be sworn in the same actions. And that no person of less sufficiency of freehold than of the yearly value xx li (£20) in the form aforesaid, shall be sworn in the King's Court upon any issue in the said *Jurors not qualified may be challenged.* actions of Attaint if he be for the same by the plaintiffs in due form challenged.

And as often as any Sheriff, Bailiff of Franchise, or Coroner do contrary to this Ordinance, he shall pay, and by this Statute be bound to pay to the King x li (£10) and to the Plaintiffs in the said actions and Writs of Attaint for their delay other x li (£10).

On a foreign plea pleaded by any of the defendants in Attaint, Judgment against him shall be final. And if any of the foreign answers and pleas be tried found against any of the said defendants that then the same judgment against the same defendants and for the said plaintiffs, shall be given by the King's Justices, and consideration of his Courts, as by the law should be given against the same defendants, in case that the grand jury in the said actions and Writs of Attaint, upon the points and articles of the same Writs, had passed against the same defendants, and with the said plaintiffs; and that by the same judgments, no other of the said defendants, but they against whom the aforesaid foreign answers and pleas be found and tried, shall be prejudiced or endamaged. And that this statute touching the Office of Sheriff, Bailiff of Franchise, and Coroner, in returning of the said persons of the sufficiency of freehold of the yearly value of xx li (£20) and that no persons of less sufficiency of freehold be sworn in the said actions and Writs of Attaint shall not extend to Cities and Boroughs within the said Realm, nor to the Inhabitants in the same: Provided always that if in any of the said counties there be not persons inhabiting, under the estate of a Baron, of Possession of lands and tenements of the yearly value of xx li (£20) in the same County, in the form aforesaid, to suffice the number to be impanelled and returned in the said actions and writs of attaint, that then the Sheriff, Bailiffs of Franchises, and Coroners of the same County, shall impanel and return in the same actions and writs, persons there inhabiting, of the most sufficient of possession[1] of yearly value of lands and tenements, within the value of xx li (£20 per annum) in the same County in the form aforesaid: and that to such persons the said challenge extends not, that they be not of the possession of lands and tenements of the yearly value of xx li (£20) in the same County: and that as often as any of the same Sheriffs, Bailiffs and Coroners do contrary to present last Article, he shall pay to the King x li (£20) and to the said plaintiff x li (£20) in the form aforesaid. [Repealed as to England by Stat. Law Rev. Act, 1863 (26 & 27 Vict. c. 125), and as to Ireland by Stat. Law (I.) Rev. Act, 1872].

Not to extend to Cities or Boroughs, as to the qualifications of Jurors.

In defect of sufficient Jurors, in Counties others may be returned.

Penalty on Sheriffs (and Coroners) for neglect.

[1] Liflode.

28 HENRY VI. c. 9.

A.D. 1444-45.

Sects. 1, 5, 13 and 14.

Sect. 1.
No Sheriff shall let his County, &c., to ferm.

Item. The King, considering the great perjury, extortion, and oppression which be and have been in this Realm by his Sheriffs, Under Sheriffs, and their clerks, Coroners, Stewards of Franchises, Bailiffs and Keepers of prisons, and other officers in divers Counties of this Realm, hath ordained by authority aforesaid[1] in eschewing of all such extortion, perjury, and oppression, that no Sheriff shall let to ferm in any manner, his County, nor any of his Bailiwicks, Hundreds, nor Wapentakes.

Sect. 5.
No fee for returns or panels.

And that the Sheriff, Under Sheriff, Sheriff's clerk, Steward or Bailiff of Franchise, Servant of Bailiff or Coroner, shall not take anything by Colour of his office, by him nor by any other person to his use, of any person for the making of any return or panel, and for the copy of any panel, but fourpence.

Sect. 13.
Sheriffs shall make deputies in the King's Courts. Penalty offending against this Act.

And also that every of the said Sheriffs shall make yearly a deputy in the King's Courts of his Chancery, the King's Bench, the Common Place, and in the Exchequer, of Record, before that they shall return any Writs, to receive all manner of Writs and Warrants to be delivered to them; and that all Sheriffs, Under Sheriffs, Clerks, Bailiffs, Gaolers, Coroners, Stewards, Bailiffs of Franchises, or any other officers or Ministers, which do contrary to this Ordinance in any point of the same, shall lose to the party in this behalf indamaged or grieved, his treble damages, and shall forfeit the sum of forty pounds at every time that they or any of them do the contrary thereof in any point of the same, whereof the King shall have the one half, to be employed to the use of his house, and in no otherwise, and the party that will sue the other half.

[1] *I.e.* by Parliament in the "recital" of the statute.

THE STATUTES. 65

And that the Justices of Assizes in their Sessions, **Sect. 14.**
Justices of the one Bench and of the other, and Justices **Justices of Assizes, &c.**
of Peace in their County shall have power to inquire hear **may inquire of offenders**
and determine, of office without special Commission, of
these Ordinances
epealed by Sheriffs
d sch. 3), and the
Coroners by the
, s. 45, sch. 3).].

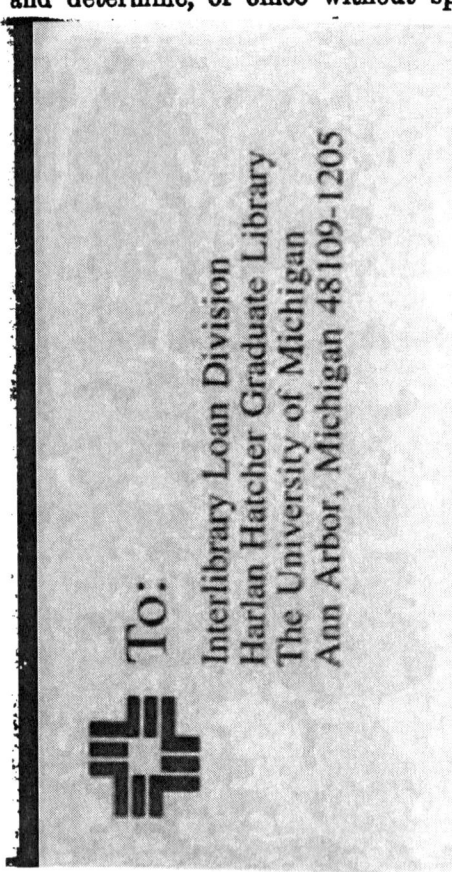

divers Sheriffs in **Sect. 1.**
of Writs to them **Extortion of Sheriffs in**
ghts of the Shires **levying wages**
of the King that **of Knights of the Shire.**
have levied more
Knights, and more
ing and retaining
use and profit, to
oss of the common
g, considering the **Sect. 2.**
ity aforesaid, that **Appointment**
me being, in the **of County Court to**
ounties, after the **assess such**
them, shall make **wages.**
and every Chief
ies, and the bailiffs
same county, and
of the Wages of
the next County
wages of the said
Knights, Sheriff, Coroners or **Sect. 3.**
Bailiffs for the time being, be there at the same time in **Penalty Sheriff,**
their proper persons, upon pain of forfeiture to the King, **for absen**

F

of every of them that maketh default, forty shillings. [Repealed as to England by the Stat. Law Rev. Act, 1863 (26 & 27 Vict. c. 125); as to Ireland by Stat. Law Ire. Rev. Act, 1872).].

---

3 HENRY VII. c. 2.[1]

A.D. 1487.

An Act against Murderers.[2]

The causes why murders be committed.

The King remembering how murders and slaying of his subjects daily increase in this land, the occasions whereof be divers, one that men in Towns where such murders hap to fall and be done, will not attach the murderer, where the law of the land is, that if any man be slain in the day, and the felon not taken, the township where the death or murder is done, shall be amerced; and if any man be wounded in peril of death, the party that so wounded should be arrested, and put in surety, till perfect knowledge be had, whether he so hurt should live or die: And the Crowner upon the View of the body dead, should inquire of him or them that had done that death or murder of their abettors and consentors, and who were present when the death or murder was done, whether man or woman, and the names of them that were present, and so found, to inrol and certify; which law by negligence is disused, and thereby great boldness is given to slayers and murderers; and over this it is used, that within the year and day after any death or murder had and done, the felon should not be determined at the King's suit, for saving of the party's suit, wherein the party is oftentimes slow, and also agreed with, and by the end of the year all is forgotten, which is another occasion of murder: And also he that will sue any appeal, must sue in proper person, which suit is long and costly, that it maketh the party appellant weary to sue: For reformation of the premisses, the King our Sovereign Lord, by the

Coroners shall exercise their office according to law.

[1] In all printed editions this forms part of Chapter I.
[2] In Lib. Scacc. Westm. xi. it is intituled "Against Coroners."

assent of the Lords Spiritual and Temporal, and the Commons, in this said parliament assembled, and by authority of the same, will that every Crowner exercise and do his office according to the law, as is afore rehearsed; and that if any man be slain or murdered, and those of the slayers, murderers, abettors, maintainers, and comforters of the same be indicted, that the same slayers and murderers and all other accessaries of the same be arraigned and determined of the same felony and murder, at any time, at the King's suit, within the year after the same felony and murder done, and not tarry the year and day for any appeal to be taken for the same felony or murder; and if it happen any person named as principal or accessary, to be acquitted of any such murder at the King's suit, within the year and day, that then the same justices afore whom he is acquitted, shall not suffer him to go at large, but either to remit him again to prison, or else to let him to bail, after their discretion, till the year and day be passed; and if it fortune the same felons or murderers, and accessaries so arraigned, or any of them, to be acquit, or the principal of the said felony, or any of them, to be attainted, the wife, or next heir to him so slain, as shall require, may take and have their appeal of the same death or murder within the year and day after the same felony and murder done against the said persons so arraigned and acquit, and all other their accessaries, or against the accessaries of the said principal, or any of them so attainted, or against the said principals so attainted, if they be then on life, and the benefit of his clergy thereof before not had: and that the Appellant have such and like advantage, as if the said acquittal or attainder had never been, the said acquittal or attainder notwithstanding: And over that, the wife, or heir of the person so slain or murdered, as case shall require, may commence their appeal in proper person, at any time within the year after the said felony done, before the Sheriff and Crowners of the County where the said felony or murder was done, or before the King in his bench, or Justices of gaol delivery; and the Appellant in any appeals of murder or death of man, where buttail by the course of the common law lieth not, (may) make

Murderers, &c., may be arraigned and tried within the year after the felony done, without waiting for appeal.

If acquitted they shall be secured to answer any appeal which may be sued against principals or accessaries, notwithstanding any such acquittal, &c.

Proceedings upon such appeals.

Appellant may appear by attorney, except where battle lieth.

Townships shall be amerced for escape of murderers by day.

their attorneys and appear by the same in the said appeals after they be commenced, to the end of the suit, and execution of the same. And if any person be slain or murdered in the day and the murderer scape untaken, that the township where the said deed is so done be amerced for the said escape, and that the Crowner have authority to inquire thereof upon the View of the body dead; and also Justices of the peace have power to inquire of such escapes, and that to certify afore the King in his bench; and that after the felony found, the Crowners deliver their inquisitions afore the justices of the next gaol-delivery in the shire where the inquisition is taken, the same justices to proceed against such murderers, if they be in the gaol, or else the same justices to put the same inquisitions afore the King in his bench.

Coroner's inquest returned to Justices of gaol delivery.

Coroner's fee on the view of the body. (Repealed 1 Hen. 8, c. 7; but see 25 Geo. 2 c. 29.)

And forasmuch as Crowners had not nor ought to have anything by the law for their office doing, which ofttimes hath been the occasion that Crowners have been remiss in doing their office, it is ordained, that a Crowner have for his fee, upon every inquisition taken upon the View of the body slain, thirteen shillings and fourpence of the goods and chattels of him that is slayer and murderer, if he have any goods and if he have no goods, then the Crowner have for his said fee, of such amerciaments as shall fortune any township to be amerced for escape of such murderer as is aforesaid.

Penalty on Coroner for neglect, five pounds.

And if any Crowner be remiss, and make not his inquisitions upon the View of the body dead, and certify not according as is afore ordained, that the Crowner for every default forfeit to the King an hundred shillings.

Justices of peace shall certify all recognisances to the next sessions.

And also it is ordained by the same authority, that every Justice of peace within this Realm that shall take any recognisance for the keeping of the peace, that the same justices do certify, send, or bring the same recognisance at the next sessions of peace, where he is or hath been Justice, that the party so bound may be called, and if the party make default, the same default then there to be recorded, and the same recognisance, with the record

THE STATUTES.

of the default, be sent and certified into the Chancery, or afore the King in his bench or into the King's exchequer. [Section 7 relating to fees extended by 25 Geo. 2, c. 29, ss. 2 and 3, but subsequently, as to County Coroners, repealed by Coroners Act, 1860 (23 & 24 Vict. c. 116, s. 3). But the whole Act, except from "and also it is ordained by the same authority" is repealed by Coroners Act, 1887 (50 & 51 Vict. c. 71, s. 45, sch. 3).].

---

1 HENRY VIII. c. 7.

A.D. 1509–10.

An Act concerning Coroners.

"Whereas by a Statute made at Westminster the "third year of King Henry VII. it was enacted that "a Coroner shall have for his fee upon every inquisition "taken upon the view of the body slain and murdered "thirteen shillings and fourpence of the goods and chattels "of him that is the slayer or murderer: Where by the "Common Law a Coroner had not nor ought not to have "any thing for their office doing as by the same statute "more plainly doth appear: Since which statute so made "the Coroners have used that if any person hath happened "to be slain by misadventure and not by no man's hand "that they will not enquire upon the view of the body "so by misadventure slain except they have for their "labour thirteen shillings and fourpence, which is contrary "to the Common Law and also to the Statute afore "rehearsed; whereby great inconvenience doth daily grow "to the King's Subjects, forasmuch as often-times the "person that is so by misadventure slain lieth long above "the ground unburied, to the great annoyance of the King's "liege people": Wherefore the King our Sovereign Lord by the assent of his Lords Spiritual and Temporal and the Commons in this present parliament assembled and by authority of the same, ordaineth, that upon a request made to a Coroner to come and inquire upon the view

Statute 3 Hen. VII. c. 1 recited.

No fee due to a Coroner on view of person slain by misadventure (but see 25 Geo. II c. 29).

of any person slain drowned or otherwise dead by misadventure, the said Coroner diligently do his office upon the view of the body of every such person or persons without anything taking theretofore upon pain to every Coroner that will not endeavour himself to do his office as afore is said or that he taketh anything for doing of his office upon any person dead by misadventure for every time Forty Shillings. And that the Justices of Assises, Justices of Peace within the County where any such default of Coroners be, have authority and power to enquire thereof and determine the same as well by examination as by presentment. [Repealed by Coroners Act, 1887 (50 & 51 Vict. c. 71, s. 45).]

Justices, &c., shall determine defaults.

---

27 HENRY VIII. c. 24, ss. 10 AND 11.

A.D. 1535-36

An Act for re-continuing certain Liberties and Franchises heretofore taken from the Crown.

Sect. 10. Jurisdiction of the King's Court and his officers within Liberties.

And over this it is ordained by authority aforesaid that in all such places wheresoever the King's Highness in his own most royal person shall come to rest, tarry, abide or make his repose, within this Realm, or any his dominions within Liberty or without, there and within the Verge limited and accustomed to his Grace's Court during the time of his abode his Grace his Steward, Marshall, Coroner and all other his Ministers shall and may keep their courts for Justice and exercise their offices as shall appertain to them according to the laws, customs and Statutes of this Realm as well within Liberties as without; and that his Grace's Clerks of the Market and none other, during the same time as well within Liberties as without, shall exercise the office of Clerk of the Market; any privilege, grant, allowance or other thing to the contrary hereof notwithstanding.

Sect. 11. Saving for the City of London.

Provided always that this article next afore rehearsed or anything therein contained be not in any wise prejudicial to the City of London, but that the same City shall have and use such liberties as they might if this article had never been made. [This Statute is still extant.]

27 HENRY VIII. c. 26, s. 3.

A.D. 1535–36.

An Act for laws and justice to be ministered in Wales in like form as it is in this Realm.

* * * * *

And that the Sheriff, Eschetours and Coroner that hereafter shall be within the said County or Shire of Monmouth shall be obliged and bounden to execute all the King's process and to make due returns thereof, and to use and exercise their offices according to the laws and Statutes of this Realm of England, in all and every thing as the Sheriffs, Eschetours and Coroners be obliged and bounden to do in all and every other Shire of this Realm of England and that Sheriff and Eschetours of the said Shire or County of Monmouth, that hereafter shall be appointed by our Sovereign Lord the King, make their accounts for their said offices in the King's Exchequer in England, in like manner and form as other Sheriffs and Eschetours do within this Realm of England, and upon such like pain and penalty as is upon the other Sheriffs and Eschetours in every other shire within this Realm of England. [Repealed by Sheriffs Act, 1887 (50 & 51 Vict. c. 55, s. 39 and sch. 3) except so far as relates to Escheators and Coroners. Also repealed by Stat. Law Rev. Act, 1887 (50 & 51 Vict. c. 59, s. 1 and sch.) except as relates to Coroners.]

The Sheriffs, Escheators, and Coroners shall execute and return Processes, and account as in England.

32 HENRY VIII. c. 12.

A.D. 1540.

Concerning Sanctuary.[1]

Sect. 1. All sanctuaries except churches and churchyards and places expressly reserved by this Act shall be abolished.

Sect. 2. Certain places declared to be Sanctuaries for all Offenders, except as after mentioned. No Sanctuaries whatever shall protect persons guilty of murder, rape, burglary, robbery, arson, sacrilege, or their accessories, &c.

Sect. 3. Persons may remain in one sanctuary forty days unless called on by the Coroner to abjure and remain in some sanctuary during his life. And be it further enacted by authority aforesaid that if at any time hereafter any person or persons do take any refuge or sanctuary in any parish church or churchyard Cathedral Church collegiate or other chapel dedicate commonly used as parish churches or in the cemetery to any of them belonging, for any offence other than such as be excepted or foreprised by this Act that then the said person or persons so taking sanctuary and refuge shall and may abide and remain there by the space of forty days as hath been aforesaid used, using himself in all points according to the laws and statutes of the realm; unless the Coroner in the meantime repair unto him for the taking of his abjuration, in which case upon repair of the said Coroner he shall and may abjure after the laws and Statutes of this realm, to any of the said territories and privileged places before named, not being full of the number as hereafter to every of the said places by this Act shall be appointed, there to abide and remain during his life, using himself in such like order condition and fashion in all things and points as heretofore hath been ordered and appointed by the statutes and laws of this realm for and concerning the good order of sanctuary persons, to be observed used and kept within privileged sanctuaries or else to lose the benefit of their said privilege and upon the penalties comprised in the said statutes.

[1] The whole of this statute is full of interest and worthy of perusal. *Vide* The Statutes of the Realm, vol. iii. pp. 756–8.

And it is further enacted that if the Coroner of the Shire or place where any person or persons shall take any refuge or sanctuary in any of the said churches or churchyards, cathedrals churches hospitals churches collegiate chapels dedicate commonly used as Parish Churches or any cemeteries to them or any of them belonging, upon reasonable request to him made do refuse to come in convenient time unto such person being in sanctuary as afore is said there to take his confession and abjuration according to the laws of this realm that then the said Coroner for every such default shall lose and forfeit to our Sovereign Lord the King one hundred shillings. [Repealed by Stat. Law Rev. Act, 1863 (26 & 27 Vict. c. 125, sch.).]

Sect. 4. Penalty on Coroners neglecting to attend and take abjurations.

---

32 HENRY VIII. c. 20, s. 7.

A.D. 1540.

The Liberties to be used.

Provided always and be it enacted by authority aforesaid that in all such of the said liberties franchises and privileged places and every of them, limited to the said Court of Augmentations and to the Surveyors Court wheresoever the King's Highness in his own most royal person shall come to rest tarry abide or make his repose within this his Realm or any of his dominions within liberty or without, there and within the Verge limited and accustomed to his Grace's Court during the time of his abode, the steward or great master of his Grace's household the Marshal, Coroner, Clerk of the Market, and all others his ministers shall and may keep their Courts for Justice, and exercise their office and offices as shall appertain to them according to the laws customs and statutes of this Realm as well within liberties and franchises as without; and that his Grace's Clerks of the Market and none other during the said time as well within the said liberties and franchises as without shall exercise the office of Clerks of the Market within the said Verge, any privilege grant

Officers of the King's household may exercise their jurisdiction within such Franchises.

allowance or other things to the contrary thereof notwithstanding. Provided alway that this article next before rehearsed or anything therein contained be not in any wise prejudiced to the City of London, but that the same City shall have and use such liberties as they might if that article had never been had nor made. [This statute is still extant.]

---

33 HENRY VIII. c. 12. ss. 1, 2 AND 9.

A.D. 1541-42.

An Act for Murder and Malicious Bloodshed within the Court.

* * * * *

Sect. 1.
All inquests on persons slain within the court shall be taken by the Coroner of the Household.

And that all inquisitions upon the view of persons slain or hereafter to be slain within any of the King's said Palaces or houses or other house or houses aforesaid, shall be by authority of this Act had and taken hereafter for ever by the Coroner for the time being of the household of our Sovereign Lord the King or his heirs without any adjoining or assisting of another Coroner of any Shire within this Realm, by the oath of twelve or more of the yeomen officers of the Kings and his heirs most honourable household, returned by the two clerk comptrollers the clerks of the Cheque and the Clerk Marshal or one of them for the time being of the said household, to whom the said Coroner of the same household shall direct his precept, which Coroner of our Said Sovereign Lord the King's household shall be from time to time named appointed and assigned by the said Lord Great Master or Lord Steward for the time being; and that the said Coroner of the said household shall from time to time for ever without delay certify under his Seal and the Seals of such persons as shall be sworn before him all such Inquisitions, Indictments and offices upon the View of all dead bodies being slain at any time since the Feast of All Saints aforesaid or which hereafter shall be slain within any the King's said Palaces or houses or other house or houses aforesaid, before the said Lord Great

THE STATUTES. 75

Master or Lord Steward, and in his absence before the Treasurer Comptroller and Steward of the Marshalsey[1] aforesaid or before two of them whereof the said Steward of the Marshalsey to be one: and that such Inquisitions and offices so certified shall be deemed judged and taken forever as good and effectual in the law to all intent construction and purposes as any Inquisition taken upon the View of the body of any person being dead by any Coroner of any County of this Realm hath been or shall be adjudged or taken.

And be it further enacted by the authority aforesaid, that the said two clerks comptrollers clerks of the cheque and clerks Marshals for the time being of the King's said household and of his heirs or one of them for ever, upon a precept to them or to any of them hereafter to be made by the said lord great master or lord steward or in the absence of the said lord great master or lord steward, by the said treasurer and comptroller of the King's most honourable household, and the said steward of the Marshalsey or by two of them, wherof the said steward of the Marshalsey to be one, shall have full power to summon warn and return the names of twenty-four persons being yeomen officers of the King's said household and of his heirs, in the said chequer-roll, to enquire of such treasons, misprisions of treasons, murders, manslaughters, and other malicious strikings by reason whereof blood is or shall be shed against the King's peace, before the said lord great master or lord steward, and in his absence before the said treasurer comptroller and steward of the Marshalsey, or before two of them at the least,

Sect. 2. How juries of the King's household shall be summoned for finding and trial of indictments for offences committed within the Court.

---

[1] Marshalsea (marshal, and sea or see, a seat). In England, formerly an ancient prison of London, originally belonging to the marshal of the royal household, described in Dickens's novel 'Little Dorrit.' Court of Marshalsea, a court formerly held before the steward and marshal of the royal house, to administer justice between the domestic servants of the king or queen. In the Marshalsea there were two courts of record: (1) The original Court of the Marshalsea, which held plea of all trespasses committed within the Verge, that is, within a circle of twelve miles round the sovereign's residence; (2) The palace-court created by Charles I. and abolished in 1849.

whereof the steward to be one. And that it shall be lawful to the said lord great master or lord steward, and in his absence, to the said Treasurer Comptroller and the said steward aforesaid or two of them whereof the said steward to be one, before whom such returns shall be so made as is aforesaid, to cause such number of the said twenty-four persons so returned, above the number of twelve persons, as to him or them shall seem expedient, to enquire of such treasons, misprisions of treasons, murders, manslaughters, and other malicious strikings, by reason whereof blood is or shall be shed, against the King's peace, within the said palaces or houses or other the said house or houses (which) sith[1] the said feast of All Saints, or at any time hereafter shall be committed or done within the said palace or houses or other the said house or houses; and if any person or persons be indicted by the said jury, so sworn before them as is aforesaid or by inquisition before the said Coroner of the said household and certified before the said lord great Master or lord Steward, or in the absence of the said lord great Master or lord Steward before the said treasurer comptroller and steward, or before two of them, whereof the said steward to be one as is aforesaid, that then immediately without delay the said lord great master or lord steward, and in his absence the said treasurer comptroller and steward or two of them, whereof the said steward to be one, before whom the said presentment inquisition or indictment shall so be found or certified by the said Coroner of the same household, shall arraign before them all and every such person and persons so indicted according to the course of the common law of this realm, and forthwith after issue joined between the King our sovereign lord his heirs or successors, and the prisoner so arraigned the same day and place or any other day and place at the pleasure of the said lord great master or lord steward, and in his absence at the pleasure of the said treasurer comptroller and steward of the Marshalsey, or two of them as is aforesaid, shall make another precept to the said clerks comptrollers clerks of the cheke and clerks

[1] Time, occasion.

marshals for the time being of the said household or to one of them, to summon and return one other jury of twenty-four persons, to appear before the said lord great Master or lord Steward, and in his absence before the said Treasurer Comptroller and Steward of the Marshalsey, or before two of them whereof the same steward to be one, at such day time and place and upon such pain as shall be then limited and appointed of the servants and gentlemen officers of the King's chamber his heirs and successors and of the said households, which now take or hereafter shall take wages by the King's chequor-roll; and that the said lord grand master or lord Steward if he be there present or in his absence the said treasurer comptroller and Steward of the said Marshalsey, or two of them, whereof the same steward to be one, before whom such jury shall be so returned, shall cause twelve of the same jury to be sworn without any manner of challenge to be had or allowed for any manner of cause, to any of the said jury (malice only excepted) truly to be tried[1] between our said sovereign lord the King and his heirs, and such person and persons as shall be so indicted and arraigned of such treasons, misprisions of treasons, murders, manslaughters, and other malicious strikings by reason whereof blood is or shall be shed against the King's peace, or any of them. And if any such person or persons so indicted or arraigned be found guilty of any treason misprision of treason, murders, or manslaughters, that then all and every such person and persons so found guilty, shall have judgment of life and member, and suffer such pains of death, and shall forfeit all their manors lands tenements goods and chattels in like manner and form, as if the same person and persons had been found guilty of any the said offences by the order of the common laws of this realm, without allowing to any such person or persons so found guilty of any of the same offences, the benefits of his or their clergy or privilege of any sanctuary: And if any person or persons so arraigned be found guilty for malicious striking by reason whereof blood is, hath been, or shall be shed against the King's peace within the

The judgment of an offender found guilty of treason, murder, &c., and his forfeiture.

[1] "To try," in the original.

said palace or house or any other house or any other the said house or houses, that then every such person or persons shall from henceforth have judgment by the said lord great master or lord steward if he be present and in his absence by the other afore named, before whom such person and persons shall be so found guilty, to have his right hand stricken off[1] before the said lord great Master or lord Steward, if he be there present, and in his absence before said treasurer comptroller and steward of the Marshalsey, or two of them at the least, whereof the said steward to be one, and at such place and time as he or they before whom such person or persons shall be so found guilty, shall appoint execution to be done; and the same execution to be done by such person as the said lord great Master or lord steward, if he be there present, and in his absence as the said treasurer comptroller and steward of the Marshalsey, or two of them, whereof the steward to be one, shall name or appoint, and also shall have judgment to have perpetual imprisonment during his life, and shall pay fine and ransom at the King's Majesty's pleasure his heirs and successors.

The judgment for striking in the King's palace, whereby blood shall be shed.

Who shall do execution.

Sect. 9. Appointment of Coroner of the King's household.

And forasmuch as before this time one Richard Staverton of Lincoln's Inn gentleman, was commanded and appointed by the King's Majesty to occupy the office of the Coroner of his said house, by force whereof he hath continued officer in the same by the space of sixteen years or more: Be it enacted by Authority aforesaid, that the said Richard Staverton shall have occupy and enjoy the said office of Coroner during his life, together with all such profits and commodities as before this time have been due and appertaining in anywise to the same; and after his decease, the said Coroner always to be made, assigned and appointed by the said lord great master or lord steward for the time being. [Section 1, as here quoted, and sect. 9 both repealed by the Coroners Act, 1887 (50 & 51 Vict. c. 71, s. 45 and sch. 3). Section 2 is still in force.]

[1] This was also the Athenian law, and Josephus mentions (De Bell. Ind. iii. 8) that in some nations the right hand of the suicide was struck off.

THE STATUTES. 79

33 HENRY VIII. c. 13 s. 1.

A.D. 1541–42.

An Act concerning certain Lordships translated from the County of Denbigh to the County of Flintshire.

* * * * *

For reformation whereof be it enacted by the King our Sovereign Lord with the assent of the Lords Spiritual and Temporal and the Commons in this present parliament assembled and by authority of the same, that the sheriff of the same County for the time being, after the feast of Easter next coming, shall be bounden to keep his Shire Court in the Shire Hall of the said County every month for ever, for determination of plaints, and actions under forty shillings, and for proclamations and callings of exigencies and other necessary causes, as is used in other Shires of this Realm of England. And that two head Coroners for the body of the said Shire shall be elected and chosen by virtue of the King's Writ de Coronatore Eligendo to be awarded out of the Exchequer of Chester; which Coroners shall be bound to sit with the said Sheriff at the said Court to give Judgment upon outlawries and to do all other things as appertaineth. [Repealed by Coroners Act, 1860 (23 & 24 Vict. c. 116, s. 7).] *(marginal note: Two Coroners shall be elected and sit with the Sheriff. (Two Coroners of the Shire of the County Palatine of Chester shall be elected by writ de Coronatore eligendo, to be awarded out of the Exchequer of Chester, and shall sit with Sheriff in cases of outlawries.))*

---

34 HENRY VIII. c. 26 s. 25.

A.D. 1542–43.

An Act for certain Ordinances in the King's Majesties Dominion and Principality of Wales.

Item. There shall be two Crowners to be elected in every of the said twelve Shires as is used in England, by virtue of the King's writ de Coronatore Eligendo, to be awarded out of the King's Chancery of England and that the said Crowners shall have like power and authority to do and exercise their offices and have like fees as is *(marginal note: Sect. XXV. Two Coroners in every Shire (Wales) shall be elected with like powers as in England.)*

80   *THE KING'S CORONER.*

limited by the laws and statutes of England: Provided always that the writ de Coronatore Eligendo, to choose the Crowners within the said County of Flint, shall be directed out of the Exchequer of Chester. [Repealed by Coroners Act, 1887 (50 & 51 Vict. c. 71, s. 45, sch. 3).]

---

2 AND 3 EDWARD VI. c. 24 s. 1.

A.D. 1548.

An Act for the Trial of Murders and Felonies in Several Counties.

Murders not punishable by law where the stroke, &c. was in one county and the death in another.

Forasmuch as the most necessary office and duty of the law is to preserve and save the life of man; and condignly[1] to punish such persons that unlawfully and wilfully murder, slay or destroy men; and also that another office and duty of Law is to punish Robbers and Thieves which daily endeavour themselves to rob and steal or give assistance to the same, and yet by craft and cautele (caution) do escape from the same without punishment: And where it often happeneth and cometh in ure[2] in sundry Counties of this Realm, that a man is feloniously stricken in one County and after dyeth in another County, in which case it hath not been founden by the laws or customs of this Realm that any sufficient Indictment thereof can be taken in any of the said two Counties, for that, that by the custom of this Realm the Jurors of the County where such party died of such stroke can take no knowledge of the said stroke being in a foreign County, although the same two Counties and places adjoin very near together, nor the Jurors of the County where the stroke was given cannot take knowledge of the death in another County, although such death most apparently come of the same stroke; so that the King's Majesty within his own realm cannot by any laws yet made or known punish such murderers and mankillers for offences in this form committed and done, nor any appeal at

[1] According to merit.   [2] Practise or fortune, destiny, chance.

sometime may lie for the same but doth also fail and the said murderer and mankillers escape thereof without punishment, as well in cases where the Counties where such offences be committed and done may join as otherwise where they may not join. And also it is a common practise among errant thieves and Robbers in this Realm, that after they have robbed or stolen in one County they will convey their spoil or part thereof so robbed and stolen unto some of their adherents into some other County, where the principal offence was not committed nor done, who knowing of such felony willingly and by false covin receiveth the same; in which case although the principal felon be after attainted in the one County the accessory escapeth by reason that he was accessory in another County and that the Jurors of the said other county by any law yet made can take no knowledge of the principal felony nor attainder in the first county, and so such accessories escape thereof unpunished and do often put in ure the same knowing they may escape without punishment: For redress and punishment of which offences and safeguard of mans life, be it enacted by authority of this present parliament, that when any person or persons hereafter shall be feloniously stricken or poisoned in one county, and die of the same stroke or poisoning in another County, that then an indictment thereof found by Jurors of the County where the death shall happen, whether it shall be founded before the coroner upon the sight of such dead body, or before the Justices of Peace or other Justices or commissioners which shall have authority to enquire of such offences shall be as good and effectual in the law as if the stroke or poisoning had been committed and done in the same county where the party shall die or where such indictment shall be so founded; any law or usage to the contrary notwithstanding.

Accessories in adjoining Counties, &c. to robberies &c., not punishable in such adjoining counties.

In cases of murder, where stroke or poisoning is in one county and the death in another, indictment thereof in the latter county shall be valid;

and be tried there, or in the King's Bench, accordingly.

And that the Justices of Gaol Delivery and Oyer and Terminer in the same county where such indictment at any time hereafter shall be taken, and also the justices of the King's Bench, after such indictment shall be removed before them, shall and may proceed upon the

82 THE KING'S CORONER.

<small>Appeals of murder may be prosecuted in the county where the party dies.</small>

same in all points as they should or ought to do in case such felonious stroke and death thereby ensuing, or poisoning and death thereof ensuing had grown all in one same county: And that such party to whom appeal of Murder shall be given by the law may commence take and sue Appeal of Murder in the same county where the party so feloniously stricken or poisoned shall die, as well against the principal and principals as against every accessory to the same offence in whatsoever county or place the accessory or accessories shall be guilty to the same; and further the Justice before whom any such appeal shall be commenced sued and taken, within the year and day after such Murder and Manslaughter committed and done shall proceed against all and every such accessory and accessories in the same county when such appeal shall be so taken, in like manner and form as if the same offence or offences of accessory or accessories had been committed or done in the same county when such appeal shall be so taken, as well concerning the trial by the Jurors or twelve men of such county where such appeal or appeals shall be hereafter taken upon the plea of not guilty pleaded by such offender or offenders as otherwise. [Repealed by 7 Geo. 4, c. 64, s. 32.]

---

1 AND 2 PHIL. AND MAR. c. 13, ss. 1, 2 AND 3.

A.D. 1554.

An Act appointing an order to Justices of Peace for the bailment of prisoners.

* * * * *

<small>Examinations before the Coroner for murder, &c. Binding witnesses to appear, &c., certificate thereof.</small>

And that every Coroner upon any inquisition before him found whereby any person or persons shall be indicted for murder or manslaughter, or as accessory or accessories to the same before the murder or manslaughter committed, shall put in writing the effect of the evidence given to the Jury before him being material; and as well the said Justices as the said Coroner shall have authority by this

Act to bind all such by Recognisance and Obligation as do declare any thing material to prove the said murder or manslaughter offences or felonies or to be accessory or accessories to the same as is aforesaid, to appear at the next general gaol delivery to be holden within the County city or town Corporate where the trial thereof shall be, then and there to give evidence against the party so indicted at the time of his trial; and shall certify as well the same evidence as such bond and bonds in writing as he shall take, together with the inquisition or indictment before him taken and found at or before the time of his said trial thereof to be had or made. And likewise the said Justices shall certify all and every such bond taken before him in like manner as before is said of Bailments and examination: And in case any Justice of Peace or Quorum or Coroner, shall after the said first day of April offend in any thing contrary to the true intent and meaning of this present Act, that then the Justices of Gaol Delivery of the Shire, City, Town or Place where such offence shall happen to be committed, upon due proof thereof by examination before them, shall for every such offence set such fine, on every of the same Justices of Peace and Coroner, as the same Justices of Gaol Delivery shall think meet; and shall estreat the same as other Fines and Amercements assessed before Justices of Gaol Delivery ought to be [Repealed by 7 Geo. 4, c. 64, s. 32]. *Justices of gaol delivery may fine for neglect of this Act.*

---

27 ELIZABETH, c. 31, ss. 1, 7 and 12.

A.D. 1584-85.

An Act for the Good Government of the City or Borough of Westminster, in the County of Middlesex.

I. Forasmuch as by erection and new building of divers houses, and by the parting and dividing of divers tenements within the City or Borough of Westminster and the liberties of the same, the people thereof are greatly increased, and being for the most part without trade or mystery, are become poor, and many of them given wholly to vice and idleness, living in contempt of all manner of officers within the said city, for that their power to correct and reform them is not so sufficient in law as in that behalf were meet and requisite: Be it therefore ordained by the Queen's most excellent Majesty the Lords Spiritual and Temporal, and the Commons in this present Parliament assembled, and by the Authority of the same, that the said City or Borough of Westminster, the Liberties, Territories and Precincts of the same, shall be and for ever hereafter continue severed and divided as it hath been accustomed into twelve several Divisions, to be called or known by the names of Wards; the same to be and continue by such Limits Meates and Divisions as heretofore hath been commonly taken or known.

Saving for the jurisdiction of the Steward, Marshall and Coroner of the Household.

VII. Provided that this Act or anything therein contained shall not be prejudicial to the Steward Marshal or Coroner of the Queen's Majesty's Household nor to the authority of Justices of Peace within the County of Middlesex, nor to the Dean and Chapter of Westminster or their successors, nor to the High Steward there or his deputy for the time being, nor to the Mayor Society and Clerk of the Staple, High Constable, Bailiff of the Liberties, Town Clerk nor to the Clerk of the Market; nor to any search to be made by any other officer in the said City or borough of Westminster now being, or that any time hereafter shall be, not being contrary to the true meaning of this present Act: And be it declared by authority of this Act that, they and every of them their Deputies and Assignees shall and may have take and enjoy all the privileges authorities benefits and profits unto them or their said office belonging, from time to time for ever hereafter in as ample wise as they or any of them have had taken and enjoyed the same at any time heretofore not being contrary to the true meaning of this present Act.

Proviso for jurisdiction of the searcher of the sanctuary.

XII. Provided also, that the Searcher for the time being, of the Sanctuary of Westminster, shall have and enjoy within the sanctuary of Westminster the execution and serving of processes commandments and warrants and the attachments and apprehensions of all manner of offenders within the sanctuary aforesaid and within the site circuit and precinct thereof, in as ample manner and form as if this Act had never been had or made. [This statute though amended and repealed in part by 24 & 25 Vict. c. 78, s. 1, section 7 remains the same.]

---

4 WILL. AND MARY, c. 22.

A.D. 1692.

An Act for Regulating Proceedings in the Crown Office of the Court of King's Bench at Westminster.

I. For rectifying the proceedings in the Crown Office in their Majesties Court of King's Bench and for the greater ease of all their Majesties Subjects who shall hereafter be prosecuted in the same be it enacted by the King and Queen's most excellent Majesties by and with the advice and consent of the Lords Spiritual and Temporal and Commons in this present Parliament assembled and by the authority of the same that no Corporation Lord or Lords of Manor or other person or persons having grants by Charter or other good conveyances who have inrolled and had the same allowed in and by the said Court shall hereafter be compelled to plead the same to any Inquisition returned by any Coroner any custom or usage to the contrary notwithstanding. And if there be any Corporations Lord or Lords of Manor or other person or persons who now have or hereafter shall have such Charters or Grants from the Crown for felons' goods deodands and other forfeitures such Corporations Lords of Manor and other persons shall not be compelled to inroll their whole Charters and Grants but bringing the same to the Clerk of the Crown of the said Court he shall inroll and enter upon record so much thereof as may express and set forth the Grants of such Felons' goods deodands and forfeitures and no more for doing whereof he shall have and receive twenty shillings for his fee and entry thereof and no more. *Fee.*

Persons and others having Grants by Charter inrolled, not bound to plead them to an Inquisition returned by Coroner.

Having Grants of Felons' Goods, &c., not bound to inrol the whole.

After inrolment not bound to plead Grant to Inquisition.

And from and after such inrollment no Corporation, Lord of Manor, or other person or persons Grantees of such goods or forfeitures shall be compelled to plead the same in the same Court to any inquisition thereafter filed therein touching any goods found thereby any usage to the contrary notwithstanding.

Penalty £5.

II. And be it further enacted by the authority aforesaid that if any Clerk of the Crown of the said Court shall hereafter issue out any process against any Corporation Lord of Manor or other person or persons grantees of such felons' goods deodand and other forfeitures after inrolment or entry as aforesaid the said Clerk of the Crown shall for every offence forfeit and pay to the Corporation or party grieved thereby the sum of five pounds to be recovered by bill plaint or information in any of Their Majesties Courts of Record at Westminster wherein no essoign privilege protection or wager of law shall be admitted nor any more than one Imparlance.

Clerk of the Crown not punishable for issuing Process against heirs, &c., before they have entered or pleaded their title.

III. And whereas divers persons having grants of felons' goods and deodands and inrolled and pleaded as aforesaid do many times alien and convey their interests therein to other person or persons or by their last Will do devise the same or by their deaths such estates do descend to their heirs whereby the Clerk of the Crown of the said Court is rendered incapable to discern where such interest lies until the person or persons to whom such estates are conveyed devised or descended shall come into the said Court and make entry of such their claim as aforesaid be it therefore hereby further enacted by the Authority aforesaid that the Clerk of the Crown of the said Court for the time being nor any succeeding clerk there shall incur any penalty mentioned in this Act for issuing process against any person or persons who shall not upon every purchase of the title of such felon's goods and deodands inrol and plead the same purchase in the said Court nor against any devisee of the like estate who shall not likewise inrol or plead such devise nor against any heir who shall not in like manner inrol his or her right by descent to the same and until after such pleas have been allowed of and approved by the said Court nor whereby any inquest of any Coroner or Coroners the goods of any felon or felons or deodands shall be by such inquest not found to be in the hands of such purchaser devisee or heir or their respective officer or officers in trust for them respectively.

IV. And whereas it is agreeable to justice that proceedings to outlawries in criminal causes should be as public and notorious as in civil causes because the consequences to persons outlawed in criminal causes are more fatal and dangerous to them and their posterities than in any other causes be it further enacted by the authority aforesaid that upon the issuing of any exigent out of any of Their Majesties' Courts against any person or persons for any criminal matter before judgment or conviction there shall (also) issue out a Writ of Proclamation bearing the same test and return to the Sheriff or Sheriffs of the County or town corporate where the person or persons in the Record of the said proceedings is or are mentioned to be or inhabit according to the form of the statute made in the one and thirtieth year of the reign of the late Queen Elizabeth of blessed memory which Writ of Proclamation shall be delivered to the said sheriff or sheriffs three months before the return of the same. *A Proclamation at the time of the exigent in criminal cases to be delivered three months before return. 31 Eliz. c. 3.*

V. Provided always and be it enacted by the Authority aforesaid that this Act shall continue and be in force for three years from the five-and-twentieth day of March one thousand six hundred ninety-three and from thence to the end of the next session of Parliament and no longer. [This statute is therefore repealed by effluxion of time under section 5. Conditionally repealed by the Stat. Law Rev. Act, 1888 (51 Vict. c. 3, s. 1, sub-s. 2).]. *Continuance of the Act.*

18 ANNE, c. 21[1] s. 1, 10 and 12.

A.D. 1713.

An Act for the preserving all such Ships and Goods thereof which shall happen to be forced on shore or stranded upon the Coasts of this Kingdom or any other of Her Majesties dominions.

Recital of Stat. 3, Ed. I. c. 4.

I. Whereas by an Act made in the third year of the Reign of King Edward the First concerning wrecks at sea it is enacted that where a Man a Dog or a Cat escape quick out of the ship that such Ship nor Barge nor any thing in them shall be adjudged a Wreck but the goods shall be saved and kept by view of the Sheriff Coroner or the King's Bailiff and delivered into the hands of such as are of the town where the goods were found so that if any sue for those goods and after prove that they were his or perished within his keeping within a year and a day they shall be restored to him without delay and if not they shall remain to the King or to such others to whom Wreck belongeth and he that otherwise doth and thereof be attainted shall be awarded to prison and make fine at the King's Will.

And of Stat. 4, Ed. I., Stat. 2.

And whereas by another Act made in the fourth year of the reign of the said King Edward the first intituled De officio Coronatoris concerning the wreck of the sea it is enacted that wheresoever it be ound if any lay hands on it he shall be attached by sufficient pledges and the price of the wreck shall be valued and delivered to the town.

Reasons for passing this Act.

And whereas great Complaints have been made by several Merchants as well Her Majesty's subjects as foreigners trading to and from this Kingdom that many ships of Trade after all their dangers at sea escaped have unfortunately near home run on shore or been stranded on the Coasts thereof and that such ships have been barbarously plundered by Her Majesty's Subjects and their Cargoes embezzled and when any part thereof has been saved it has been swallowed up

---

[1] This is Chapter xviii. 12 Ann Stat. 2. in the Common printed Editions.

by exorbitant demands for salvage to the great loss of Her Majesty's Revenue and to the much greater damage of Her Majesty's trading subjects. For remedy whereof: Be it enacted by the Queen's Most excellent Majesty by and with the Advice and Consent of the Lords Spiritual and Temporal and Commons in this present Parliament assembled and by the authority of the same: That the Sheriffs Justices of the Peace of every County or County of a City or Town and also all Mayors, Bailiffs and other Head Officers of Corporations and Port Towns near adjoining to the sea and all Constables, Headboroughs Tithingmen and Officers of the Customs in all and every such places shall upon Application made to them, or any of them by or on behalf of any Commander or Chief Officer of any Ship or Vessel of any of Her Majesty's Subjects or others being in danger of being stranded or run on shore or being stranded or run on shore are hereby empowered and required to command the Constables of the several ports within Her Majesty's Dominions nearest to the sea coasts where any such ship or vessel shall be in danger as aforesaid to summon and call together as many men as shall be thought necessary to the assistance and for the preservation of such Ship or Vessel so in distress as aforesaid and their cargoes and that if there shall be any ship or vessel either Man of War of Merchants Ship belonging to Her Majesty or any of Her Subjects riding at Anchor near the place where such ship or vessel is in distress or danger as aforesaid the Officers of the Customs and Constables above mentioned or any of them are hereby empowered and required to demand of the superior Officers of such ship or vessel so riding at anchor as aforesaid assistance by their boats and such hands as they can conveniently spare for the said service and preservation of the said ship or vessel so in distress as aforesaid and that in case such superior officer of such ship or vessel riding at anchor as aforesaid shall refuse or neglect to give such assistance he shall forfeit for the same the sum of One hundred pounds to be recovered by the Superior Officer of the said ship or vessel so in distress as aforesaid together with their costs of suit in

Sheriffs, Mayors, &c., and Custom House Officers to summon men to assist ships in distress.

King's ships and other ships to assist.

Penalty on superior officer of £100.

any of Her Majesty's Courts of Record by Action Debt Bill Plaint or Information wherein no essoign Wager of Law or Protection shall be allowed.

<small>Act to commence 1st Aug., 1714, and to be read four times in the year on Sundays in seaport towns.</small>

X. And it is hereby further enacted that this Act and the several clauses herein contained shall take effect from and after the first day of August in the year of our Lord One thousand seven hundred and fourteen and that for the better observing of the same this Act shall be read four times in the year in all the parish churches and chapels of every seaport town and upon the sea coast in this Kingdom upon the Sundays next before Michaelmas-day Christmas-day Lady-day and Midsummer-day in the morning immediately after the prayers and before the sermon.

<small>Continuance of the Act.</small>

XII. Provided, that this Act shall continue in force for the space of three years and from thence to the end of the next session of Parliament and no longer. [Repealed by Merchant Shipping Act (17 & 18 Vict. c. 120, s. 4, and sch.).]

---

2 GEORGE II. c. 21.

A.D. 1729.

An Act for the trial of murders, in cases where either the stroke or death only happens within that part of Great Britain called England.

For preventing any failure of justice and taking away all doubts touching the trial of murders in the cases herein after mentioned: Be it enacted by the King's Most Excellent Majesty, by and with the Advice and Consent of the Lords Spiritual and Temporal, and Commons, in this present Parliament assembled, and by the Authority of the same, that where any person, at any time after the twenty-fourth day of June in the year of our Lord one thousand seven hundred and twenty-nine, shall be feloniously stricken or poisoned upon the sea, or at any place out of that part of the Kingdom of Great Britain

<small>Persons feloniously stricken or poisoned on the sea, &c. An indictment found by jurors shall be good against principal and accessaries.</small>

called England and shall die of the same stroke or poisoning within that part of the Kingdom of Great Britain called England; or where any person, at any time after the twenty-fourth day of June in the year of our Lord one thousand seven hundred and twenty-nine, shall be feloniously stricken or poisoned at any place within that part of Great Britain called England, and shall die of the same stroke or poisoning upon the sea, or at any place out of that part of the Kingdom of Great Britain called England; in either of the said cases an indictment thereof found by the jurors of the County in that part of the Kingdom of Great Britain called England, in which such death, stroke or poisoning shall happen respectively as aforesaid, whether it shall be found before the Coroner upon the View of such dead body, or before the justices of the peace, or other justices or Commissioners, who shall have authority to enquire of murders, shall be as good and effectual in the law, as well against the principals in any such murder, as the accessaries thereunto, as if such felonious stroke and death thereby ensuing, or poisoning and death thereby ensuing, and the offence of such accessaries, had happened in the same county where such indictment shall be found; and that the Justices of gaol delivery and oyer and terminer in the same county where such indictment shall be found, and also any Superior Court, in case such indictment shall be removed into such superior court, shall and may proceed upon the same in all points as well against the principals in any such murder, as the accessaries thereto, as they might or ought to do, in case such felonious stroke and death thereby ensuing, or poisoning and death thereby ensuing, and the offence of such accessaries, had happened in the same county where such indictment shall be found; and that every such offender, as well principal as accessary, shall answer upon their arraignments, and have the like defences, advantages and exceptions (except challenges for the Hundred) and shall receive the like trial, judgment, order and execution, and suffer such forfeitures, pains and penalties, as they ought to do, if such felonious stroke and death thereby ensuing, or

Justices of gaol delivery shall proceed thereon.

And offender shall answer and receive the like trial, &c., as if the murder had happened in the county. See 25 Geo. II., c. 87.

poisoning and death thereby ensuing, and the offence of such accessaries had happened in the same county where such indictment shall be found. [Repealed by 9 George IV. c. 31, s. 1.]

---

25 GEORGE II. c. 29.

(A.D. 1751–52.)

An Act for giving a proper reward to Coroners for the due execution of their office; and for amoval of Coroners upon a lawful conviction for certain misdemeanors.

3 Hen. VII., c. 1.
"I. Whereas the office of Coroner is a very ancient and "necessary office: And whereas by an Act made in the "third year of the reign of King Henry the Seventh, "reciting that Coroners had not, nor ought to have, any- "thing by the law for their office doing; which oft time "had been the occasion that coroners had been remiss "in doing their office: It was ordained, that a coroner "should have for his fee, upon every inquisition taken "upon the view of the body slain, thirteen shillings and "four pence, of the goods and chattels of him that is the "slayer and murderer, if he have any goods; and if he "have no goods, of such amerciaments as should fortune "any township to be amerced, for the escape of the "murderer: And whereas the said thirteen shillings and "four pence, due only upon an inquisition taken upon the "view of a body slain or murdered, and payable only out "of the goods and chattels of the slayer or murderer, or "out of the amerciaments imposed upon the township, "if the murderer escape, is not an adequate reward for "the general execution of the said office:"

To the intent thereof that coroners may be encouraged to execute their office with diligence and integrity: Be it enacted by the King's Most Excellent Majesty by and with the advice and consent of the Lords Spiritual and Temporal, and Commons, in this present Parliament assembled, and by the authority of the same, that for every inquisition, not taken upon the view of a body dying in gaol or prison, which from and after the twenty-fourth day of June one thousand seven hundred and fifty-two, shall be duly taken within that part of Great Britain called England, by any coroner or coroners, in any township or place, contributory to the rates directed by an Act made in the twelfth year of the reign of his present Majesty, intituled, "An Act for the more easy assessing, collecting, and levying of county rates," the sum of twenty shillings; and for every mile which he or they shall be compelled to travel, from the usual place of his or their abode, to take such inquisition, the further sum of nine pence, over and above the said sum of twenty shillings, shall be paid to him or them out of any monies arising from the rates before mentioned, by order of the justices of the peace in their general or quarter sessions assembled, for the County, Riding, Division, or Liberty where such inquisition shall have been taken, or the major part of them; which Order the said justices of the peace so assembled, or the major part of them, are hereby authorized and directed to make; for which Order no fee or reward shall be paid to the clerk of the peace or any other officer.

Coroner to be paid 20s. for every inquisition taken in any township contributing to the County rates, and 9d. for every mile, to be paid out of the County rates.

II. And be it further enacted by the Authority aforesaid, that for every inquisition, which from and after the said twenty fourth day of June one thousand seven hundred and fifty-two, shall be duly taken upon the view of a body dying in any gaol or prison, within that part of Great Britain called England, by any Coroner or Coroners of a county, so much money not exceeding the sum of twenty shillings, shall be paid to him or them, as the justices of the peace in their general or quarter sessions assembled for the County, Riding, or Division wherein such gaol or prison is situate, or the major part of them, shall think fit to allow, as a recompence for his or their labour, pains, and charges in taking such inquisition, to be paid in like manner by Order of the said justices, or the major part of them, out of any monies arising from the said rates; which Order the said justices of the peace

And for every inquisition on bodies dying in gaol, as justices shall think fit;

so assembled, or the major part of them, are hereby authorized and directed to make; for which Order no fee or reward shall be paid to the clerk of the peace or any other officer.

<small>and for inquisitions on a body slain 13s. 4d. over and above.</small>

III. Provided nevertheless, that over and above the recompence hereby limited and appointed for inquisitions taken as aforesaid, the Coroner or Coroners who shall take an inquisition upon the View of a body slain or murdered, shall also have the fee of thirteen shillings and four pence, payable by Virtue of the said Act made in the third year of the reign of King Henry the Seventh, out of the goods and chattels of the slayer or murderer, or out of the amerciaments imposed upon the township, if the slayer and murderer escape; anything in this Act contained to the contrary thereof in any wise notwithstanding.

<small>Coroners taking more, guilty of extortion.</small>

IV. Provided also, and be it declared and enacted by the Authority aforesaid, that no coroner to whom any benefit is given by this Act, shall, by colour of his office, or upon any pretext whatsoever, take for his office doing, in case of the death of any person, any fee or reward, other than the said fee of thirteen shillings and fourpence, limited as is aforesaid by the said Act made in the third year of the reign of King Henry the Seventh, and other than the recompence hereby limited and appointed, upon pain of being deemed guilty of extortion.

<small>Coroners for particular places excepted.</small>

V. Provided likewise, and be it further enacted by the Authority aforesaid, that no coroner of the King's Household, and of the Verge of the King's Palaces, nor any coroner of the Admiralty, nor any coroner of the County Palatine of Durham, nor any coroner of the City of London and borough of Southwark, or of any franchises belonging to the said City; nor any coroner of any city, borough, town, liberty, or franchise which is not contributory to the rates directed by the said Act, made in the twelfth year of the reign of his present Majesty, or within which such rates have not been usually assessed, shall be entitled to any fee, recompence, or benefit given to or provided for coroners by this Act; but that it shall and may be lawful for all such coroners as are last mentioned, to have and receive all such fees, salaries, wages, and allowances as they were entitled to by law before the making of this Act, or as shall be given or allowed to them by the person or persons by whom they have been or shall be appointed.

VI. And be it further enacted by the Authority aforesaid, that if any coroner who is not appointed by Virtue of an annual election or nomination, or whose office of coroner is not annexed to any other office, shall, from and after the said twenty-fourth day of June one thousand seven hundred and fifty-two, be lawfully convicted of extortion, or wilful neglect of his duty, or misdemeanour in his office, it shall be lawful for the Court before whom he shall be so convicted to adjudge that he shall be amoved from his office; and thereupon, if such coroner shall have been elected by the freeholders of any county, a writ shall issue for the amoving him from his office, and electing another coroner in his stead, in such manner as writs for the amoval or discharge of coroners, and for electing coroners in their stead, are in any cases already directed by law: And if the coroner so convicted shall have been appointed by the Lord or Lords of any liberty or franchise, or in any other manner than by the election of the freeholders of any county, the Lord or Lords of such liberty or franchise, or the person or persons entitled to the nomination or appointment of any such coroner, shall, upon notice of such judgment of amoval, nominate and appoint another person to be coroner in his stead. [Section 3 in part (as relates to coroner for County Palatine of Durham) repealed by 1 Vict. c. 64, s. 3. Sections 1 and 3 concerning fees, allowances, and mileage to County Coroners repealed by County Coroners Act, 1860 (23 & 24 Vict. c. 116, s. 3). Sections 1–4 repealed by Stat. Law Rev. Act, 1867 (30 & 31 Vict. c. 59). The remainder is repealed by Coroners Act, 1887 (50 & 51 Vict. c. 71, s. 45, sch. 3).]

Coroner convicted of misdemeanour in his office to be removed.

38 GEO. III. c. 52.

An Act to regulate the Trial of Causes, Indictments, and other Proceedings, which arise within the Counties of certain Cities and Towns Corporate within this Kingdom. [1st June, 1798.]

Preamble. — Whereas there at present exists, in the Counties of Cities and of Towns Corporate within this Kingdom, an exclusive Right, that all Causes and Offences which arise within their particular Limits should be tried by a Jury of Persons residing within the Limits of the County of such City or Town Corporate; which ancient Privilege, intended for other and good Purposes, has in many Instances been found, by Experience, not to conduce to the Ends of Justice: And whereas it will tend to the more effectual Administration of Justice, in certain Cases, if Actions, Indictments, and other Proceedings, the Causes of which arise within the Counties of Cities and Towns Corporate, were tried in the next adjoining Counties: In order therefore to remedy this Mischief for the future, be it enacted:

Indictments found by a Grand Jury of any City or Town Corporate, or Inquisitions taken before the Coroner, may be ordered to be filed with the proper Officer of the next adjoining County, and the Defendants removed to the Gaol thereof, etc. — III. And be it further enacted by the Authority aforesaid, That if it shall appear to any Court of Oyer and Terminer or General Gaol Delivery for the County of any City or Town Corporate, that any Indictment found by any Grand Jury of the County of such City or Town Corporate, or any Inquisition taken before the Coroner or Coroners of the County of such City or Town Corporate, or other Franchise, is fit and proper to be tried by a Jury of any next adjoining County, that it shall and may be lawful for the said Court of Oyer and Terminer or General Gaol Delivery, at the Prayer of any Defendant, to order such Indictment or Inquisition, and the several Recognizances, Examinations, and Depositions, relative to such Indictments and Inquisitions, to be filed with the proper Officer, to be by him kept among the Records of the Courts of Oyer or Terminer and General Gaol Delivery for such next adjoining County, and to cause the Defendant or Defendants in such Indictment to be removed, by Writ of *Habeas Corpus*, to the Gaol of such next adjoining County; which Writ the said Court is hereby directed and authorized to issue, if such Defendant or Defendants be in the Prison of such City or Town Corporate; and if he, she, or they be not in such Prison, to commit such Defendant or Defendants to the Gaol of such next adjoining County, and to cause the Prosecutors and Witnesses against such Defendant or Defendants, to enter into a Recognizance or Recognizances, to prosecute and give Evidence against such Defendant or Defendants at the Sessions of Oyer and Terminer and General Gaol Delivery for such next adjoining County; and that the same Proceedings and Trial shall be had, and the same Judgement shall be given, in such last-mentioned Court of Oyer and Terminer or General Gaol Delivery, as would and might be had and given in Cases of Indictments or Inquisitions for the like Offences, committed within such next adjoining Counties.

IV. And be it further enacted by the Authority aforesaid, That it shall and may be lawful for any of the Judges of His Majesty's Court of King's Bench, or any of the Justices of Oyer and Terminer or General Gaol Delivery, for such next adjoining or other County as aforesaid, on the Application of any such Prosecutor or Prosecutors Ten Days next before the holding of any Sessions of Oyer and Terminer, or General Gaol Delivery, for such last-mentioned County, by proper Writs of *Habeas Corpus*, which they are hereby empowered and authorized to issue, to cause any Person or Persons who may be in the Custody of any Sheriff or Sheriffs, or of the Keepers of any Gaol or Prison, charged with any Offence or Offences committed within the County of any such City or Town Corporate, to be removed into the Custody of the Sheriff of such next adjoining County, in order that he, she, or they may, for such Offence or Offences as aforesaid be tried in such last-mentioned County, and by order under the Hand of any One of the said Judges or Justices of Oyer and Terminer and General Gaol Delivery, to

The Judges of the Court of King's Bench, etc., may cause Persons in Custody for Offences committed within the County of any City or Town Corporate, to be removed into the Custody of the Sheriff of the next adjoining County, for Trial; and direct Coroners to return to the Court of Oyer and Terminer Inquisitions, etc.

direct the Coroner or Coroners of the County of any such City or Town Corporate, or other Franchise, to return to the next Court of Oyer and Terminer or General Gaol Delivery, to be holden for such next adjoining County any Inquisition or Inquisitions, Examination or Deposition taken touching the Death of any Person or Persons within the Limits of his or their Jurisdictions; and that whenever, in pursuance of this Act, any Bill or Bills of Indictment shall be found by such Grand Jury as aforesaid, against any Person or Persons, for any Offence or Offences committed, or charged to be committed, within the County of any City or Town Corporate, that it shall and may be lawful for the said Courts of Oyer and Terminer and General Gaol Delivery, to issue Process for apprehending the Person or Persons against whom such Bill or Bills of Indictment shall be found, if not in Custody, and to compel the Attendance of Witnesses upon the Trial of such Indictments, in like Manner as in Cases of Indictments found in any such Court of Oyer and Terminer or General Gaol Delivery, for Offences committed within such adjoining Counties.

---

51 GEO. III. c. 86.

An Act to facilitate the Execution of Justice within The Cinque Ports. [25th May 1811.]

Giving the Coroners of Essex Cognizance within the Parish of Brightlingsea. VI. And be it hereby further enacted, That from and after the Fifth Day of *July* one thousand eight hundred and eleven, the Coroners for the County of *Essex* shall have Cognizance of all Matters and Things whereof it appertaineth to the Office of Coroner to have Cognizance, which shall happen or fall out within the said Parish of *Brightlingsea*, and shall do and execute all Matters and Things appertaining to the Office of Coroner to do and execute within the said Parish of *Brightlingsea*, and be paid for the same in such and the same Manner as they ought and should have done and been paid in case the said Parish of *Brightlingsea* was to all Intents and Purposes Part of the said County of *Essex*, and was not or had not been annexed to, or did not form, or had not formed Part of the Liberties of the Town and Port of *Sandwich* aforesaid.

VII. And be it hereby further enacted, That from and after the Fifth Day of *July* One thousand eight hundred and eleven, all Offenders to be committed or imprisoned for any Offence committed within the said Parish of *Brightlingsea*, shall be committed to, and imprisoned and delivered at such Place and Places, Time and Times, as they would have been committed to, imprisoned in and delivered at, in case the said Parish of *Brightlingsea* was Part of the said County of *Essex*, and that such Offenders shall be maintained and kept in such Place or Places, and conveyed to and from Trial at the Expence of the said County of *Essex*; and that the Treasurer or Treasurers of the said County of *Essex* shall, and he and they is and are hereby respectively authorized to demand and receive of the Overseers of the Poor of the said Parish of *Brightlingsea*, such Sum and Sums as they shall respectively pay to any Coroner of the said County of *Essex*, for any Matter or Thing done by such Coroner within the said Parish of *Brightlingsea*, and such further Sum and Sums as the Justices of the said County of *Essex* shall, at the Sessions to be holden by them next after the Clause of *Easter* in each Year, determine to be Double the Average Amount of the Expence *per* Day of feeding and clothing a Prisoner in their County Gaol, for each Day any Offender shall be so confined or imprisoned in any Place of Confinement within their County, in lieu and Satisfaction of all Contribution from the said Parish of *Brightlingsea* to the Rate of the said County; and the Treasurer or Treasurers of the said County of *Essex* shall have the same Remedy and Remedies for receiving and enforcing the Payment of such Sum and Sums, as he or they now have for recovering or enforcing the Payment of the County Rate from any Parish of the said County; and the said Overseers are hereby required to pay the same accordingly,

How the Maintenance, etc., of Offenders, committed to or imprisoned in the County Gaol of Essex, from Brightlingsea, shall be defrayed.

out of the Rates to be made and collected within the said Parish for the Relief of the Poor thereof: Provided always, that nothing herein contained shall extend or be construed to extend to deprive the Mayor and Jurats of *Sandwich* to raise or levy any Rate, Cess, or Impost, they are now authorized to raise or levy within the said Parish of *Brightlingsea*, or on the Inhabitants thereof, other than and except for any Expence to be incurred for the Rebuilding, Sustentation or Repair, of any Gaol or Place of Confinement of Offenders within the said Town and Port of *Sandwich*, or the Liberties thereof, or in the Maintenance, Clothing or keeping of any Offenders therein, or the Trials of any such Offenders.

Coroners of Kent to have Cognizance within Beakesbourne and Grange otherwise Grench.

IX. And be it hereby further enacted, That from and after the Fifth Day of *July* One thousand eight hundred and eleven, the Coroners for the County of *Kent* shall have Cognizance of all Matters and Things whereof it appertaineth to the Office of Coroner to have Cognizance, which shall happen or fall out within the said Parish of *Beakesbourne*, or Hamlet of *Grange* otherwise *Grench*, and and shall do and execute all Things appertaining to the Office of Coroner to do and execute within the said Parish of *Beakesbourne* and Hamlet of *Grange* otherwise *Grench* and be paid for the same in such and the same Manner as they ought and should have done and been paid, in case the said Parish of *Beakesbourne* and Hamlet of *Grange* otherwise *Grench* was to all Intents and Purposes Part of the said County of *Kent*, and was not and had not been annexed to, and did not form, and had not formed Part of the Liberties of the Town and Port of *Hastings*.

How the Expences of Maintenance, Clothing, and Trial of Offenders committed or imprisoned in the County of Kent, from Beakesbourne or Grench, shall be defrayed.

X. And be it hereby enacted, That from and after the Fifth Day of *July* One thousand eight hundred and eleven all Offenders to be committed or imprisoned for any Offence committed within the Parish of *Beakesbourne*, or the Hamlet of *Grange* otherwise *Grench*, shall be committed or imprisoned in such Place or Places, and delivered at such Time or Times, Place or Places, as they would have been committed to, imprisoned in and delivered at, in case the said Parish of *Beakesbourne*, and Hamlet of

Grange otherwise *Grench*, were respectively Part of the said County of *Kent*, and that such Offenders shall be maintained and kept in such Place or Places, and conveyed to and from Trial at the Expence of the said County of *Kent*, and that the Treasurer of the said County of *Kent*, or the Treasurers of the Divisions of the said County of *Kent*, shall, and he and they is or are hereby respectively authorized to demand and receive of the Overseer or Overseers of the Poor of the said Parish of *Beakesbourne*, or Hamlet of *Grange* otherwise *Grench* respectively, such Sum or Sums as they shall respectively pay to any Coroner of the said County of *Kent*, for any Matter or Thing done by such Coroner within the said Parish of *Beakesbourne*, or the Hamlet of *Grange* otherwise *Grench*, and such further Sum and Sums as the Justices of the Divisions of which such Treasurer shall be the Treasurer, shall, at the Sessions to be by them holden next after the Clause of *Easter* in each Year, determine to be double the average Amount of the Expence *per* Day of feeding and clothing a Prisoner in the Gaol of their respective Divisions, for each Day any Offender shall be so confined or imprisoned in any Place of Confinement within such respective Divisions, in lieu and Satisfaction of all Contribution from the said Parish of *Beakesbourne*, or Hamlet of *Grange* otherwise *Grench*, to the Rate of the said County; and the said Treasurer or Treasurers shall have the same Remedy and Remedies for recovering and enforcing the Payment of such Sum and Sums, as he or they now have respectively for recovering and enforcing the Payment of the County Rate from any Parish of the said County; and the said Overseer and Overseers is and are hereby required to pay the same accordingly out of the Rates to be respectively made and collected within the said Parish and Hamlet for the Relief of the respective Poor thereof accordingly: Provided always, that nothing herein contained shall extend or be construed to extend to deprive the Mayor and Jurats of *Hastings* of any Power to raise or levy any Rate, Cess, or Impost, they are now authorized to raise or levy within the said Parish of *Beaksbourne*, or the Hamlet of *Grange* otherwise *Grench*, or either of them, or on the Inhabitants of them or either of them, other than and except for any Expence to be incurred for the Rebuilding, Sustentation or Repair of any Gaol or Place of Confinement of Offenders within the said Town and Port of *Hastings*, or the Liberties thereof, or in the Maintenance, clothing and keeping of any Offenders therein, or in regard to the Trial of any such Offenders. [Conditionally repealed as to certain places by 18 & 19 Vict. c. 48, s. 5. (Breaksbourne and Grench severed from Dover. Ratepayers may petition for inclusion in County and from date of issue of Order or grant of Charter, Act repealed).]

---

58 GEO. III. c. 95.

An Act to regulate the Election of Coroners for Counties.
[10th June 1818.]

Whereas there are no sufficient Regulations for the Election of Coroners for Counties; be it therefore enacted by the King's most Excellent Majesty, by and with the Advice and Consent of the Lords Spiritual and Temporal, and Commons, in this present Parliament assembled, and by the Authority of the same, That from and after the passing of this Act, upon every Election to be made of any Coroner or Coroners of any County in *England* and *Wales*, the Sheriff of the County where such Election shall be made shall hold his County Court for the same Election at the most usual Place or Places of Election of Coroners within the said County, and where the same have most usually been held for Forty Years last past, and shall there proceed to Election at the next County Court, unless the same fall out to be held within Six Days after the Receipt of the Writ *de Coronatore eligendo*, or upon the same Day; and then shall adjourn the same Court to some convenient Day, not exceeding Fourteen Days, giving Ten Days' Notice of the Time and Place of Election; and in case the said Election be not determined upon the View, with the Consent of the Freeholders there present,

[Marginal note: Sheriff to hold his County Court for the Election of Coroner at the Usual Place of Election;]

but that a Poll shall be demanded for Determination thereof, then the said Sheriff, or in his Absence his Under Sheriff, with such others as shall be deputed by him, shall forthwith there proceed to take the said Poll, in some public Place, by the same Sheriff, or his Under Sheriff as aforesaid in his absence, or others appointed for the taking thereof as aforesaid; and every such Poll shall commence on the Day upon which the same shall be demanded, and be duly and regularly proceeded in from Day to Day (*Sunday* excepted) until the same be finished; but so as that no Poll for such Election shall continue more than Ten Days at most (*Sundays* excepted), and the said Poll shall be kept open Seven Hours at the least each Day, between the hours of Nine in the Morning and Five at night: And for the more due and orderly proceeding in the said Poll, the said Sheriff, or in his Absence his Under Sheriff, or such as he shall depute, shall appoint such Number of Clerks as to him shall seem meet or convenient for the taking thereof; which Clerks shall all take the said Poll in the Presence of the said Sheriff or his Under Sheriff, or such as he shall depute; and before they begin to take the said Poll, every Clerk so appointed shall by the said Sheriff or his Under Sheriff, or such as he shall depute as aforesaid, be sworn truly and indifferently to take the same Poll, and to set down the Names of each Freeholder, and the Place of his Abode and Freehold, and the Name of the Occupier thereof, and for whom he shall poll, and to poll no Freeholder who is not sworn, if required to be sworn by the Candidates or either of them, and which Oaths of the said Clerks, the said Sheriff or his Under Sheriff, or such as he shall depute, are hereby empowered to administer; and the Sheriff, or in his Absence his Under Sheriff as aforesaid shall appoint for each Candidate such One Person as shall be nominated to him by each Candidate, to be Inspector of every Clerk who shall be appointed for taking the Poll; and every Freeholder, before he is admitted to poll at the same Election, shall, if required by the Candidates or any of them, first take the Oath herein after mentioned which Oath the said Sheriff by himself or his Under

and if Election not determined on View, then to proceed to take a Poll.

Commencement and Duration of Poll.

Poll Clerks to be appointed and sworn.

Inspector of Poll Clerk to be appointed.

Freeholder, if required, to be sworn before he polls.

Sheriff, or such sworn Clerk by him appointed for taking the said Poll as aforesaid, is hereby authorized to administer; *videlicet,*

The Oath of Qualification.

" You swear [*or,* being one of the People called *Quakers,* "you solemnly affirm] That you are a Freeholder of the " County of   and have a Freehold Estate, " consisting of   lying at " within the said County; and that such Freehold Estate " has not been granted to you fraudulently, on purpose " to qualify you to give your Vote at this Election; and " that the Place of your Abode is at   [*and* "*if it be a Place consisting of more Streets or Places than* "*One, specifying what Street or Place;*] that you are Twenty-" one Years of Age, as you believe, and that you have not " been before polled at this Election."

Punishment against Perjury, or Subornation of Perjury.

And in case any Freeholder or other Person taking the said Oath or Affirmation hereby appointed to be taken by him as aforesaid shall thereby commit wilful and corrupt Perjury, and be thereof convicted, and if any Person shall unlawfully or corruptly procure or suborn any Freeholder or other Person to take the said Oath or Affirmation in order to be polled, whereby he shall commit such wilful and corrupt Perjury, and shall be thereof convicted, he and they for every such Offence shall incur such Pains and Penalties as are declared in and by Two Acts of Parliament, the one made in the

5 Eliz. c. 9.

Fifth Year of the late Queen *Elizabeth,* intituled *An Act for Punishment of such as shall procure or commit any wilful Perjury;* and the other made in the Second Year

2 G. 2. c. 25.

of His late Majesty King *George* the Second, intituled *An Act for the more effectual preventing and further Punishment of Forgery, Perjury, and Subornation of Perjury, and to make it a Felony to steal Bonds, Notes, or other Securities for Payment of Money;* and by any other Law or Statute now in force for the Punishment of Perjury or Subornation of Perjury.

Mortgagor and Cestuique Trust to vote.

II. And be it further enacted, That no Person or Persons shall be allowed to have any Vote at such Elections for Coroner or Coroners of any County in *England* and *Wales* as aforesaid, for or by reason of any Trust Estate or Mortgage, unless such Trustee or Mortgagee be in actual Possession or Receipt of the Rents and Profits of such Estate; but that the Mortgagor or *Cestuique* Trust in Possession shall and may vote for the same Estate, notwithstanding such Mortgage or Trust; and that all Conveyances of any Messuages, Lands, Tenements, and Hereditaments, in order to Multiply Voices, or to split or divide the Interest in any Houses or Lands among several Persons, to enable them to vote at Elections for a Coroner of any County as aforesaid, are hereby declared to be void and of none Effect.

III. And be it further enacted, That all the reasonable Costs, Charges, and Expences, the said Sheriff or his Under Sheriff or other Deputy shall expend or be liable to in and about the providing of Poll Books, Booths, and Clerks (such Clerks to be paid not exceeding One Pound and One Shilling each *per Diem*) for the Purpose of taking the Poll at any such Election, shall be borne, sustained, and paid by the several Candidates at such Election, in equal Proportions. [Repealed by 7 & 8 Vict. c. 92, s. 1.] *Expences of Sheriff and Poll Clerks to be paid by the Candidates.*

---

4 GEO. IV. c. 52.

8TH JULY 1823.

An Act to alter and amend the Law relating to the Interment of the Remains of any Person found Felo de se.

Whereas it is expedient that the Laws and Usages relating to the Interment of the Remains of Persons, against whom a finding of *Felo de se* shall be had, should be altered and amended: Be it therefore enacted by the King's most Excellent Majesty, by and with the advice and consent of the Lords Spiritual and Temporal, and Commons, in this present Parliament assembled, and by the Authority of the same, that from and after the passing

Remains of persons against whom a finding of Felo de se is had to be privately buried in the parish churchyard.

of this Act it shall not be lawful for any Coroner, or other officer having authority to hold inquests, to issue any warrant or other Process directing the interment of the remains of persons, against whom a finding of *Felo de se* shall be had, in any public Highway, but that such Coroner or other officer shall give directions for the private interment of the remains of such person *Felo de se*, without any stake being driven through the body of such person, in the churchyard or other burial ground of the parish or place in which the remains of such person might by the laws or custom of *England* be interred if the Verdict of *Felo de se* had not been found against such person; such interment to be made within twenty-four hours from the finding of the inquisition, and to take place between the hours of nine and twelve at night.

II. Provided nevertheless, that nothing herein contained shall authorize the performing of any of the rites of Christian burial on the interment of the remains of any such person as aforesaid; nor shall anything hereinbefore contained be taken to alter the laws or usages relating to the burial of such persons, except so far as relates to the interment of such remains in such churchyard or burial ground at such time and in such manner as aforesaid. [The whole Act repealed by Interments (Felo de se) Act, 1882 (45 & 46 Vict. c. 19, s. 1).]

---

6 GEO. IV. c. 50.

THE COUNTY JURIES ACT, 1825.

An Act for consolidating and amending the Laws relative to Jurors and Juries. [22nd June 1825.]

Exemptions from serving on Juries (See 1 W. & M. c. 18, s. 11; 19 G. 3, c. 44; 31 G. 3, c. 32, s. 8; 52 G. 3, c. 155, s. 9).

2. Provided always and be it further enacted: That all Peers all Judges of the King's Courts of Record at Westminster and of the Courts of Great Session in Wales, all Clergymen in Holy Orders, all Priests of the Roman Catholic Faith who shall have duly taken and subscribed

the Oaths and Declarations required by Law, all persons who shall teach or preach in any congregation of Protestant Dissenters whose place of Meeting is duly registered, and who shall follow no Secular Occupation except that of a Schoolmaster, producing a Certificate of some Justice of the Peace of their having taken the Oaths and subscribed the Declaration required by Law, all Serjeants and Barristers at Law actually practising, all Members of the Society of Doctors of Law and Advocates of the Civil Law actually practising, all Attornies, Solicitors and Proctors duly admitted in any Court of Law or Equity or of Ecclesiastical or Admiralty Jurisdiction in which Attornies, Solicitors and Proctors have usually been admitted actually practising and having duly taken out their annual Certificates, all officers of any such Courts actually exercising the Duties of their respective offices, all Coroners, Gaolers and Keepers of Houses of Correction, all Members and Licentiates of the Royal College of Physicians in London actually practising, all Surgeons being Members of one of the Royal Colleges of Surgeons in London, Edinburgh or Dublin, and actually practising, all Apothecaries certificated by the Court of Examiners of the Apothecaries' Company and actually practising, all officers in His Majesty's Navy or Army on Full Pay, all Pilots licensed by the Trinity House of Deptford, Stroud, Kingston-upon-Hull, or Newcastle-upon-Tyne and all Masters of Vessels in the Buoy and Light Service employed by either of those Corporations, and all Pilots licensed by the Lord Warden of the Cinque Ports or under any Act of Parliament or Charter for the regulation of Pilots in any other Port, all the Household Servants of his Majesty his Heirs and Successors, all officers of Customs and Excise, all Sheriffs' Officers, High Constables and Parish Clerks, shall be and are hereby absolutely freed and exempted from being returned, and from serving upon any Juries or Inquests whatsoever, and shall not be inserted in the Lists to be prepared by Virtue of this Act as hereinafter mentioned, Provided also that all Persons exempt from serving upon Juries in any of the Courts aforesaid by virtue of any Prescription Charter, Grant or Writ, shall continue to have and enjoy such

See 5 H. 8, c. 6; 18 G. 2, c. 15, s. 10.

See 6 & 7 W. & M. c. 4; 55 G. 3, c. 194.

Proviso.

Exemption in as ample a manner as before the passing of this Act, and shall not be inserted in the Lists hereinafter mentioned.

<small>Juries to be returned from Juror's Book by Sheriff, and by Coroners and Elisors.
Proviso.</small>

14. And be it further enacted, That every Sheriff upon the receipt of every such Writ of Venire Facias and Precept for the Return of Jurors shall return the names of men contained in the Juror's Book for the then current year and no others, and that where process for returning a Jury for the Trial of any of the Issues aforesaid shall be directed to any Coroner, Elisor or other Minister he shall have free access to the Juror's Book for the current year, and shall in like manner return the names of men contained therein and no others, Provided always that if there shall be no Juror's Book in existence for the current year it shall be lawful to return Jurors from the Juror's Book for the year preceding.

<small>No money taken to excuse Persons from Serving (See 3 G. 2, c. 25, s. 6).

None to be summoned but those named in Warrant.

Officer offending.</small>

43. And be it further enacted, That no Sheriff, Under Sheriff, Coroner, Elisor, Bailiff or other officer or person whatsoever shall directly or indirectly take or receive any money or other reward or promise of money or reward to excuse any man from serving or from being summoned to serve on Juries or be under any such Colour or pretence, and that no Bailiff or other Officer appointed by any Sheriff, Under Sheriff, Coroner or Elisor to summon Juries shall summon any men to serve thereon other than those whose names are specified in a Warrant or Mandate signed by such Sheriff, Under Sheriff, Coroner, or Elisor and directed to such Bailiff or other officer, and if any Sheriff, Under Sheriff, Coroner, Elisor, Bailiff or other officer shall wilfully transgress in any of the cases aforesaid, or shall summon any Juror not being a Special Juror, less than Ten Days before the day on which he is to attend, or shall summon any Special Juror less than three days before the day on which he is to attend, except in the cases hereinbefore excepted, the Court of Assize, Nisi Prius, Oyer and Terminer, Gaol Delivery, Great Sessions, or Superior Court of the said Counties Palatine, or Court of Sessions of the Peace within whose Jurisdiction the offence shall

have been committed, may and is hereby required on Examination and proof of such offence, in a summary way, to set such a Fine upon every person so offending, as the Court shall think meet, according to the Nature of the offence.

Penalty.

52. And be it further enacted, That no man shall be liable to be summoned or impannelled to serve as a Juror in any county in England or Wales or in London, upon any Inquest or Inquiry to be taken or made by or before any Sheriff or Coroner by virtue of any Writ of Inquiry or by or before any Commissioners appointed under the Great Seal, or the Seal of the Court of Exchequer, or the Seals of the Courts of the said Counties Palatine, or the Seals of the Courts of Great Session of Wales, who shall not be duly qualified according to this Act to serve as a Juror upon Trials at Nisi Prius in such County in England or Wales, or in London respectively. Provided always that nothing herein contained shall extend to any Inquest to be taken by or before any Coroner of a County by virtue of his office, or to any Inquest or Inquiry to be taken or made by or before any Sheriff or Coroner of any Liberty, Franchise, City, Borough or Town Corporate not being Counties, or of any City, Borough or Town being respectively counties of themselves, but that the Coroners in all Counties, when acting otherwise than under a Writ of Inquiry, and the Sheriffs and Coroners in all such places as are herein mentioned shall and may respectively take and make all Inquests and Inquiries by Jurors of the same description as they have been used and accustomed to do before the passing of this Act.

Qualification of Jurors on Inquests, etc.

Proviso for certain Inquests hereinmentioned.

53. And be it further enacted, That if any man having been duly summoned and returned to serve as a Juror in any County in England or Wales, or in London upon any Inquest or Inquiry before any Sheriff or Coroner, or before any of the Commissioners aforesaid[1] shall not, after being openly called three times, appear and serve as such Juror, every such Sheriff, or in his absence the Under Sheriff or

Sheriffs, Coroners and Commissioners appointed as mentioned in sect. 52 ante, may fine Jurors for non-attendance.

---

[1] *Vide* section 52, *ante.*

Secondary, and such Coroner and Commissioners respectively, are hereby authorized and required (unless some reasonable Excuse shall be proved on Oath or Affidavit) to impose such Fine upon every man so making default as they shall respectively think fit, not exceeding Five pounds, and every such Sheriff, Under Sheriff, Secondary, Coroner and Commissioners respectively shall make out and sign a Certificate containing the Christian and Surname, the Residence and Trade or calling of every man so making default, together with the amount of the Fine imposed, and the cause of such Fine, and shall transmit such Certificate to the Clerk of the Peace of the County, Riding or Division in which every such Defaulter shall reside, on or before the first day of the Quarter Sessions next ensuing, and every such Clerk of the Peace is hereby required to copy the Fines so certified on the Roll on which all Fines and Forfeitures imposed at such Quarter Sessions shall be copied, and the same shall be estreated, levied and applied in like manner, and subject to the like powers, provisions and penalties in all respects as if they had been part of the Fines imposed at such Quarter Sessions.

Certificate thereof.

See 3 G. 4, c. 46.

62. And be it further enacted, That those parts of this Act which relate to the issuing of warrants and precepts for the return of jury lists, the preparation, production, reformation and allowance of those lists, the holding of the petty sessions for those purposes, the formation of a Juror's Book, and the delivery thereof to the Sheriff, and the preparation of a list of special jurors, and of parchments or cards, in the manner hereinbefore mentioned, shall commence and take effect so soon after the passing of this Act as the proper periods for doing those things shall occur; and that the rest of this Act shall commence and take effect on the first day of January in the year one thousand eight hundred and twenty-six; And that from and after the commencement of the several parts of this Act respectively, so much of the provisions made in the forty-third year of the reign of King Henry the Third, as relates to Exemption from Assizes, Juries and Inquests; and so much of a Statute made in the fifty-second year of

Repeal of 43 Hen. III.; 52 Hen. III. c. 14.

the same reign, as relates to the like exemptions; and so much of the same statute as provides that all, being twelve years of age, ought to appear at inquests for the death of man; and so much of the statutes made in the twelfth year of the reign of King Edward the First, intituled *Statuta Walliæ* as relates to persons of twelve years of age being summoned upon Coroners' inquests; . . . and so much of a statute made in the twenty-eighth year of the same reign, intituled *Articuli super Cartus* as declares how inquests and juries are to be impannelled; . . . and so much of a statute made in the thirty-fourth year of the same reign (34 Edw. III. c. 4) as accords that panels of inquests shall be of the neighbourhood, and so much thereof as directs the proceedings against jurors taking a reward to give their verdict; and so much thereof as relates to the qualification of jurors on inquests of escheat. [Sect. 2 repealed by the Stat. Law Rev. Act, 1875 (38 & 39 Vict. c. 66, Sch.). Sect. 14 repealed in part (the words "Writ of *Venire facias*"), and Sect. 52 repealed in part (from "or the seals of the Court" to "Session of Wales") by Stat. Law Rev. Act (No. 2), 1888 (51 & 52 Vict. c. 57). Sect. 53 repealed as far as it relates to a coroner upon an inquest, by Coroners' Act, 1887 (50 & 51 Vict. c. 71, and s. 45 & Sch. 3). Sect. 62 repealed by Stat. Law Rev. Act, 1874 (37 & 38 Vict. c. 35, & Sch.).]

12 Ed. I.

84 Ed. III. c. 4.

---

7 GEO. IV. c. 64.

An Act for improving the Administration of criminal Justice in England. [26th May 1826.]

IV. And be it further enacted, That every Coroner, upon any Inquisition before him taken, whereby any person shall be indicted for Manslaughter or Murder, or as an Accessory to Murder before the fact, shall put in Writing the Evidence given to the Jury before him, or as much thereof as shall be material; and shall have Authority to bind by Recognisance all such Persons as know or declare anything material touching the said

Duty of Coroner. (1 & 2 P. & M. c. 13, s. 5.)

Manslaughter or Murder, or the said Offence of being accessory to Murder, to appear at the next Court of Oyer and Terminer, or Gaol Delivery, or Superior Criminal Court of a County Palatine, or Great Sessions, at which the Trial is to be, then and there to prosecute or give Evidence against the Party charged, and every such Coroner shall certify and subscribe the same Evidence, and all such Recognizances, and also the Inquisition before him taken, and shall deliver the same to the proper Officer of the Court in which the Trial is to be, before or at the Opening of the Court.

Penalty on Justices and Coroners. (1 & 2 P. & M. c. 13, s. 5.) V. And be it further enacted, That if any Justice or Coroner shall offend in anything contrary to the true Intent and Meaning of these Provisions, the Court to whose Officer any such Examination, Information, Evidence, Bailment, Recognizance, or Inquisition ought to have been delivered, shall, upon Examination and Proof of the Offence in a summary Manner, set such Fine upon every Justice or Coroner, as the Court shall think meet.

Provisions to apply to all Justices and Coroners. (1 & 2 P. & M. c. 13, s. 6.) VI. And be it further enacted, That all these Provisions relating to Justices and Coroners shall apply to the Justices and Coroners not only of Counties at large, but also of all other Jurisdictions. [Sect. 4 and so much of Sects. 5 and 6 as relate to a Coroner, repealed by Coroners Act, 1887 (50 & 51 Vict. c. 71, s. 45, Sch. 3).]

---

4 & 5 WILL. IV. c. 36.

An Act for establishing a new Court for the Trial of Offences committed in the Metropolis and Parts adjoining. [25th July 1834.]

His Majesty, by Order in Council, to appoint the Places of Confinement for Prisoners. V. And whereas, for the more convenient Distribution of Prisoners, as well before Trial as after, and also for rendering more effectual the Punishment of Imprisonment, it may be expedient that Power should be given to appoint from Time to Time in what Places of Confinement within the Limits of this Act such Prisoners shall be kept in Custody; be it therefore further enacted, That it shall be lawful for His Majesty, by and with the Advice of His Privy Council, from Time to Time to order and direct in what Gaol, House of Correction, or other Prison, being within the Limits of this Act, any Person or Persons charged with or convicted of Offences committed or alleged to have been committed within the Limits of this Act shall be imprisoned or kept in Custody; and that when and so often as His Majesty, by and with the Advice of His Privy Council, shall be pleased to give such Orders and Directions, the said Justices and Judges of Oyer and Terminer and Gaol Delivery, and all Justices of the Peace, Coroners, and other Magistrates acting within the Limits of this Act, shall commit all persons charged or convicted before them to such Gaol, House of Correction, or other Prison as in such Orders or Directions shall be expressed and commanded, any Law, Usage, or Custom to the contrary notwithstanding; provided nevertheless, and it is hereby declared, that the City, County, or Place in which the offence of such Person or Persons was committed or alleged to have been committed shall be liable to and charged with the Expence of supporting and maintaining such Prisoner during his Imprisonment in such Gaol, House of Correction, or other Prison, at and after such Rate as His Majesty, by and with the Advice of His Privy Council, shall order and direct, and shall be paid by the Treasurer of the said City, Council, or Place in which such Offence was committed or alleged to have been committed: Provided nevertheless, that the County of *Middlesex* and City of *Westminster* and Liberty of the *Tower* of *London* shall not be liable to any Charge for the Support and Maintenance of any Prisoner charged with any offence in the said County, City, or Liberty, who shall be committed to His Majesty's Gaol of *Newgate*.

X. And be it further enacted, That until His Majesty shall be pleased, by and with the Advice of His Privy Council, to order and direct in what Gaol, House of Correction, or other Prison Persons charged with or {Justices and Coroners in Essex and Kent to commit Offenders to Newgate,} *and Justices and Coroners in Surrey to commit Offenders to Horsemonger Lane, and certify Examinations to the Court.*

convicted of Offences committed or alleged to have been committed within the Limits of this Act shall be imprisoned or kept in Custody, it shall be lawful for any Justice of the Peace or Coroner acting in and for the said Counties of *Essex* or *Kent*, so far as relates to the said several Parishes lying within their respective Counties, to commit any Person or Persons charged with any of the Offences aforesaid cognizable by the said Justices and Judges of Oyer and Terminer and Gaol Delivery by virtue of this Act to His Majesty's Gaol of *Newgate;* and also for any Justice of the Peace or Coroner acting in and for the said County of *Surrey*, so far as relates to the several Parishes above mentioned lying within the said County of *Surrey*, to commit any Person charged with any of the Offences aforesaid cognizable by the Justices and Judges of Oyer and Terminer and Gaol Delivery by virtue of this Act to His Majesty's Gaol of *Horsemonger Lane* or *Newington* in and for the County of *Surrey*.

Justices and Coroners to specify that Persons are committed under this Act, and to take Examinations, etc., as required under 7 G. 4, c. 64.

XI. And be it further enacted, That every Justice or Coroner acting within the Limits of this Act shall specify in the Commitment that the Person or Persons charged are committed under the Authority of this Act; and such Justice or Coroner shall in all such Cases take the like Examinations, Informations, Bailments, and Recognizances, and certify the same to the said Justices of Oyer and Terminer and Gaol Delivery, as they are required by an Act passed in the Seventh Year of the Reign of His late Majesty King *George* the Fourth, intituled *An Act for improving the Administration of Criminal Justice in* England; and any Justice of the Peace or Coroner, in default of so doing, shall be liable to the same Fines and Penalties to be imposed by the said Justices and Judges

Power to remove Prisoners from County Gaol of Surrey to Newgate.

of Oyer and Terminer and Gaol Delivery in the same Manner as is mentioned in the said Act: and when any Person or Persons shall be committed to His Majesty's Gaol for the County of *Surrey* for any Offence cognizable by the said Justices and Judges of Oyer and Terminer and Gaol Delivery by virtue of this Act, by a Commitment specifying that such Person or Persons is or are committed under the Authority of this Act, the Sheriff of the said County of *Surrey*, or the Keeper of the Gaol for the said County, shall, Six Days at least before the Sitting of the next Court of Oyer and Terminer and Gaol Delivery appointed under the Authority of this Act, or at such other Time as the said Justices and Judges of Oyer and Terminer and Gaol Delivery, or any Two or more of them, shall from Time to Time direct, cause such Person and Persons, with their Commitments and Detainers, to be safely moved from the Gaol of the said County of *Surrey*, without the issuing of any Writ of Habeas Corpus, or other Writ, to the said Gaol of *Newgate*, there to remain until delivered by due Course of Law. [Sects. 10 and 11 in part repealed by (and may be cited with) Central Criminal Court (Prisons) Act, 1881 (44 & 45 Vict. c. 64, ss. 1 & 2, ss. 4).]

---

5 & 6 WILL. IV. c. 76.

An Act to provide for the Regulation of Municipal Corporations in England and Wales. [9th September 1835.]

Sect. 62. In certain Boroughs, Council to appoint a Coroner.

And be it enacted, That the Council of every borough in which a separate court of quarter sessions of the peace shall be holden, as is hereinafter provided, shall, within ten days next after the Grant of the said Court shall have been signified to the Council of such borough, appoint a fit person, not being an alderman or councillor, to be coroner of such borough so long as he shall well behave himself in his office of coroner, and shall fill up every vacancy of the office of coroner of the borough, by death, resignation, or removal, within ten days next after such vacancy shall have occurred, and none thereafter shall take any inquisition which belongs to the office of coroner within such borough save only the coroner so from time to time to be appointed; and every such coroner, for every inquisition which he shall duly take within such borough, shall be entitled to have the sum of twenty shillings, and also the sum of nine pence for every mile exceeding two miles which he shall be compelled to travel from his usual place of abode to take such inquisition, to be paid by the treasury out of the borough fund of such borough, by order of the court of quarter sessions for such borough.

Sect. 63. Coroners to make returns to Secretary of State.

And be it further enacted, that on and before the first day of February in every year after the passing of this Act every coroner appointed in any borough shall make and transmit to one of His Majesty's principal Secretaries of State a return in writing, according to such form as the said Secretary of State from time to time shall direct, of all the cases in which he may have been called upon to hold an inquest touching the cause of death of any person during the year ending on the thirty-first day of December immediately preceding.

Sect. 64. County Coroner to act in other boroughs.

And be it enacted, that in every borough in and for which no separate court of quarter sessions of the peace shall be holden no person from and after the end of this present year shall take any inquisition which belongs to the office of Coroner within such borough, save only the coroner for the county or district in which such borough is situated; and the coroner of such county or district for every inquisition which he shall duly take within any place or precinct within any such borough, shall be entitled to have such rateable fees and salary as would be allowed and due to him, and to be allowed and paid in like manner, as for any other inquisition taken by him within such county. Provided always, that nothing in this Act contained shall extend or be construed to annul, diminish, or affect the Authority of the Lord High Admiral, or of the Commissioners for executing the office of Lord High Admiral of the United Kingdom for the time being, or of the Judge of the High Court of Admiralty of England, as the Lieutenant of the Lord High Admiral in the said Court, to appoint Coroners to act within the jurisdiction of the Admiralty in the several ports and havens and on the sea coast of England, and to take inquisitions touching deaths happening within the said jurisdiction, as hath heretofore been done. [The whole of this Act is repealed by the Municipal Corporations' Act 1882 (45 & 46 Vict. c. 50, s. 5, Sch. 1, part 1.)]

6 & 7 WILL. IV. c. 86.

An Act for registering Births, Deaths, and Marriages in England. [17th August 1836.]

XIX. And be it enacted, That the Father or Mother of any Child born, or the Occupier of every House or Tenement in *England* in which any Birth or Death shall happen, after the said First Day of *March,* may, within Forty-two Days next after the Day of such Birth or within Five Days after the Day of such Death respectively, give Notice of such Birth or Death to the Registrar of the District; and in case any new-born Child or any dead Body shall be found exposed, the Overseers of the Poor in the Case of the new-born Child, and the Coroner in the Case of the dead Body, shall forthwith give Notice and Information thereof, and of the Place where such Child or dead Body was found, to the Registrar; and for the Purposes of this Act the Master or Keeper of every Gaol, Prison, or House of Correction, or Workhouse, Hospital, or Lunatic Asylum, or public or charitable Institution, shall be deemed the Occupier thereof. *[Parents or Occupiers of Houses in which Births or Deaths happen, and Overseers and Coroners in Cases of Foundlings or exposed dead Bodies, to give Notice to the Registrar.]*

XXV. And be it enacted, That some Person present at the Death or in attendance during the last Illness of every Person dying in *England* after the said First Day of *March,* or in case of the Death, Illness, Inability, or Default of all such Persons, the Occupier of the House or Tenement, or if the Occupier be the Person who shall have died, some Inmate of the House or Tenement in which such Death shall have happened, shall, within Eight Days next after the Day of such Death, give Information, upon being requested so to do, to the said Registrar, according to the best of his or her Knowledge and Belief, of the several Particulars hereby required to be known and registered touching the Death of such Person: Provided always, that in every Case in which an Inquest shall be held on any dead Body the Jury shall inquire of the Particulars herein required to be registered concerning the Death, and the Coroner shall inform the *[Some Person present at Death, or Occupier of House, required to give Particulars of Death, so far as known. Registrar to make Entry of Finding of Jury upon Coroner's Inquests.]*

Registrar of the Finding of the Jury, and the Registrar shall make the Entry accordingly.

Registrar to give Certificate of Registry of Death to Undertaker, who shall deliver the same to the Minister or officiating Person.

XXVII. And be it enacted, That every Registrar, immediately upon registering any Death, or as soon thereafter as he shall be required so to do, shall, without Fee or Reward, deliver to the Undertaker or other Person having Charge of the Funeral, a Certificate under his Hand, according to the Form of Schedule (E) to this Act annexed, that such Death has been duly registered, and such Certificate shall be delivered by such Undertaker or other Person to the Minister or officiating Person who shall be required to bury or to perform any religious Service for the Burial of the dead Body, and if any dead Body shall be buried for which no such Certificate shall have been so delivered, the Person who shall bury or perform any Funeral or any religious Service for the Burial shall forthwith give Notice thereof to the Registrar:

Coroner may order Body to be buried, and give Certificate thereof.

Provided always, that the Coroner, upon holding any Inquest, may order the Body to be buried, if he shall think fit, before Registry of the Death, and shall in such Case give a Certificate of his Order in Writing under his Hand, according to the Form of Schedule (F) to this Act annexed, to such Undertaker or other Person having Charge of the Funeral, which shall be delivered as aforesaid; and every Person who shall bury or perform any Funeral or any religious Service for the Burial of any dead Body for which no Certificate shall have been duly made and delivered as aforesaid, either by the Registrar or Coroner, and who shall not within Seven Days give notice thereof to the Registrar, shall forfeit and pay any Sum not exceeding Ten Pounds for every such Offence. [Sects. 19, 25 & 27, and Sch. F., repealed by Registration of Births and Deaths Act, 1874 (37 & 38 Vict. c. 88, s. 54).]

No dead Body to be buried without Certificate of Registry or of Inquest, Penalty, 10l.

SCHEDULE (F).

I *James Smith*, Coroner for the County of *Dorset*, do hereby order the Burial of the Body now shown to the Inquest Jury as the Body of *John Jones*. Witness my Hand this *Eighth* Day of *March*, 1836.

James Smith, Coroner.

6 & 7 WILL. IV. c. 87.

An Act for extinguishing the Secular Jurisdiction of the Archbishop of York *and the Bishop of* Ely *in certain Liberties in the Counties of* York, Nottingham, *and* Cambridge.   [17th August 1836.]

Be it enacted, That all the Secular Authority of the Archbishop of *York* in the said Liberty of *Ripon*, and in the said Liberty of *Cawood, Wistow,* and *Otley*, and in the said Soke of *Southwell*, shall, from and after the passing of this Act, cease and determine, and shall become and be transferred to and vested in His Majesty, His Heirs and Successors. *{Secular Jurisdiction of Archbishop of York in the Places herein mentioned to cease.}*

X. And be it further enacted, that the present Coroner of the Liberty of *Ripon* shall continue Coroner during his Life, or so long as he shall well behave himself; and upon the Death, Removal, or Resignation of such Coroner, and upon every future Vacancy of the Office, a Coroner shall be chosen by the Freeholders of the said Liberty of *Ripon* in like Manner as Coroners are chosen in the Case of other Counties or Divisions of Counties in *England*. *{Coroner for Ripon.}*

XVI. And be it enacted, That the present Coroners of the said *Isle of Ely* shall continue Coroners respectively during their respective lives, or so long as they shall respectively well behave themselves; and that upon the Death, Removal, or Resignation of either of them, and upon every future Vacancy of the Office, a Coroner shall be chosen by the Freeholders of the said Isle in like Manner as Coroners are chosen in the Case of other Counties or Divisions of Counties of *England*; and the said Coroners for the Time being shall be entitled to demand and take the same Fees, Recompence, and Benefit as are given to or provided for the Coroners by an Act made and passed in the Twenty-fifth Year of the Reign of His late Majesty King *George* the Second, intituled *An Act for giving a proper Reward to Coroners for the due Execution of their Office, and for the Removal of Coroners* *{Present Coroners of Ely continued and future Vacancies provided for.}* *{25 G. 2, c. 29.}*

on lawful Conviction of certain Misdemeanors, and shall as such Coroners be subject to all the Provisions of the said Act. [Sec. 10 as far as it relates to Coroners, and Sec. 16 wholly, repealed by Coroners Act, 1887 (50 & 51 Vict. c. 71, s. 45, and Sch. 3).]

---

6 & 7 WILL. IV. c. 89.

An Act to provide for the Attendance and Remuneration of Medical Witnesses at Coroner's Inquests.

[17th August 1836.]

Whereas it is expedient to provide for the Attendance of Medical Witnesses at Coroner's Inquests, also Remuneration for such Attendance, and for the Performance of post-mortem examinations at such Inquests; be it therefore enacted by the King's most Excellent Majesty, by and with the Advice and Consent of the Lords Spiritual and Temporal, and Commons, in this present Parliament assembled, and by the Authority of the same, That from and after the passing of this Act, whenever upon the summoning or holding of any Coroner's Inquest it shall appear to the Coroner that the deceased Person was attended at his Death or during his last Illness by any legally qualified Medical Practitioner, it shall be lawful for the Coroner to issue his Order, in the Form marked (A) in the Schedule hereunto annexed, for the Attendance of such Practitioner as a Witness at such Inquest; and if it shall appear to the Coroner that the deceased Person was not attended at or immediately before his Death by any legally qualified Medical Practitioner, it shall be lawful for the Coroner to issue such Order for the Attendance of any legally qualified Medical Practitioner being at the Time in actual Practice in or near the Place where the Death has happened; and it shall be lawful for the Coroner, either in his Order for the Attendance of the Medical Witness, or at any Time between the issuing of such Order and the Termination of the Inquest, to direct the Performance of a post-mortem Examination, with or

[margin: Coroner empowered to summon Medical witnesses, and to direct the Performance of a post-mortem Examination.]

without an Analysis of the Contents of the Stomach or Intestines, by the Medical Witness or Witnesses who may be summoned to attend at any Inquest; provided that if any Person shall state upon Oath before the Coroner that in his or her Belief the Death of the deceased Individual was caused partly or entirely by the improper or negligent Treatment of any Medical Practitioner or other Person, such Medical Practitioner or other Person shall not be allowed to perform or assist at the post-mortem Examination of the Deceased.

II. And be it further enacted, That whenever it shall appear to the greater Number of the Jurymen sitting at any Coroner's Inquest, that the Cause of Death has not been satisfactorily explained by the Evidence of the Medical Practitioner or other Witness or Witnesses who may be examined in the first instance, such greater Number of the Jurymen are hereby authorized and empowered to name to the Coroner in Writing any other legally qualified Medical Practitioner or Practitioners, and to require the Coroner to issue his Order, in the Form herein-before mentioned, for the Attendance of such last-mentioned Medical Practitioner or Practitioners as a Witness or Witnesses, and for the Performance of a post-mortem Examination, with or without an Analysis of the Contents of the Stomach or Intestines, whether such an Examination has been performed before or not; and if the Coroner, having been thereunto required, shall refuse to issue such Order, he shall be deemed guilty of a Misdemeanor, and shall be punishable in like Manner as if the same were a Misdemeanor at Common Law. *A Majority of the Jury may require the Coroner to summon additional Medical Evidence if the first be not satisfactory.*

III. And be it further enacted, That when any legally qualified Medical Practitioner has attended upon any Coroner's Inquest in obedience to any such Order as aforesaid of the Coroner, the said Practitioner shall for such Attendance at any Inquest in *Great Britain* be entitled to receive such Remuneration or Fee as is mentioned in the Table marked (B) in the Schedule hereunto annexed; and for any Inquest held in *Ireland*, *Fees to Medical Witnesses;*

the said Practitioner shall be paid in the Manner provided by the Laws in force in that Part of the United Kingdom; and the Coroner is hereby required and commanded to make, according to the form marked (C) in the Schedule hereunto annexed, his Order for the Payment of such Remuneration or Fee, when the Inquest shall be held in *Great Britain,* and such Order may be addressed and directed to the Churchwardens and Overseers of the Parish or Place in which the Death has happened; and such Churchwardens and Overseers, or any One of them, is and are hereby required and commanded to pay the Sum of Money mentioned in such Order of the Coroner to the Medical Witness therein mentioned, out of the Funds collected for the Relief of the Poor of the said Place.

to be paid out of Funds collected for Relief of the Poor.

IV. Provided nevertheless, and be it further enacted, That no Order of Payment shall be given, or Fee or Remuneration paid, to any Medical Practitioner for the Performance of any post-mortem Examination which may be instituted without the previous Direction of the Coroner.

No fee for a post-mortem Examination instituted without Order from the Coroner.

V. Provided also, and be it further enacted, That when any Inquest shall be holden on the Body of any Person who has died in any public Hospital or Infirmary, or in any Building or Place belonging thereto, or used for the Reception of the Patients thereof, or who has died in any County or other Lunatic Asylum, or in any public Infirmary or other public Medical Institution, whether the same be supported by Endowments or by voluntary Subscriptions, then and in such Case nothing herein contained shall be construed to entitle the Medical Officer whose Duty it may have been to attend the deceased Person as a Medical Officer of such Institution as aforesaid to the Fees or Remuneration herein provided.

Inquests on Bodies of Persons dying in public Institutions.

VI. And be it further enacted, That where any Order for the Attendance of any Medical Practitioner as aforesaid shall have been personally served upon such Practitioner, or where any such Order not personally served

Penalty on Medical Practitioner for neglecting to attend.

shall have been received by any Medical Practitioner in sufficient Time for him to have obeyed such Order, or where any such Order has been served at the Residence of any Medical Practitioner, and in every Case where any Medical Practitioner has not obeyed such Order, he shall for such Neglect or Disobedience forfeit the Sum of Five Pounds Sterling upon Complaint thereof made by the Coroner or any Two of the Jury before any Two Justices having Jurisdiction in the Parish or Place where the Inquest under which the Order issued was held, or in the Parish where such Medical Practitioner resides; and such Two Justices are hereby required, upon such Complaint, to proceed to the Hearing and Adjudication of such Complaint, and, if such Medical Practitioner shall not show to the said Justices a good and sufficient Cause for not having obeyed such Order to enforce the said Penalty by Distress and Sale of the Offender's Goods, as they are empowered to proceed by any Act of Parliament for any other Penalty or Forfeiture.

VII. And be it enacted, That nothing in this Act contained shall extend to *Scotland*. [Sect. 3 repealed in part by 1 Vict. c. 68, s. 2. Remainder of Act (except as to Ireland) repealed by Coroners Act, 1887 (50 & 51 Vict. c. 71, s. 45, and Sch. 3).] *Act not to extend to Scotland.*

SCHEDULE TO WHICH THIS ACT REFERS.

(A)

Form of Summons.

CORONER'S INQUEST at   upon the Body of

By virtue of this my Order as Coroner for   you are required to appear before me and the Jury at   on the Day of   One thousand eight hundred and , at   of the Clock, to give Evidence touching the Cause of Death of   [*and then add, when the Witness is required to make or assist at a post-mortem Examination*, and make or assist in making a post-mortem Examination of the Body, with [*or without*] an Analysis, *as the Case may be*], and report thereon at the said Inquest.

             (Signed)   Coroner.

To   Surgeon [*or M.D., as the Case may be.*]

(B.)

Table of Fees.

1. To every legally qualified Medical Practitioner for attending to give Evidence under the Provisions of this Act at any Coroner's Inquest whereat no post-mortem Examination has been made by such Practitioner, the Fee or Remuneration shall be One Guinea.
2. For the making of a post-mortem Examination of the Body of the Deceased, either with or without an Analysis of the Contents of the Stomach or Intestines, and for attending to give Evidence thereon, the Fee or Remuneration shall be two Guineas.

(C.)

Coroner's Order for the Payment of Medical Witnesses.

By virtue of an Act of Parliament passed in   Session of   holden in the   intituled   I,   the Coroner of and for   do order you, the Overseers of the Parish [*or* Township, *as the Case may be*], to pay to   the Sum of [One Guinea, *or* Two Guineas, *as the Case may be*], being the Fee [*or* Fees] due to him for having attended as a Medical Witness at an Inquest holden before me this   Day of   upon the Body of   about the Age of   who was found dead at   [*or other Particulars or Description*], and at which said Inquest the Jury returned a Verdict of

       (Signed)   Coroner.

Witnessed by me   of

To the Overseers, *et cætera*.

---

6 & 7 WILL. IV. c. 105.

An Act for the better Administration of Justice in certain Boroughs. [20th August 1836.]

Coroner may appoint a Deputy in case of Illness or unavoidable Absence.
VI. be it enacted, That in case of Illness or unavoidable Absence the Coroner for the Time being of any Borough, Town, or City named in the said Act shall be empowered and he is hereby required, by Writing under his Hand and Seal, to appoint a fit Person, being a Barrister at Law

or an Attorney of one of His Majesty's Courts at *Westminster*, and not being an Alderman or Councillor of such Borough, Town, or City, to act for him as Deputy Coroner during the Illness or unavoidable Absence of such Coroner, but no longer or otherwise: Provided always, that the Mayor or two Justices of such Borough, Town, or City, shall on each Occasion certify under their Hands and Seals the Necessity for the Appointment of such Deputy Coroner; and such Certificate shall state the Cause of Absence of the Coroner, and shall be openly read to every Inquest Jury summoned by such Deputy Coroner; and the Particulars of every Inquest holden before any Deputy Coroner shall be included in the Return to be made by the Coroner to the Secretary of State, as provided by the said Act. Proviso.

X. And be it enacted, That so much of the said Act as provides that the Courts of Quarter Sessions of the Peace of the Towns and Ports of *Hastings, Sandwich, Dover,* and *Hythe,* and of the ancient Town of *Rye,* or of such of the said Towns and Ports and ancient Town to which His Majesty shall grant a separate Court of Quarter Sessions of the Peace, shall have Jurisdiction over Offences and Matters committed, arising, and happening within the Towns named in the Schedule to the said Act which are ancient Corporate Members and Liberties of the said Towns and Ports and ancient Town respectively, and to which His Majesty shall not grant a separate Court of Quarter Sessions of the Peace, and also provides that any or either of the said Towns and Ports of *Hastings, Sandwich, Dover,* and *Hythe,* and ancient Town of *Rye,* to which His Majesty shall not grant a separate Court of Quarter Sessions of the Peace, and their or its Members and Liberties, shall, for all Purposes relating to the Jurisdiction of Courts of Quarter Sessions of the Peace, be respectively within the jurisdiction of the Courts of Quarter Sessions of the Peace of the nearest other of the said Towns and Ports or ancient Town to which His Majesty shall grant a separate Court of Quarter Sessions of the Peace, is hereby repealed; and it is hereby enacted, that, until other Provision shall be made Repeal of Part of 5 & 6 W. 4, c. 76, as to Courts of Quarter Sessions for the Cinque Ports, and new Provision made.

by Parliament in that Behalf, Courts of General Sessions of the Peace and Gaol Delivery shall and may be holden in and for the said Towns and Ports of *Hastings, Sandwich, Dover,* and *Hythe,* and ancient Town of *Rye,* or such of the said Towns and Ports and ancient Town to which His Majesty shall not grant a separate Court of Quarter Sessions of the Peace, and for the ancient Members and Liberties thereof, not being Corporate, and also in and for the Towns of *Deal, Faversham, Folkestone,* and *Tenterden,* or such of the said Towns to which His Majesty shall not grant a separate Court of Quarter Sessions of the Peace, before the Person who at the Time of the passing of the said Act was or acted as Recorder or Steward or Assessor, or by whatsoever other Name he was called, of the said Towns and Ports, ancient Town and Towns respectively, or in case of his Death or Resignation or Absence, or in case there was no such Recorder or Steward or Assessor, then before any Barrister at Law, of not less than Five Years' Standing, whom His Majesty shall appoint to hold the same, in the same Manner in other respects, and with the same Powers and Authorities, as before the passing of the said Act, except as regards the Trial of Capital Felonies; and so long as such Courts of General Sessions of the Peace and Gaol Delivery shall be holden the Offices of Clerk of the Peace and Coroner shall be holden and exercised by the same Persons, or by the same Officers of such of the said Towns and Ports, ancient Town and Towns respectively, to which His Majesty shall not grant a separate Court of Quarter Sessions, by whom or by which the same were holden at the Time of the passing of the said Act, or in case of their Death or Resignation, or there being no longer such Officers, then by such Persons as the Councils of such Towns and Ports, ancient Town and Towns respectively, shall appoint to hold the same, with the same Powers and Authorities as before the passing of the said Act; and the Non-corporate Members and Liberties of the said Towns and Ports of *Hastings, Sandwich, Dover,* and *Hythe,* and the said ancient Town of *Rye,* shall and may be chargeable and charged by the Courts of General or Quarter Sessions of the Peace holden for the same respectively with a due Proportion of the Expences of such Towns and Ports and ancient Town respectively, and the Non-corporate Members and Liberties thereof, to the Payment of which Expences Rates in the Nature of County Rates are applicable, and the same shall and may be assessed and levied in the manner in which rates of that description were assessed and levied before the passing of the said Act; and a due proportion of Inhabitant Householders to serve as Grand Jurors and Jurors at the Courts of General or Quarter Sessions of the Peace of the said Towns and Ports of *Hastings, Sandwich, Dover*, and *Hythe*, and of the said ancient Town of *Rye*, shall be summoned by the Clerks of the Peace of the said Towns and Ports and ancient Town from the Non-corporate Members and Liberties thereof respectively, and the Attendance of such Jurors shall be enforced and their Defaults punished in the Manner by the said Act directed with respect to Jurors in Boroughs. [Repealed by Municipal Corporations Act, 1882 (45 & 46 Vict. c. 50, s. 5, Sch. 1).]

---

1 VICT. c. 64.

An Act for regulating the Coroners of the County of Durham. [15th July 1837.]

Whereas by an Act passed in the last Session of Parliament, intituled *An Act for separating the Palatine Jurisdiction of the County Palatine of* Durham *from the Bishoprick of* Durham, the Palatine Jurisdiction, Power and Authority heretofore vested in and belonging to the Bishop of *Durham* was separted from the Bishoprick of *Durham*, and was transferred to and vested in His late Majesty King *William* the Fourth, His Heirs and Successors: And whereas previously to the passing of the said Act the Coroners for the said County of *Durham* were appointed by the said Bishop, and it is necessary that Provision should be made for the future Appointment of the Coroners of the said County, and for their due Remuneration: Be it therefore enacted by the Queen's

6 & 7 W. 4, c. 19.

most Excellent Majesty, by and with the Advice and Consent of the Lords Spiritual and Temporal, and Commons, in this present Parliament assembled, and by the Authority of the same, That the present Coroners of the Four Wards, respectively called *Easington* Ward, *Chester* Ward, *Stockton* Ward, and *Darlington* Ward, in the said County of *Durham*, shall continue Coroners of the same Wards respectively during their respective Lives, or so long as they shall respectively well behave themselves; and that upon and after the Death, Removal, or Resignation of the Coroner either of *Easington* Ward or of *Chester* Ward (which Two Wards form the Northern Division of the said County of *Durham*) a Coroner shall be chosen for each of such Wards in the Place of the Coroner making a Vacancy, and so from Time to Time on every future Vacancy of the Office of Coroner of either of the said Wards, the Coroner of each of the said Wards to be chosen by its own Freeholders in like Manner as Coroners are chosen in the Case of other Counties or Divisions of Counties in *England*; and that after the Death, Removal, or Resignation of the Coroner either of *Stockton* Ward or of *Darlington* Ward (which two Wards form the Southern Division of the said County of *Durham*) a Coroner shall be chosen for each of such last-mentioned Wards in the Place of the Coroner making a Vacaucy, and so from Time to Time on every future Vacancy of the Office of Coroner of either of the said last-mentioned Wards, the Coroner of each of such Wards to be chosen by its own Freeholders in like Manner as Coroners are chosen in the case of other Counties or Divisions of Counties in *England*: Provided always, that on every Vacancy of the Office of Coroner in any of the said Wards, and until the Appointment of another Coroner in his Place, it shall be lawful for any of the remaining Coroners to act as Coroner for the Ward in which such Vacancy may have occurred.

Present Coroners to continue.

Election of future Coroners.

In case of Vacancy.

Coroners liable to be removed.

II. And be it enacted, That the Coroners of the said County of *Durham* shall be liable to be removed from their respective Offices in the same manner as Coroners of the other Counties in *England* and *Wales*.

III. And be it enacted, That from and after the passing of this Act the Coroners of the said County of *Durham* shall be entitled to all the same Fees and Emoluments as the Coroners of the other Counties in *England* and *Wales*; and so much of an Act passed in the Twenty-fifth Year of the Reign of His Majesty King *George* the Second, intituled *An Act for giving a proper Reward to Coroners for the due Execution of their Office, and for the Removal of Coroners on lawful Conviction of certain Misdemeanors*, as provides that no Coroner of the County Palatine of *Durham* shall be entitled to any Fee, Recompence, or Benefit given to or provided for Coroners by that Act, shall be and the same is hereby repealed. [Repealed by Coroners Act, 1887 (50 & 51 Vict. c. 71, s. 45, & Sch. 3).] Coroners to be entitled to usual Fees and Emoluments.
25 G. 2 c. 29.

---

1 VICT. c. 68.

An Act to provide for Payment of the Expences of holding Coroner's Inquests. [15th July 1837.]

Whereas the holding of Coroner's Inquests on dead Bodies is attended with divers necessary Expences, for the Payment whereof no certain Provision is made by Law, and such Expences have usually been discharged without any lawful Authority for that Purpose out of the Monies levied for the Relief of the Poor; and it is expedient to make adequate legal Provision for the Payment of such Expences: Be it therefore enacted by the Queen's most Excellent Majesty, by and with the Advice and Consent of the Lords Spiritual and Temporal, and Commons, in this present Parliament assembled, and by the Authority of the same, That the Justices of the Peace for every County, Riding, Division, or District in *England* and *Wales*, in General or Quarter Sessions assembled, shall, at the General or Quarter Sessions of the Peace to be holden next after the passing of this Act or at some subsequent General or Quarter Sessions, and the Town Council of every Borough having a Coroner shall at the Schedule to be made of Fees payable on holding Inquests.

on lawful Conviction of certain Misdemeanors, and shall as such Coroners be subject to all the Provisions of the said Act. [Sec. 10 as far as it relates to Coroners, and Sec. 16 wholly, repealed by Coroners Act, 1887 (50 & 51 Vict. c. 71, s. 45, and Sch. 3).]

---

6 & 7 WILL. IV. c. 89.

An Act to provide for the Attendance and Remuneration of Medical Witnesses at Coroner's Inquests.

[17th August 1836.]

Whereas it is expedient to provide for the Attendance of Medical Witnesses at Coroner's Inquests, also Remuneration for such Attendance, and for the Performance of post-mortem examinations at such Inquests; be it therefore enacted by the King's most Excellent Majesty, by and with the Advice and Consent of the Lords Spiritual and Temporal, and Commons, in this present Parliament assembled, and by the Authority of the same, That from and after the passing of this Act, whenever upon the summoning or holding of any Coroner's Inquest it shall appear to the Coroner that the deceased Person was attended at his Death or during his last Illness by any legally qualified Medical Practitioner, it shall be lawful for the Coroner to issue his Order, in the Form marked (A) in the Schedule hereunto annexed, for the Attendance of such Practitioner as a Witness at such Inquest; and if it shall appear to the Coroner that the deceased Person was not attended at or immediately before his Death by any legally qualified Medical Practitioner, it shall be lawful for the Coroner to issue such Order for the Attendance of any legally qualified Medical Practitioner being at the Time in actual Practice in or near the Place where the Death has happened; and it shall be lawful for the Coroner, either in his Order for the Attendance of the Medical Witness, or at any Time between the issuing of such Order and the Termination of the Inquest, to direct the Performance of a post-mortem Examination, with or

Coroner empowered to summon Medical witnesses, and to direct the Performance of a post-mortem Examination.

without an Analysis of the Contents of the Stomach or Intestines, by the Medical Witness or Witnesses who may be summoned to attend at any Inquest; provided that if any Person shall state upon Oath before the Coroner that in his or her Belief the Death of the deceased Individual was caused partly or entirely by the improper or negligent Treatment of any Medical Practitioner or other Person, such Medical Practitioner or other Person shall not be allowed to perform or assist at the post-mortem Examination of the Deceased.

II. And be it further enacted, That whenever it shall appear to the greater Number of the Jurymen sitting at any Coroner's Inquest, that the Cause of Death has not been satisfactorily explained by the Evidence of the Medical Practitioner or other Witness or Witnesses who may be examined in the first instance, such greater Number of the Jurymen are hereby authorized and empowered to name to the Coroner in Writing any other legally qualified Medical Practitioner or Practitioners, and to require the Coroner to issue his Order, in the Form herein-before mentioned, for the Attendance of such last-mentioned Medical Practitioner or Practitioners as a Witness or Witnesses, and for the Performance of a post-mortem Examination, with or without an Analysis of the Contents of the Stomach or Intestines, whether such an Examination has been performed before or not; and if the Coroner, having been thereunto required, shall refuse to issue such Order, he shall be deemed guilty of a Misdemeanor, and shall be punishable in like Manner as if the same were a Misdemeanor at Common Law. *A Majority of the Jury may require the Coroner to summon additional Medical Evidence if the first be not satisfactory.*

III. And be it further enacted, That when any legally qualified Medical Practitioner has attended upon any Coroner's Inquest in obedience to any such Order as aforesaid of the Coroner, the said Practitioner shall for such Attendance at any Inquest in *Great Britain* be entitled to receive such Remuneration or Fee as is mentioned in the Table marked (B) in the Schedule hereunto annexed; and for any Inquest held in *Ireland*, *Fees to Medical Witnesses;*

said, over and above all other Fees and Allowances to which he is now by Law entitled; and the Treasurer of any County, Riding, Division, or District on whom any such Order shall be made shall, out of the Monies in his Hands arising from the County Rates, and the Treasurer of any Borough on whom any such Order shall be made shall, out of the Monies in his Hands on account of the Borough Fund, pay to the said Coroner the Sum mentioned in · such Order, without any Abatement or Deduction whatever; and every such Treasurer shall, on passing his Accounts, be allowed all Sums which he shall pay in pursuance of any such Order as aforesaid.

Act applicable to London.

IV. And be it enacted, That this Act and the several Provisions herein contained shall extend and be applicable to the City of *London* and the Town and Borough of *Southwark*.

Act may be altered.

V. And be it enacted, That this Act may be altered or repealed by any Act in this present Session of Parliament. [Sect. 3, as to fees and allowances to County Coroners, repealed by County Coroners Act, 1860 (23 & 24 Vict. c. 116, s. 3). Sect. 5 repealed by Stat. Law Rev. Act (No. 1), 1874 (37 & 38 Vict. c. 35, s. 1, & Sch.). Remainder of Act repealed by Coroners Act, 1887 (50 & 51 Vict. c. 71, s. 45, and Sch. 3).]

---

1 & 2 VICT. c. 105.

An Act to remove Doubts as to the Validity of certain Oaths. [14th August 1838.]

All Persons to be bound by the Oath administered in the Form, etc., which such Persons may declare binding.

Be it declared and enacted, That in all Cases in which an Oath may lawfully be and shall have been administered to any Person, either as a Juryman or a Witness, or a Deponent in any Proceeding, Civil or Criminal, in any Court of Law or Equity in the United Kingdom, or on Appointment to any Office or Employment, or on any

Occasion whatever, such Person is bound by the Oath administered, provided the same shall have been administered in such Form and with such Ceremonies as such Person may declare to be binding; and every such Person in case of wilful false swearing, may be convicted of the Crime of Perjury, in the same Manner as if the Oath had been administered in the Form and with the Ceremonies most commonly adopted.

---

3 VICT. c. 87.

An Act to authorize the Appointment of additional Coroners for the County Palatine of Chester.

[19th June 1840.]

Whereas by an Act passed in the Thirty-third Year of the Reign of His Majesty King *Henry* the Eighth, Chapter Thirteen, intituled *An Act concerning certain* 33 Hen. 8, *Lordships translated from the Countie of* Denbighe *to the* c. 18. *Countie of* Flinte, it was enacted, that the Shyryf of the said Countie of *Chester* for the Tyme being, after the Feaste of *Easter* next coomyng, shoulde be bounde to keepe his Shyre Courte in the Shyre Hall of the saide Countye everye Monethe for ever for Determinacon of Plaints and Accōns under xlˢ., and for Proclamacōns and calling of Exigends and other necessarye Causes as was used in other Shyres of this Realme of *Englande*, and that Twoo Heade Coroners for the Bodye of the said Shyre shoulde be elected and chosen by vertue of the King's Wrytt De coronatore eligend to be awardyd oute of the Exchequiere of *Chester*, whiche Coroners shouldde be bounde to sitt with the said Shyryff at the saide Courts to gyve Iudgements uppon Otlaryes and to doo all other Things as appteyned: And whereas an Act was passed in the Fifty-eighth Year of the Reign of His Majesty King *George* the Third, intituled *An Act to regulate the Election* 58 G. 2, c. 95. *of Coroners for Counties:* And whereas by an Act passed in the First Year of the Reign of His late Majesty King *William* the Fourth, intituled *An Act for the more effectual*

11 G. 4 & 1 W. 4, c. 70.

Administration of Justice in England *and* Wales, it was amongst other things enacted, that from and after the Commencement of that Act His Majesty's Writ should be directed and obeyed, and the Jurisdiction of His Majesty's Courts of King's Bench, Common Pleas, and Exchequer respectively, and the several Judges and Barons thereof, should extend and be exercised over and within the County of *Chester*, and the County of the City of *Chester*, and the several Counties in *Wales*, in like Manner, to the same Extent, and to and for all Intents and Purposes whatsoever as the Jurisdiction of such Courts respectively was then exercised in and over the Counties of *England* not being Counties Palatine, any Statute theretofore passed to the contrary notwithstanding, and that all original Writs to be issued into the said several Counties of *Chester*, City of *Chester*, and *Wales* should be issued by the Cursitors for *London* and *Middlesex*, and the Process and Proceedings should be issued by and transacted with such of the Officers of the several Courts of King's Bench and Common Pleas as should be named for the Purpose by the Chief Justices of such Courts respectively, each naming for his own Court; and it was by the same Act further enacted, that all the Power, Authority, and Jurisdiction of His Majesty's Court of Session of the said County Palatine of *Chester*, and of the Judges thereof, and of his Court of Exchequer of the said County Palatine, and of the Chamberlain and Vice Chamberlain thereof, and also of his Judges and Courts of Great Sessions, both in Law and Equity, in the Principality of *Wales*, should cease and determine: And whereas the Population of the said County of *Chester* has greatly increased since the passing of the first-recited Act, and Two Head Coroners are not now sufficient to discharge the duties which devolve upon Coroners within the said County, whereby the holding of Inquests is frequently delayed and great public Inconvenience sustained: And whereas Doubts have arisen whether any additional Head Coroners can be appointed for the said County of *Chester*: And whereas it is expedient that such Doubts should be removed, and that the Lord Chancellor should be empowered, upon the Application of the Justices of the Peace of the said County in Quarter Sessions assembled, to issue One or more Writ or Writs De coronatore eligendo, for the Election of One or more additional Head Coroner or Coroners for the said County: And whereas by reason of the great Extent of the said County of *Chester* the Expence necessarily attendant upon Elections for Coroners is very great, and it would be very beneficial to the County at large if the same were for the Purposes of such Elections divided into Divisions, to be settled and described by the Justices of the Peace for the said County in Quarter Sessions assembled: And whereas the beneficial Purposes aforesaid cannot be effected without the Aid and Authority of Parliament: May it therefore please Your Majesty that it may be enacted; and be it enacted by the Queen's most Excellent Majesty, and by and with the Advice and Consent of the Lords Spiritual and Temporal, and Commons, in this present Parliament assembled, and by the Authority of the same, That from and immediately after the passing of this Act it shall be lawful for the Lord High Chancellor, From Time to Time upon the Application or Representation of the Justices of the Peace for the said County of *Chester* in Quarter Sessions assembled, or at any Adjournment thereof, to issue or cause to be issued Her Majesty's Writ De coronatore eligendo for the Election of One or more additional Head Coroner or Coroners for the said County of *Chester*, as in any such Application or Representation shall be required, any thing in the said first-recited Act to the contrary thereof in any wise notwithstanding.

The Lord Chancellor authorized to issue Writs De coronatore eligendo for the Election of additional Head Coroners.

II. And be it enacted, That the Justices of the Peace for the said County assembled at the Quarter Sessions to be holden in the Month of *October* in the present Year, or at some Adjournment thereof, or at some special Sessions to be appointed by them so assembled as aforesaid, shall divide the said County (with the Exception of that District or Portion of the County which is commonly called or known by the Name of *Halton Fee*) into Three or more Divisions, and shall set out and determine the

The Justices of the Peace assembled in Quarter Sessions authorised to divide the County into Three or more Divisions, and fix the Place of Election for each Division.

Extent of Limits of such Divisions, and what Parishes Townships, Extra-parochial Places, and other Portions of the said County shall be included therein respectively, and shall fix and determine at what Place, within each Division, the Court for the Election of Head Coroner for such Division shall be holden, and shall cause an Instrument to be prepared, under the Hands and Seals of the Justices so assembled as aforesaid, or the major Part of them, describing the Divisions into which the said County is to be divided, and the Name by which each such Division is to be distinguished, and the Parishes, Townships, Extra-parochial Places, and other Portions of the said County intended to be included therein respectively, and the Place at which the Court for the Election of the Head Coroner for such Division is to be held, a Copy of which Instrument shall be published in the *London Gazette*, and also in Two or more Newspapers published or usually circulated within the said County, and the Original thereof shall be deposited with the Clerk of the Peace for the said County, to be by him safely kept amongst the public Records of the said County, and the said County shall, after such Publication as aforesaid, be deemed to be divided into such Divisions as shall be so determined and set out as aforesaid, and such Divisions shall continue and be in force until the same shall be altered by the Authority and in the Manner herein-after mentioned.

Justices may assign the present Head Coroners and apply for Writs for the Election of others.

III. And be it enacted, That it shall be lawful for the said Justices, so assembled as aforesaid, to fix and determine to which of the Divisions into which the said County shall be so divided the present Head Coroners, or the Head Coroners for the Time being of the said County at the Time of such Division, shall be assigned, and within which they shall act, for the Purpose of holding Inquests, and to apply to the Lord High Chancellor to issue One or more Writ or Writs De coronatore eligendo for the Election of a Head Coroner or Coroners for the remaining Division or Divisions.

IV. And be it enacted, That if the Justices of the

Peace for the said County assembled at the Quarter Sessions, or at any Adjournment thereof, shall at any Time hereafter think it expedient that the Divisions into which the said County may at that Time happen to be divided should be increased or augmented by the Creation of an additional Division or Divisions, or be in any Manner varied or altered, or that the places for the Time being appointed for holding the Courts for the Election of Head Coroners for such Divisions, or any of them, should be altered or changed, it shall be lawful for such Justices so assembled as aforesaid, or at some special Sessions to be appointed by them for that Purpose, to increase the Number of Divisions into which the said County may for the Time being be divided, and to set out and determine the Extent and Limits of such additional Division or Divisions, and the Parishes, Townships, Extra-parochial Places, and other Portions of the said County to be included therein respectively, and the Place or Places within such additional Division or Divisions at which the Court for the Election of Head Coroners for such Division or Divisions shall be holden, and, either with or without increasing the Number of Divisions, to alter and vary the Division into which the County may for the Time being be divided, and the Parishes, Townships, Extra-parochial Places, and other Portions of the County to be included therein, and to vary or alter the Places at which the Courts for the Election of Head Coroners for any such Division or Divisions shall be holden; and whenever any such additional Division or Divisions shall be made, or any such Alteration as aforesaid shall be made, the said Justices shall cause an Instrument to be prepared, under the Hands and Seals of the Justices so assembled as aforesaid, or the major Part of them, describing the additional Division or Divisions, and the Name by which each is to be distinguished, and the Parishes, Townships, Extra-parochial Places, and other Portions of the said County intended to be included therein, and the Place at which the Court for the Election of the Head Coroner for such Division is to be held, and the Alteration which shall be made in

Justices may alter or increase the Divisions of the County, and if increased, apply to the Lord Chancellor to issue Writs for the Election of Coroners for the new Divisions.

the existing Divisions of the County, and the Variation or Alteration which shall be made in the Places at which the Court for the Election of Head Coroners shall be held, and any other Alteration which shall from Time to Time be made; and a Copy of such Instrument shall be published in the *London Gazette*, and in Two Newspapers printed or usually circulated within the said County, and the Original thereof shall be deposited with the Clerk of the Peace for the said County, to be by him safely kept amongst the public Records of the said County, and the said County shall, after such Publication, be deemed to be divided into such Divisions as shall be so determined and set out as last aforesaid, or as the same shall be so altered or varied, and such Divisions shall continue and be in force until the same shall be again varied or altered in the Manner herein-before directed; and when and as soon as any additional Division or Divisions shall be made, under the Authority herein-before contained, the said Justices so assembled as aforesaid shall fix and determine to which of the Divisions of the said County the Head Coroners for the Time being shall be assigned, and within which they shall act for the Purpose of holding Inquests, and shall apply to the Lord High Chancellor to issue One or more Writ or Writs De coronatore eligendo for the Election of a Head Coroner or Coroners for such additional Division or Divisions.

Instruments dividing Counties, etc., to be open to Inspection.

V. And be it enacted, That the said Instruments under the Hands and Seals of the Justices aforesaid, herein-before directed to be deposited with the Clerk of the Peace for the County, shall be at all reasonable Times open to the Inspection of all Persons interested therein, who shall be at liberty to make Extracts therefrom or Copies thereof respectively, paying to the said Clerk of the Peace for every Inspection the Sum of Six Shillings and Eight-pence, and for Copies of or Extracts from the said Instruments or any of them after the Rate of Sixpence for every One hundred Words; and the said several Instruments, or any of them, or true Copies thereof respectively, or so much thereof respectively as shall relate to any Matter in question, certified by the said Clerk of the Peace, shall be and are hereby declared to be good Evidence in all Courts of Law or elsewhere.

VI. And be it enacted, That the Head Coroners for the said County shall no longer be elected by the Freeholders of the County at large, but every future Head Coroner shall be elected by the Freeholders of the Division of the County within which it is intended that he shall hold Inquests, in the same Manner as if such Division were a separate County, and (except where otherwise provided by this Act) in the same Manner in all respects as is directed by the said recited Act of the Fifty-eighth Year of the Reign of His Majesty King *George* the Third, or any other Law or Statute now in force regulating the Election of Coroners; and the Court for the Election of a Head Coroner for each Division of the said County shall be holden at the Place to be from Time to Time appointed for that Purpose by the Magistrates for the said County in the Manner herein-before directed.

Head Coroners to be no longer elected by the Freeholders of the County at large, but by the Freeholders of the Division within which they are to hold Inquests.

VII. And be it enacted, That upon every Election of a Head Coroner for any Division of the said County the Sheriff of the said County, or his Under Sheriff or Deputy, shall hold a Court in the Nature of a County Court for the same Election at such a Place as shall from Time to Time be appointed in the Manner herein-before directed for that Purpose, and shall there proceed to Election on some convenient Day, not exceeding Fourteen Days from the Receipt of the Writ De coronatore eligendo of which Day Ten Days' Notice shall be given; and in case the said Election be not determined upon the View with the Consent of the Freeholders there present, but a Poll shall be demanded for the Determination thereof, then the said Sheriff, or in his Absence his Under Sheriff or Deputy, with such others as shall be deputed by him, shall take the said Poll, on such Days, at such Times, and in such Manner as are herein-after provided.

Upon the Election of Head Coroner the Sheriff to hold a Court for that Purpose within the Division for which the Election is to take place.

VIII. And be it enacted, That for more conveniently taking the Poll at all Elections of Head Coroners for the

The Polling Places in Elections for

several Divisions of the said County, in pursuance of the Provisions of this Act, the Poll for the Election of Head Coroner in each Division shall be taken at the Place to be appointed for holding the Court for such Election, and at such other Places within the same Division as may for the Time being be appointed as the Places for taking the Poll at Elections of a Knight or Knights of the said Shire of *Chester* to serve in Parliament, and the District which shall or may be assigned to every such Polling Place for the Purpose of such Election of a Knight or Knights of the Shire, or so much of such District as shall be within the Division of the County for which such Election of Head Coroner is to be made, shall be considered as the District assigned to every such Polling Place for the Purposes of this Act.

<small>Knights of the Shire to be Polling Places for taking the Poll at Elections for Head Coroners.</small>

IX. And be it enacted, That at every contested Election of Head Coroner for any Division of the said County, the Sheriff, Under Sheriff, or Sheriff's Deputy shall, if required, by or on the Behalf of any Candidate on the Day fixed for the Election, and if not so required may, if it shall appear to him expedient, cause a Booth or Booths to be erected for taking the Poll at the Court or principal Place of Election, and also at each of the Polling Places within the said Division herein-before directed to be used for the Purposes of such Election, and shall cause to be affixed on the most conspicuous Part of each of the said Booths the Names of the several Parishes, Townships, and Places for which such Booth is respectively allotted; and no Person shall be admitted to vote at any such Election in respect of any Property situate in any Parish, Township, or Place, except at the Booth so allotted for such Parish, Township, or Place, and if no Booth shall be so allotted for the same, then at any of the Booths for the same District; and in case any Parish, Township, or Place, or Part of any Parish, Township, or Place, shall happen not be included in any of the Districts, the Votes in respect of Property situate in any Parish, Township, or Place, or any Part of any Parish, Township, or Place, so omitted, shall be taken

<small>The Sheriff may erect Polling Booths for taking the Poll at.</small>

<small>No Voter to Poll out of the District where his Property lies.</small>

at the Court or principal Place of Election for such Division of the said County.

X. And be it enacted, That at every contested Election of Head Coroner for any Division of the said County the polling shall commence at Nine o'Clock in the Forenoon of the next Day but Two after the Day fixed for the Election, unless such next Day but Two shall be *Saturday* or *Sunday*, and then on the *Monday* following, the principal Place of Election, and also at the several Places within the same District herein-before directed to be used for taking Polls at such Elections, and such Polling shall continue for Two Days only, such Two Days being successive Days; that is to say, for Seven Hours on the first Day of polling, and for Eight Hours on the Second Day of Polling; and no Poll shall be kept open later than Four o'Clock in the Afternoon of the Second Day, the said recited Act of the Fifty-eighth Year of the Reign of King *George* the Third or any other Statute to the contrary notwithstanding.

Commencement and Continuance of the Poll.

XI. And be it enacted, That the Sheriff of the said County shall have full Power to appoint Deputies to preside and Clerks to take the Poll at the Court or principal Place of Election, and also at the several Places for taking the Poll for any Division of the said County; and that the Poll Clerks employed at those several Places shall at the close of each Day's Poll enclose and seal their several Books, and shall publicly deliver them, so enclosed and sealed, to the Sheriff, Under Sheriff, or Sheriff's Deputy presiding at such Poll, who shall give a Receipt for the same, and shall, on the Commencement of the Poll on the Second Day, deliver them back, so enclosed and sealed, to the Persons from whom he shall have received them; and on the final Close of the Poll every such Deputy who shall have received any such Poll Book shall forthwith deliver or Transmit the same, so enclosed and sealed, to the Sheriff or his Under Sheriff, who shall receive and keep all the Poll Books unopened until the re-assembling of the Court on the Day next but one after

Sheriff to appoint Deputies, Poll Clerks, etc.

Delivery and Custody of Poll Books.

the close of the Poll, unless such next Day but one shall happen on *Sunday*, and then on the *Monday* following, when he shall openly break the Seals thereon and cast up the Number of Votes as they appear on the said several Books, and shall openly declare the State of the Poll, and shall make Proclamation of the Head Coroner chosen not later than Two o'Clock in the Afternoon of the same Day.

Final Declaration of the Poll.

The Sheriff may act in Places of exclusive Jurisdiction.

XII. And be it enacted, That in all Matters relative to the Election of a Head Coroner for any Division of the said County the Sheriff of the said County, or his Under Sheriff, or any lawful Deputy of such Sheriff, shall have Power to act in all Places within such Division having any exclusive Privilege or Jurisdiction whatsoever, in the same Manner as such Sheriff, Under Sheriff, or Deputy may act within any Part of such Sheriff's ordinary Jurisdiction.

Polling Booths to be erected at the Expence of the Candidates.

XIII. And be it enacted, That at every Election of Head Coroner for any Division of the said County all Booths erected for the Convenience of taking Polls at such Elections shall be erected at the joint and equal Expence of the several Candidates, and the same shall be erected by Contract with the Candidates, if they shall think fit to make such Contract, or if they shall not make such Contract then the same shall be erected by the Sheriff at the Expence of the several Candidates as aforesaid, subject to such Limitation as is herein-after next mentioned (that is to say), that the Expence to be incurred for the Booth or Booths to be erected at the principal Place of Election for any such Division of the said County or at any of the Polling Places within the said Division to be used for taking the Poll at such Election, shall not exceed the Sum of Forty Pounds in respect of any One such principal Place of Election, or any One such Polling Place, and that all Deputies appointed by the Sheriff shall be paid each Two Guineas by the Day, and all Clerks employed in taking the Poll shall be paid One Guinea each by the Day, at the Expence of the Candidates at

Limitation of Expence.

such Election, who shall also defray the reasonable Costs and Expence of providing Poll Books: Provided always, that if any Person shall be proposed without his Consent, then the Person so proposing him shall be liable to defray his Share of the said Expences in like Manner as if he had been a Candidate: Provided also, that the Sheriff may, if he shall think fit, instead of erecting such Booth or Booths as aforesaid, procure or hire and use any Houses or other Buildings for the Purpose of taking the Poll therein, subject always to the same Regulations, Provisions, Liabilities, and Limitations of Expence as are hereinbefore mentioned with regard to Booths for taking the Poll.

Persons proposing a Candidate without his Consent, to be at the Expence. Houses may be hired for polling instead of Booths.

XIV. And be it enacted, That in every Election for a Head Coroner for any Division of the said County, every Deputy of the Sheriff shall have the same Power of administering the Oaths and Affirmations required by Law, and of appointing Commissioners or Sworn Clerks for administering such Oaths and Affirmations, as may by Law be administered by Commissioners or Sworn Clerks, as the Sheriff of the said County of *Chester* has by virtue of this Act, or of any Law now in force with relation to the Election of Coroners, and subject to the same Regulations and Provisions in every respect as such Sheriff.

Sheriff's Deputy to have the same Power as the Sheriff.

XV. And be it enacted, That the said recited Act of the Fifty-eighth Year of the Reign of King *George* the Third, and all other Laws, Statutes, and Usages now in force respecting the Election of Coroners, shall be and remain, and are hereby declared to be and remain, in full Force, and shall apply to the Election of Head Coroners for the several Divisions of the said County hereby empowered to elect Head Coroners, as fully and effectually as if such Divisions respectively had heretofore elected Head Coroners, except so far as the said recited Act, or any of the said Laws, Statutes, or Usages, are repealed or altered by this Act, or are inconsistent with the Provisions thereof.

The Act 58 G. 3, c. 95, and all Laws relating to the Election of Coroners to remain in force, except where superseded by this Act.

Writs De coronatore eligendo to be directed to the Sheriff.

XVI. And be it enacted, That all Writs De coronatore eligendo to be issued for the Election of a Head Coroner for any Division of the said County shall be directed to the Sheriff of the said County; and all Mandates, Precepts, Instruments, Proceedings, and Notices consequent upon such Writs shall be and the same are hereby authorized to be framed and expressed in such Manner and Form as may be necessary for the carrying the Provisions of this Act into effect.

Head Coroners although elected by Freeholders of Division shall for all Purposes, except holding Inquests, be considered as Coroners for the whole County.

XVII. And be it enacted, That every Head Coroner to be elected under the Authority of this Act, although such Coroner may be designated as the Coroner for any particular Division of the said County, and may be elected by the Freeholders of such Division, and not by the Freeholders of the County at large, shall for all Purposes whatsoever, except as herein-after mentioned, be considered as a Coroner for the whole County, and shall and may have and exercise the same Jurisdiction, Rights, Powers, and Authorities throughout the said County as if he had been elected one of the Head Coroners of the said County by the Freeholders of the County at large, and as the present Head Coroners for the said County, or either of them, now have or had and exercised.

Present and future Coroners, except during Illnesses, etc. of Coroner for another Division, or in case of Vacancy in the Office, to hold Inquests only within the Division to which they shall have been assigned or elected.

XVIII. And be it enacted, That the present and all future Head Coroners for the said County, or any Division thereof, after they shall, in pursuance of the Provisions of this Act, have been assigned to or elected by the Freeholders of any particular Division of the said County, shall, except during the Illness or Incapacity, or necessary Absence through unavoidable Business, of any Head Coroner for any Division, or during a Vacancy in the Office of Head Coroner for any Division, hold Inquests only within the Division to or for which they shall have been respectively assigned or elected: Provided always, that the Coroner who shall hold any Inquest in any other Division or District of the said County save that to which he shall have been assigned or elected as aforesaid shall in the Inquisition to be returned on such Inquest, certify the Cause of his Attendance and holding such Inquest, which Certificate shall be conclusive Evidence of the Illness or Incapacity, or necessary Absence through unavoidable Business, of the Head Coroner in whose Place and Stead he shall so attend, or of there being a Vacancy in the Office of Head Coroner for the Division in which such Inquest shall be holden.

XIX. And be it enacted, That the present Head Coroners, or the Head Coroner for the Time being of the said County, after they shall have been assigned to any of the Divisions into which the said County may, under the Authority of this Act, be divided, and also every Head Coroner to be elected for any Division of the said County, shall be entitled to receive and shall receive and be paid the like Fees and Allowances on holding Inquests, either within the Division of the County for which he shall be Head Coroner, or within any other Division thereof, during the Illness, or Incapacity, or necessary Absence through unavoidable Business, of the Head Coroner thereof, or during a Vacancy in the Office of Head Coroner thereof, as other Coroners in *England* and *Wales* are by Law entitled to.

Head Coroners to receive the same Fees upon Inquests held within Divisions as other Coroners in England and Wales are entitled to.

XX. And be it enacted, That at every Inquest which, after the passing of this Act, shall be held within the said County, or any Division thereof, upon any dead Human Body which may have been picked up floating in the Sea or in any Inlet, Bay, or Creek, it shall be lawful for the Head or other Coroner before whom such Inquest shall be held, if he shall think proper so to do, but not otherwise, to pay to the Person by whom such Body shall have been picked up the Sum of Five Shillings for his Trouble, and the Money so paid by such Head or other Coroner shall be considered as Part of the Expences attendant upon holding such Inquest, and shall be included by him in the Account of such Expences, and shall be repaid to him, at the Time and in the Manner directed by an Act passed in the Seventh Year of the Reign of His late Majesty King *William* the Fourth and the First Year

Coroner may reward Persons for picking up dead Bodies at Sea.

L

of the Reign of Her present Majesty, intituled *An Act to provide for Payment of the Expences of Holding Coroners Inquests.*

7 W. 4 & 1 Vict. c. 68.

In case the Fees and Emoluments of the Coroners shall be reduced by any Division of the County under the Authority of this Act, the Justices in Quarter Sessions assembled may make them Compensation out of the County Rate.

XXI. And whereas by reason of the Division of the said County, in pursuance of the Provisions of this Act, the Fees and other Emoluments to which, according to Usage, the present Head Coroners of the said County are entitled, will probably be reduced, and in like Manner, upon any new Division of the said County, the Fees and other Emoluments to which the Head Coroners for the Time being may be entitled will also probably be reduced, and such Division being for the public Benefit, it is reasonable and just that the present Head Coroners, and other Head Coroners for the Time being, of the said County should not be prejudiced thereby; be it therefore enacted, That upon the Division of the said County into Divisions, in pursuance of the Provisions of this Act, and in like Manner upon any subsequent new Division thereof, under the Authority herein-before contained, it shall be lawful for the Justices of the Peace for the said County in Quarter Sessions assembled, or at any Adjournment thereof, or any special Sessions held for that Purpose, to make a Compensation out of the County Rate to each of the present Head Coroners, whose Fees or Emoluments may be reduced by the County being so divided as aforesaid, and in like Manner to each and every of the Head Coroners for the Time being whose Fees and Emoluments may be reduced by the Alteration of the Division to which he may have been appointed or elected in pursuance of the Authority herein-before contained, and for that Purpose such Justices, so assembled as aforesaid, shall cause a Calculation to be made of the average Annual Amount of Fees and Emoluments received by any such Head Coroner, during the Three Years preceding such Division or Alteration, for or in respect of Inquests held by him within that Portion of the County, or of the Division, as the Case may be, which shall be taken from him, or in which he shall no longer have or be entitled to the holding of Inquests, and after ascertaining such average Amount of Fees during such preceding Three Years it shall be lawful for such Justices so assembled as aforesaid, if they shall think proper so to do, but not otherwise, to direct the Treasurer of the said County, yearly and every Year, during the Remainder of the Life of the Head Coroner whose Fees or Emoluments shall be so reduced, or during such Period as he shall continue Head Coroner, or during such shorter Period as such Justices shall think proper, to pay to such Head Coroner such Sum or Sums of Money, not exceeding such yearly Average amount of Fees, as such Justices shall think reasonable, which Sum or Sums of Money so directed to be paid to such Head Coroner shall be paid by the Treasurer of the said County out of any Public Money in his Hands, and he shall be allowed all such Payments in his Accounts.

XXII. And be it enacted, That the Costs, Charges, and Expences incident to or attending the applying for, obtaining, and passing this Act shall be defrayed and paid by and out of the Monies to be raised by the general Rates and Assessments made and to be assessed and levied in the said County by virtue of the several Statutes for the Time being in force for the assessing, collecting, and levying of County Rates, and the Justices of the Peace for the said County assembled at any General or Quarter Sessions to be held after the passing of this Act, or at any Adjournment of such Sessions, shall order the Treasurer of the said County to pay the same Costs, Charges, and Expences, and such Treasurer shall be allowed such Payments in his Accounts. *The Expences of this Act to be paid, upon the Order of the Justices, out of the County Rate.*

XXIII. Provided always, and be it enacted, That nothing in this Act contained shall extend, or be deemed or construed to extend, to prejudice or alter or in any Manner affect the Right or Privilege of the Lord of the Manor of *Halton Fee* to appoint a Coroner for that District or Portion of the said County of *Chester* which is commonly called or known by the Name of *Halton Fee*, or the Right or Privilege of any Coroner appointed by the Lord of the *Saving Right of Lord of the Manor of Halton Fee.*

148 *THE KING'S CORONER.*

said Manor to hold Inquests in the Townships or Places included within the same District.

The Act 5 & 6 W. 4, c. 76, not to be altered by this Act.

XXIV. Provided also, and be it enacted, That nothing in this Act contained shall be construed to repeal, vary, or alter the Provisions of an Act passed in the Fifth and Sixth Years of His late Majesty King *William* the Fourth, intituled *An Act for the Regulation of Corporations in* England *and* Wales, as to the Appointment of Coroners for any of the Municipal Boroughs in the said County in which separate Courts of Quarter Sessions of the Peace shall be holden.

Public Act.

XXV. And be it enacted, That this Act shall be deemed and taken to be a Public Act, and shall be judicially taken notice of as such by all Judges, Justices, and others. [Except Sect. 21 (as regards Head Coroners now in office for the three divisions in which the County is divided), repealed by County Coroners Act, 1860 (23 & 24 Vict. c. 116. s. 7).]

---

5 & 6 VICT. c. 55.

An Act for the better Regulation of Railways, and for the Conveyance of Troops. [30th July 1842.]

Meaning of the Words "Railway" and "Company."

XXI. And be it enacted, That whenever the Word "Railway" is used in this or in the said recited Act it shall be construed to apply to all Railways used or intended to be used for the Conveyance of Passengers in or upon Carriages drawn or impelled by the Power of Steam or by any other mechanical Power; and whenever the Word "Company" is used in this or in the said recited Act it shall be construed to extend to and include the Proprietors for the Time being of any such Railway, whether a Body Corporate or Individuals, and their Lessees, Executors, Administrators, and Assigns, unless in either of the above Cases the Subject or Context be repugnant to such Construction.

6 VICT. c. 12.

An Act for the more convenient holding of Coroners Inquests. [11th April 1843.]

Whereas it often happens that it is unknown where Persons lying dead have come by their Deaths, and also that such Persons may die in other Places than those in which the Cause of Death happened: Be it enacted by the Queen's most Excellent Majesty, by and with the Advice and Consent of the Lords Spiritual and Temporal, and Commons, in this present Parliament assembled, and by the Authority of the same, That the Coroner only within whose Jurisdiction the Body of any Person upon whose Death an Inquest ought to be holden shall be lying dead shall hold the Inquest, notwithstanding that the Cause of Death did not arise within the Jurisdiction of such Coroner; and in the Case of any Body found dead in the Sea, or any Creek, River, or navigable Canal within the flowing of the Sea, where there shall be no Deputy Coroner for the Jurisdiction of the Admiralty of *England*, the Inquest shall be holden only by the Coroner having Jurisdiction in the Place where the Body shall be first brought to Land. *(Coroner only within whose Jurisdiction the Body is lying dead shall hold the Inquest.)*

II. And be it enacted, That for the Purpose of holding Coroners Inquests every detached Part of a County, Riding, or Division shall be deemed to be within that County, Riding, or Division by which it is wholly surrounded, or, where it is partly surrounded by Two or more Counties, Ridings, or Divisions, within that one with which it has the longest common Boundary. *(Provision for detached Parts of Counties.)*

III. And be it declared and enacted, That if a Verdict of Murder or Manslaughter, or as Accessary before the Fact to any Murder, shall be found by the Jury at any such Inquest, against any Person or Persons, the Coroner holding the said Inquest, and the Justices of Oyer and Terminer and Gaol Delivery for the County, City, District, or Place in which such Inquest shall be holden, *(Parties may be tried on Verdicts of Murder or Manslaughter.)*

and all other Persons, shall have the same Powers respectively for the Commitment, Trial, and Execution of the Sentence of the Person or Persons so charged as they now by Law possess with regard to the Commitment, Trial, and Execution of the Sentence upon any Person or Persons committed and tried within the Jurisdiction where the Death happened.

Deodands may be levied on Verdicts.

IV. And be it declared and enacted, That if a Verdict of Accidental Death shall be found by the Jury at any such Inquest, the Coroner and Jury, and the Sheriff and Court of Exchequer, and all other persons whosoever, shall have the same Powers respectively with regard to the finding, returning, and levying of Deodands as they now possess in Cases where the Death and the Cause of Death happened within the same Jurisdiction.

Act may be amended or repealed.

V. And be it enacted, That this Act may be amended or repealed by any Act to be passed in this Session of Parliament. [Sec. 4 repealed by Stat. Law Rev. Act, 1861 (24 & 25 Vict. c 101); Sec. 5 by Stat. Law Rev. Act (No. 2), 1874 (37 & 38 Vict. c. 96), and remainder (so far as relates to England) repealed by Coroners Act, 1887 (50 & 51 Vict. c 71, s 45, and Sch. 3).]

---

6 & 7 VICT. c. 83.

An Act to amend the Law respecting the Duties of Coroners.
[22nd August 1843.]

Whereas the Coroners of Boroughs and Liberties are empowered and directed by Law to appoint Deputies to act in their Stead in certain Cases: And whereas the Coroners of Counties have no sufficient Authority of the Law for making such appointments: And whereas it is expedient to prevent unnecessary Expence and Delay in the holding of Inquests in Counties: Be it therefore enacted by the Queen's most Excellent Majesty, by and with the Advice and Consent of the Lords Spiritual and Temporal, and Commons, in this present Parliament assembled, and by the Authority of the same, That from and after the passing of this Act it shall be lawful for every Coroner of any County, City, or Riding, Liberty, or Division, and he is hereby directed, by writing under his Hand and Seal, to nominate and appoint from Time to Time a fit and proper Person, such Appointment being subject to the Approval of the Lord High Chancellor, Lord Keeper or Lords Commissioners of the Great Seal, to act for him as his Deputy in the holding of Inquests; and all Inquests taken and other Acts performed by any such Deputy Coroner under and by virtue of any such Appointment shall be deemed and taken, to all Intents and Purposes whatsoever, to be the Acts and Deeds of the Coroner by whom such Appointment was made: Provided always, that a Duplicate of such Appointment shall be forthwith transmitted to the Clerk of the Peace for the County, City, Riding, Liberty, or Division in which such Coroner shall reside, to be filed among the Records of the said County, City, Riding, Liberty, or Division: Provided also, that no such Deputy shall act for any such Coroner as aforesaid except during the Illness of the said Coroner, or during his Absence from any lawful or reasonable Cause: Provided also, that every such Appointment may at any Time be cancelled and revoked by the Coroner by whom the same was made.

Coroners of Counties, etc., may appoint Deputies, subject to the Approval of the Lord Chancellor.

Duplicate of Appointment to be transmitted to Clerk of the Peace.

Deputy to act only during Illness, etc.

II. And whereas by an Act passed in the Seventh Year of the Reign of King *George* the Fourth certain Provisions were made for preventing the quashing of Indictments on technical Grounds: And whereas it is expedient to make Provisions for supporting Coroners Inquisitions, and for preventing the same from being quashed on account of technical Defects; Be it therefore enacted, That from and after the passing of this Act no Inquisition found upon or by any Coroner's Inquest, nor any Judgment recorded upon or by virtue of any such Inquisition, shall be quashed, stayed, or reversed for Want of the Averment therein of any Matter unnecessary to be proved, nor for the Omission of the Words "with Force and Arms," or of the Words "against the Peace," or of

Inquisitions, etc., not to be quashed on account of technical Defects.

the Words "against the Form of the Statute," nor for the Omission or Insertion of any other Words or Expressions of mere Form or Surplusage, nor for the Insertion of the Words "upon their Oath," instead of the Words "upon their Oaths," nor for omitting to state the Time at which the Offence was committed, when Time is not the Essence of the Offence, nor for stating the Time imperfectly, nor because any Person or Persons mentioned in any such Inquisition is or are designated by a Name of Office or other descriptive Appellation, instead of his, her, or their proper Name or Names, nor by reason of the Non-insertion of the Names of the Jurors in the Body of any such Inquisition, or of any Difference in the Spelling of the Names of any of the Jurors in the Body of any such Inquisition and the Names subscribed thereto, nor because any Juror or Jurors shall have set his or their Mark or Marks to any such Inquisition, instead of subscribing his or their Name or Names thereto, nor because any such Mark or Marks is or are unattested, provided the Name or Names of such Juror or Jurors is or are set forth, nor because any Juror or Jurors has or have signed his or their Christian Name or Names by means of an Initial or partial Signature only, and not at full Length, nor because of any Erasures or Interlineations appearing in any such Inquisition, unless the same shall be proved to have been made therein after the same was signed, nor for Want of a proper Venue, where the Inquest shall appear or purport to have been taken by a Coroner of or for the County, Riding, City, Borough, Liberty, Division, or Place in which it shall appear or purport to have been taken, nor (except only in Cases of Murder or Manslaughter) for or by reason of any such Inquisition not being duly sealed or written upon Parchment, nor by reason of any such Inquisition having been taken before any Deputy instead of the Coroner himself, nor because the Coroner and Jury did not all view the Body at one and the same Instant, provided they all viewed the Body at the first Sitting of the Inquest; and in all or any of such Cases of technical Defect as are herein-before mentioned it shall be lawful for any Judge of either of Her Majesty's Courts at

Westminster, or any Judge of Assize or Gaol Delivery, if he shall so think fit, upon the Occasion of any such Inquisition being called in question before him, to order the same to be amended in any of the respects aforesaid, and the same shall forthwith be amended accordingly.

III. And be it enacted, That this Act shall extend only to that Part of the United Kingdom called *England* and *Wales*. {Extent of Act.}

IV. And be it enacted, That this Act may be amended or repealed by any Act to be passed in this present Session of Parliament. [Sec. 4 repealed by Stat. Law Rev. Act (No. 2), 1874 (37 & 38 Vict. c 96), and remainder repealed by Coroners' Act, 1887 (50 & 51 Vict. c 71, s. 45, and Sch. 3).] {Act may be amended, etc.}

---

6 & 7 VICT. c. 85.

An Act for improving the Law of Evidence.
[22nd August 1843.]

I. Whereas the Inquiry after Truth in Courts of Justice is often obstructed by Incapacities created by the present Law, and it is desirable that full information as to the Facts in Issue, both in Criminal and in Civil Cases, should be laid before the Persons who are appointed to decide upon them, and that such Persons should exercise their Judgment on the Credit of the Witnesses adduced and on the Truth of their Testimony: Now therefore be it enacted, That no Person offered as a Witness shall hereafter be excluded by reason of Incapacity from Crime or Interest from giving Evidence, either in Person or by Deposition, according to the Practice of the Court, on the Trial of any Issue joined, or of any Matter or Question or on any Inquiry arising in any Suit, Action, or Proceeding, Civil or Criminal, in any Court, or before any Judge, Jury, Sheriff, Coroner, Magistrate, Officer, or Person having, by Law or by Consent of Parties, {Witnesses not to be excluded from giving Evidence by Incapacity from Crime or Interest.}

Authority to hear, receive, and examine Evidence; but that every Person so offered may and shall be admitted to give Evidence on Oath, or solemn Affirmation in those Cases wherein Affirmation is by Law receivable, notwithstanding that such Person may or shall have an Interest in the Matter in question, or in the Event of the Trial of any Issue, Matter, Question, or Injury, or of the Suit, Action, or Proceeding in which he is offered as a Witness, and notwithstanding that such Person offered as a Witness may have been previously convicted of any Crime or Offence: &c. &c. [Proviso in Sec. 1 (which does not relate to Coroners) repealed by Stat. Law Rev. Act (No. 2), 1874 (37 & 38 Vict. c 96).]

---

7 & 8 VICT. c. 92.

An Act to amend the Law respecting the Office of County Coroner. [9th August 1844.]

Whereas the Regulations for the Elections of Coroners for Counties are insufficient: And whereas such Elections are made with much Inconvenience, and are attended with great and unnecessary Expence: And whereas, for Remedy of such Grievances, it is expedient that an Alteration should be made in the Manner of making such Elections.[1] Be it therefore enacted by the Queen's most Excellent Majesty, by and with the Advice and Consent of the Lords Spiritual and Temporal, and Commons, in this present Parliament assembled, and by the Authority of the same, That an Act passed in the Fifty-eighth Year of the Reign of His late Majesty King George the Third, intituled *An Act to regulate the Elections of Coroners for Counties*, shall be repealed.

58 G. 3, c. 95, repealed.

II.[2] And be it enacted, That when and as often as

---

[1] The election of County Coroners by freeholders is entirely abolished by the Local Government Act, 1888.

[2] See s. 48 of the Coroners Act, 1887, and as to transfer of powers of justices to County Council, see s. 3, par. xi. of the Local Government Act, 1888 (51 & 52 Vict. c. 41).

it shall seem expedient to the Justices of any County that such County should be divided into Two or more Districts for the Purposes of this Act, or that any Alteration should be made of any Division theretofore made under this Act, it shall be lawful for the said Justices, in General or Quarter Session assembled, to resolve that a Petition shall be presented to Her Majesty, praying that such Division or Alteration be made, and thereupon to adjourn the further Consideration of such Petition until Notice thereof shall be given to the Coroner or Coroners of such County as herein-after provided. *Petition for Division of Counties.*

III. And be it enacted, That the Clerk of the Peace shall give Notice of any such Resolution to every Coroner for such County, and of the Time when the Petition will be taken by the said Justices into consideration, and the Justices shall confer with every such Coroner, who shall attend the Meeting of the Justices for that Purpose, touching such Petition, having due Regard to the Size and Nature of each proposed District, the Number of the Inhabitants, the Nature of their Employments, and such other Circumstances as shall appear to the Justices fit to be considered in carrying into execution the Provisions of this Act; and such Petition, with a Description of the several proposed Districts, and of the Boundaries thereof, with the Reasons upon which the Petition is founded, shall be certified to Her Majesty under the Hands and Seals of Two or more of the Justices present when such Petition shall be agreed to, and the Clerk of the Peace for such County shall forthwith give or send a true Copy of such Petition, certified under his Hand, to every Coroner for such County. *Preparation of Petition.*

IV. And be it enacted, That it shall be lawful for Her Majesty, if She shall think fit, with the Advice of Her Privy Council, after taking into consideration any such Petition, and also any Petition which may be presented to Her by any Coroner of the same County concerning such proposed Division or Alteration, or whenever it shall seem fit to Her Majesty to direct the Issue of a Writ De *Division of the County into Districts.*

coronatore eligendo, for the Purpose of authorizing the Election of an additional Coroner above the Number of those who have been theretofore customarily elected in such County, to order that such County shall be divided into such and so many Districts, for the Purposes of this Act, as to Her Majesty, with the Advice aforesaid, shall seem expedient, and to give a Name to each of such Districts, *and to determine at what Place within each District the Court for the Election of Coroner for such District shall be holden as hereinafter provided*,[1] and every such Order shall be published in the *London Gazette*.

Districts to be assigned to Coroners.

V. And be it enacted, That the Justices in General or Quarter Session assembled shall assign one of such Districts to each of the Persons holding the Office of Coroner in such County, and upon the Death, Resignation, or Removal of any such Person each of his Successors, and also every other Person thereafter elected into the Office of Coroner in such County, *shall be elected to and*[1] shall exercise the Office of Coroner, according to the Provisions of this Act, and shall reside within the District in and for which he shall be *so*[1] elected, or in some Place wholly or partly surrounded by such District, or not more than Two Miles beyond the outer Boundary of such District.

Provision for Coroners already acting in Districts.

VI. And be it enacted, That whenever it shall appear to Her Majesty, with the Advice aforesaid, and shall be set forth in the said Order in Council, that any such County has been customarily divided into Districts for the Purpose of holding Inquests during the Space of Seven Years before the passing of this Act, and it shall seem expedient to Her Majesty, with the Advice aforesaid, that the same Division of the County be made under this Act, each of such Districts shall be assigned to the Coroner usually acting in and for the same District 'before the passing of this Act; but if it shall appear expedient to Her Majesty, with the Advice aforesaid, that a different Division of such County be made, and any such Coroner shall present a Petition to Her Majesty, praying for Com-

---

[1] Words in italics repealed by Stat. Law Rev. Act, 1891.

pensation to him for the loss of his Emoluments arising out of such Change, it shall be lawful for Her Majesty, with the Advice aforesaid, to order the Lord High Treasurer or Commissioners of Her Majesty's Treasury to assess the Amount of Compensation which it shall appear to him or them ought to be awarded to such Coroner, and the Amount of such Compensation shall be paid by the Treasurer of the County to such Coroner, his Executors or Administrators, out of the County Rate.

[*VII. And be it enacted, That such Justices so assembled as aforesaid shall order a List to be prepared by the Clerk of the Peace for their respective Counties of the several Parishes, Townships, or Hundreds, as the Case may be, in each and every of the several Districts into which the respective Counties shall be divided under the Authority of this Act, specifying in such List the Place within each District at which the Court for the Election of Coroner is to be holden, and also the Place or Places at which the Poll shall be taken, inserting the Parishes, Townships, and Places for each of such Polling Places, and shall cause such Order to be enrolled among the Records of the County.—Repealed by Stat. Law Rev. Act, 1891.*] *List of Places in each District to be made.*

VIII. And be it enacted, That all isolated or detached Parts of Counties shall be considered, for the Purposes of this Act, as forming a Part of that County, Riding, or Division respectively whereby such isolated or detached Parts shall or may be wholly surrounded, but if any such isolated or detached Part shall be surrounded by Two or more Counties, Ridings, or Divisions, then as forming Part of that County, Riding, or Division with which such isolated or detached Part shall have the longest common Boundary. *Detached Parts to form Parts of Counties by which they are surrounded.*

IX. And be it enacted, That from and after the Time when any County shall have been so as aforesaid divided every Election of a Coroner for any such District shall be held at some Place within the District in which he shall be elected to serve the Office of Coroner; and that every Person to be so elected shall be chosen by a Majority of such Persons *Election to be held in the District; who to elect.*

residing within such District as shall at the Time of such Election be duly qualified to vote at the Elections of Coroners for the said County.

Sheriff to hold a Special County Court for Election of Coroner.

X. And be it enacted, That from and after the Division of any Counties as aforesaid into Coroners Districts, upon every Election to be made of any Coroner or Coroners for any County the Sheriff of the County where such Election shall be made shall hold a Court for the same Election at some convenient Place within the District for which the Election of Coroner shall take place, on some Day to be by him appointed, which Day shall not be less than Seven Days nor more than Fourteen Days after the Receipt of the Writ

If Election not determined on the View, then to proceed to take a Poll.

De coronatore eligendo; and in case the said Election be not then determined upon the View, with the Consent of the Electors there present, but that a Poll shall be demanded for Determination thereof, then the said Sheriff, or in his Absence his Under Sheriff, shall adjourn the same Court to Eight of the Clock in the forenoon of the next Day but one, unless such next Day but one shall be Saturday or Sunday, and then of the Monday following; and the said Sheriff, or in his Absence the Under Sheriff, with such others as shall be deputed by him shall then and there proceed to take the said Poll in some public Place or Places by the same Sheriff, or his Under Sheriff as aforesaid in his Absence, or others appointed for the taking thereof as aforesaid; and such

Duration of Poll.

Polling shall continue for Two Days only, for Eight Hours in each Day; and no Poll shall be kept open later than Four of the Clock in the Afternoon of either of the said Days.

Places for taking the Poll at Elections for Coroners.

XI. And be it enacted, That for more conveniently taking the Poll at all Elections of Coroners under the Authority of this Act the Poll for the Election of the Coroner in each District shall be taken at the Place to be appointed for holding the Court for such Election, and at such other Places within the same District as may for the Time being be appointed by the Quarter Sessions.

Sheriff may erect Polling Booths for

XII. And be it enacted, That at every contested Election of Coroner for any District of the said County the Sheriff,

Under Sheriff, or Sheriff's Deputy shall, if required by or on the Behalf of any Candidate on the Day fixed for the Election, and, if not so required, may, if it shall appear to him expedient, cause a Booth or Booths to be erected for taking the Poll at the Court or principal Place of Election, and also at each of the Polling Places within the District herein-before directed to be used for the Purposes of such Election, and shall cause to be affixed on the most conspicuous Part of each of the said Booths the Names of the several Parishes, Townships, and Places for which such Booth is respectively allotted; and no Person shall be admitted to vote at any such Election in respect of any Property situate in any Parish, Township, or Place, except at the Booth so allotted for such Parish, Township, or Place, and if no Booth shall be allotted for the same, then at any of the Booths for the same Districts; and in case any Parish, Township, or Place, or Part of any Parish, Township, or Place, shall happen not to be included in any of the Districts, the Votes in respect of Property situate in any Parish, Township, or Place, or any Part of any Parish, Township, or Place, so omitted, shall be taken at the Court or principal Place of Election for such District of the said County. taking the Poll at.

No Voter to poll out of the District where his Property lies.

In case of a Parish not included in any District.

XIII. And for the more due and orderly proceeding in the said Poll, be it enacted, That the said Sheriff, or in his Absence the Under Sheriff, or such as he shall depute, shall appoint such Number of Clerks as to him shall seem meet and convenient for the taking thereof, which Clerks shall take the said Poll in the Presence of the said Sheriff or his Under Sheriff, or such as he shall depute; and before they begin to take the said Poll every Clerk so appointed shall by the said Sheriff or his Under Sheriff, or such as he shall depute as aforesaid, be sworn truly and indifferently to take the same Poll, and to set down the Names of each Elector, and the Place of his Residence, and for whom he shall poll, and to poll no Elector who is not sworn, if required to be sworn by the Candidates or either of them; and which Oaths of the said Clerks, the said Sheriff or his Under Sheriff, or such as he shall depute, shall have Authority to Poll Clerks to be appointed and sworn.

Inspector of Poll Clerk.

Electors to be sworn.

administer; and the Sheriff, or in his Absence his Under Sheriff, as aforesaid, shall appoint for each Candidate such one Person as shall be nominated to him by each Candidate to be Inspector of every Clerk who shall be appointed for taking the Poll; and every Elector, before he is admitted to poll at the same Election, shall, if required by or on behalf of any Candidate, first take the Oath herein-after mentioned; which Oath the said Sheriff, by himself or his Under Sheriff, or such sworn Clerk by him appointed for taking the said Poll as aforesaid, shall have Authority to administer; (that is to say,)

Oath.

"*I swear* [or, being one of the People called Quakers, or "entitled by Law to make Affirmation, *solemnly affirm*].
" *That I am a Freeholder of the County of*
" *and have a Freehold Estate, consisting of* lying
" *at* *within the said County; and that such*
" *Freehold Estate has not been granted to me fraudulently or*
" *colourably on purpose to qualify me to give my Vote at*
" *this Election; and that the Place of my Abode is at*
" [*and, if it be a Place consisting of more*
" *Streets or Places than One, specifying what Street or*
" *Place*]; *that I am Twenty-one Years of Age, as I believe;*
" *and that I have not been before polled at this Election*
" [*adding, except in Cases of solemn Affirmations*]
                              " *So help me GOD.*"

Punishment for Perjury.

XIV. And be it enacted, That every Elector or other Person who shall wilfully and falsely take the said Oath or Affirmation hereby appointed to be taken by the Electors as aforesaid shall for every such Offence incur the Penalties by Law inflicted on Persons guilty of Perjury; and every Person who shall unlawfully and corruptly procure or suborn any Freeholder or other Person wilfully and falsely to take the said Oath or Affirmation in order to be polled shall for every such Offence incur such Pains and Penalties as are by Law inflicted on Persons guilty of Subornation of Perjury.

Custody of Poll Books, and Final

XV. And be it enacted, That the Poll Clerks shall, at the Close of the Poll, enclose and seal their several Books, and *shall publicly deliver them, so enclosed and sealed, to the Sheriff, Under Sheriff, or Sheriff's Deputy presiding at such Poll, who shall give a Receipt for the same; and every such Deputy who shall have received any such Poll Books shall forthwith deliver or transmit the same, so enclosed and sealed, to the Sheriff or his Under Sheriff, who shall receive and keep all the Poll Books unopened until the reassembling of the Court on the Day next but one after the Close of the Poll, unless such next Day but one shall be* Sunday, *and then on the* Monday *following, when he shall openly break the seals thereon, and cast up the Number of Votes as they appear on the said several Books, and shall openly declare the State of the Poll, and shall make Proclamation of the Person chosen, not later than Two of the Clock in the Afternoon of the said Day.* — Declaration of the Poll.

XVI. *And be it enacted, That all the reasonable Costs, Charges, and Expences which the said Sheriff, or his Under Sheriff or other Deputy, shall expend or be liable to in and about the providing of Poll Books, Booths, and Clerks (such Clerks to be paid not more than One Guinea each for each Day), for the Purpose of taking the Poll at any such Election, shall be borne and paid by the several Candidates at such Election in equal Proportions.* — Expences of Sheriff, etc., to be paid by the Candidates.

XVII. *And whereas great Difficulty and Delay is frequently occasioned by the Nonattendance of Jurors and Witnesses summoned to attend the Coroner on taking an Inquest; be it therefore enacted, That if any Person, having been duly summoned as a Juror or Witness to give Evidence upon any Coroner's Inquest, as well of Liberties and Franchises contributing to the County Rates, as of Counties, Cities, and Boroughs, shall not, after being openly called Three Times, appear and serve as such Juror, or appear and give Evidence on such Inquest, every such Coroner shall be empowered to impose such Fine upon every Person so making default as he shall think fit, not exceeding Forty Shillings; and every such Coroner shall make out and sign a Certificate, containing the Name and Surname, the Residence, and Trade or Calling of every such Person so making* — Coroners may compel attendance of Jurors and Witnesses. Coroner to certify Defaulters to the Clerk of the Peace;

default, together with the Amount of the Fine imposed, and the Cause of such Fine, and shall transmit such Certificate to the Clerk of the Peace for the County, Riding, Division, or Place in which such Defaulter shall reside, on or before the First day of the Quarter Session of the Peace then next ensuing, and shall cause a Copy of such Certificate to be served upon the Person so fined, by leaving it at his Residence Twenty-four Hours at the least before the First Day of the said next Quarter Session of the Peace; and every such Clerk of the Peace shall copy the Fine or Fines so certified on the Roll on which all Fines and Forfeitures imposed at such Quarter Session of the Peace shall be copied, *who shall enter them on the Roll of Fines.* *and the same shall be estreated, levied, and applied in like Manner, and subject to the like Powers, Provisions, and Penalties in all respects, as if such Fine or Fines had been Part of the Fines imposed at such Quarter Session:*

Proviso. *Provided always, that nothing herein contained shall be construed to affect any Power now by Law vested in the Coroner for compelling any Person to appear and give Evidence before him on any Inquest or other Proceeeding, or for punishing any Person for Contempt of Court in not so appearing and giving Evidence, or otherwise.*

Coroner not to act professionally in Prosecutions where he shall have sat as Coroner in the same Case.

XVIII *And be it enacted, That from and after the passing of this Act, in all Cases in which any Person shall be charged by any Coroner's Inquisition with the Commission of any Crime, and shall be subsequently put upon his Trial, either on such Inquisition, or in pursuance of any Bill of Indictment found for the same, the Coroner before whom such Inquisition shall have been found shall be wholly incompetent to act as an Attorney in Prosecution or Defence of such Person for such Crime, either by himself or his Partner (directly or Indirectly); and that in all Cases in which it shall appear to the Judge before whom such Person shall be tried that any Coroner shall have so acted contrary to the Provision and Intention of this Act, such Judge shall impose upon every Coroner so offending such Penalty, not exceeding Fifty Pounds, as the said Judge shall in his Discretion think fit.* [Sects. 8–18 repealed by Coroners Act, 1887.]

XIX. And be it enacted, That every Coroner elected under the Authority of this Act, although such Coroner may be designated as the Coroner for any particular District of a County, *and may be elected by the Electors of such District, and not by the Freeholders of the County at large*,[1] shall for all Purposes whatsoever, except as hereinafter mentioned, be considered as a Coroner for the whole County, and shall have the same Jurisdiction, Rights, Powers, and Authorities throughout the said County as if he had been elected one of the Coroners of the said County *by the Freeholders of the County at large.*[1]

Coroner, although elected for a District, shall be considered as Coroner for the whole County, except, etc.

XX. And be it enacted, That, except as aforesaid, every Coroner for any County, or any District thereof, or his Deputy, after he shall, in pursuance of the Provisions of this Act, have been assigned to *or elected by the Electors of*[1] any particular District, shall, except during Illness or Incapacity or unavoidable Absence as aforesaid of any Coroner for any other District, or during a Vacancy in the Office of Coroner for any other District, hold Inquests only within the District to or for which he shall have been assigned *or elected*:[1] Provided always, that the Coroner who shall, by himself or Deputy, hold any Inquest in any other District, save that to which he shall have been assigned *or elected*[1] as aforesaid, shall in his Inquisition to be returned on such Inquest, certify the Cause of his Attendance and holding such Inquest; which Certificate shall be conclusive Evidence of the Illness or Incapacity or unavoidable Absence as aforesaid of the Coroner in whose Stead he shall so attend, or of there being a Vacancy in the Office of Coroner for the District in which such Inquest shall be holden.

Present and future Coroners (except during Illness, etc., of Coroner for another District, or in case of Vacancy in the Office,) to hold Inquests only within the District to which they shall have been assigned or elected.

XXI. And whereas Doubts have arisen as to the Power of the Justices to order the Payment of Allowances for travelling in any Case where an Inquisition has not been taken, although such Coroner has been compelled to travel from his usual Place of Abode for the Purpose of taking

Coroners to be paid travelling Expences where Inquisition shall not be taken.

[1] Words in italics repealed by Stat. Law Rev. Act, 1891; as to Chester, see 23 & 24 Vict. c. 116, s. 7.

an Inquisition; be it therefore enacted, That it shall and may be lawful for the Justices of the Peace in their General or Quarter Sessions assembled for the County, Riding, Division, or Liberty where such Inquisition would have been taken, or the major Part of them, if they shall see fit, to order the Payment of such Allowances for travelling to any Coroner who shall show, to the Satisfaction of the said Justices, that he had been compelled, in the Discharge of his Office, to travel from his usual Place of abode for the Purpose of taking an Inquisition, but which, in the Exercise of his Discretion, he deemed to be unnecessary, and declined to take.

Coroners to be paid when they act for Sheriffs.

XXII. And whereas, in Cases where the Sheriff is a Party, or otherwise disqualified to act, and in various other Cases, Writs and Processes in civil Actions and Suits, and also Extents and other Process where the Queen is interested, are frequently directed to and executed by the Coroner in the Place and Stead of the Sheriff, but the Coroner is not in any such Case allowed any Fee or Reward for the Execution of any such Writs, Process, or Extents; be it therefore enacted, That in all Cases where any Writ, Process, or Extent whatsoever shall be directed to and executed by any Coroner or Coroners in the Place or Stead of any Sheriff or Sheriffs, such Coroner or Coroners shall have and receive such and the same Poundage Fees or other Compensation or Reward for executing the same as the Sheriff or Sheriffs, if he or they had executed the same, would have been entitled to receive for so doing, and shall also have such and the same Right to retain, and all other Remedies for the Recovery of the same, as the Sheriff or Sheriffs would have had in whose Place and Stead such Coroner or Coroners shall have been substituted; and if the Fees or Compensation payable to the Sheriffs shall at any Time after the passing of this Act be increased by Act of Parliament or otherwise, that in every such Case the Coroner or Coroners shall be entitled to such increased Fees or Compensation.

Coroners for detached Places to con-

XXIII. And whereas by an Act passed in the Sixth Year of the Reign of Her Majesty Queen Victoria, *intituled*

An Act for the more convenient holding of Coroners Inquests, *it was enacted, that for the Purpose of holding Coroners Inquests every detached Part of a County, Riding, or Division shall be deemed to be within that County, Riding, or Division by which it is wholly surrounded, or where it is partly surrounded by Two or more Counties, within that one with which it has the longest common Boundary: And whereas as to some such detached Parts of Counties, Ridings, or Divisions there were at the Time of the passing of the last-mentioned Act Coroners appointed expressly for and having Jurisdiction in such detached Parts only, and Doubts have arisen whether such last-mentioned Coroners were superseded by such last-mentioned Act; be it therefore enacted, That as to every such detached Part of any County for which at the Time of the passing of the said last-mentioned Act there was a Coroner appointed for and acting in such detached Part such last-mentioned Coroner shall (if now living, and not having resigned, or been removed from his Office otherwise than by the Operation of the said Act,) continue to hold and exercise his former Office and Jurisdiction within such detached Part for so long a Time and in such Manner as such Coroner would have held and exercised the said Office and Jurisdiction if the said last-mentioned Act had not passed.*

tinus to hold Inquests.
6 & 7 Vict. c. 12.

XXIV. *And be it enacted, That the Treasurer of every County shall keep an Account of all Expences occasioned to such County by any Inquest in or with respect to any such detached Part of any other County, and shall twice in every Year send a Copy of such Account to the Treasurer of the other County to which such detached Part belongs; and the Treasurer of such other County shall, out of the Monies in his Hands as Treasurer, pay the same to the Order of the Treasurer sending the Account, with all reasonable Charges of making and sending the Account; and in case any Difference shall arise concerning the said Account, and such Difference shall not be adjusted by Agreement, it shall be lawful for either of the Parties to apply to the Justices of Assize of the last preceding Circuit or of the next succeeding Circuit, or to one of such Justices, who shall, by Writing*

Expences of Inquests occasioned to any County with respect to any detached Part of any other County.

under their or his Hands or Hand, nominate a Barrister at Law, not having any Interest in the Question, to arbitrate between the Parties; and such Arbitrator may, if he shall see fit, adjourn the Hearing from Time to Time, and require all such further Information to be afforded by either of the Parties as shall appear to him necessary and shall by his Award in Writing, determine the Matters in difference, and his award shall be final and conclusive between the Parties; and such Arbitrator shall also assess the Costs of the Arbitration, and shall direct by whom and out of what Fund the same shall be paid.

Coroners for particular Places excepted out of this Act.

XXV. *And be it enacted, That no Coroner of the Queen's Household and the Verge of the Queen's Palaces, nor any Coroner of the Admiralty, nor any Coroner of the City of* London *and Borough of* Southwark, *or of any Franchises belonging to the said City, nor any Coroner of any City, Borough, Town, Liberty, or Franchise which is not contributory to the County Rates, or within which such Rates have not been usually assessed, shall be entitled to any Fee, Recompence, or Benefit given to or provided for Coroners by this Act; but that it shall be lawful for all such Coroners as are last mentioned to have and receive all such Fees, Salaries, Wages, and Allowances as they were entitled to by Law before the making of this Act, or as shall be given or allowed to them by the Person or Persons by whom they have been or shall be appointed.*

Provisions of Act as to Expences to extend to the Cinque Ports.

XXVI. *And be it enacted, That the Provisions of this Act touching the Allowance for the travelling Expences of Coroners shall be deemed and taken to extend to Coroners appointed and acting for the Jurisdiction of the Cinque Ports, any thing herein-before contained to the contrary notwithstanding.* [Sects. xxii.–xxvi. repealed by Coroners Act, 1887.]

To what Places this Act shall not extend.

XXVII. *And be it enacted, That nothing in this Act contained touching the Divisions of Counties into Districts, or the Appointment or Election or Coroners, shall extend* to *the County of Chester,*[1] *or any County Palatine,* City, Borough, Town, Liberty, Franchise, Part, or Place the Appointment or Election of Coroner whereof takes place by Law otherwise than under the Writ De coronatore eligendo.

XXVIII. And be it enacted, That in construing this Act the Word "County" shall be taken to mean County, Riding, or Division of a County in and for which a separate Coroner hath been customarily elected; *and that in the Counties of* York *and* Lincoln *all things herein-before directed to be done by and with respect to the Justices in General or Quarter Sessions assembled, and by their Clerk, shall be done by and with respect to the Justices of the said Counties of* York *and* Lincoln *in General Gaol Sessions assembled, and by their Clerk.*[1]

<small>Meaning of "County."</small>

XXIX. Provided always, and be it declared and enacted, That nothing herein contained shall be construed to abridge or affect the Royal Prerogative, or the Authority of the Lord Chancellor, for issuing a Writ De coronatore eligendo, as fully as if this Act had not been passed.

<small>Not to affect the Royal Prerogative.</small>

XXX. And be it enacted, That this Act shall extend only to England. [Repealed by Coroners Act, 1887.]

<small>Act to extend only to England.</small>

XXXI. And be it enacted, That this Act may be amended or repealed by any Act to be passed during the present Session of Parliament. [Ext. to all Counties and Secs., 10 in part, 21 and 27 in part, repealed by County Coroners' Act, 1860 (23 & 24 Vict. c. 116, ss. 1, 2, 3, and 7).

<small>Act may be amended this Session.</small>

Sects. 1, 23 and 31 repealed by Stat. Law Rev. Act (No. 2), 1874 (37 & 38 Vict. c. 96).

Sects. 8–18, 22–26, and 30 repealed by Coroners Act, 1887 (50 & 51 Vict. c. 71, s. 45, Sch. 3).]

[*Vide* Local Government Act, 1888 (51 & 52 Vict. c. 41, s. 3) as to transfer to County Councils of administrative business of Justices.]

[1] Words in italics repealed by Stat. Law Rev. Act, 1891; as to Chester, see 23 & 24 Vict. c. 116, s. 7.

8 VICT. c. 18.

An Act for consolidating in One Act certain Provisions usually inserted in Acts authorising the taking of Lands for Undertakings of a public Nature.

[8th May 1845.]

Warrant for summoning Jury to be addressed to the Sheriff.

XXXIX. In every Case in which any such Question of disputed Compensation shall be required to be determined by the Verdict of a Jury the Promoters of the Undertaking shall issue their Warrant to the Sheriff, requiring him to summon a Jury for that Purpose, and such Warrant shall be under the Common Seal of the Promoters of the Undertaking if they be a Corporation, or if they be not a Corporation under the Hands and Seals of such Promoters or any Two of them; and if such Sheriff be interested in the Matter in dispute such Application shall be made to some Coroner of the County in which the Lands in question, or some Part thereof, shall be situate, and if all the Coroners of such County be so interested, such Application may be made to some Person having filled the Office of Sheriff or Coroner in such County, and who shall be then living there, and who shall not be interested in the Matter in dispute; and with respect to the Persons last mentioned Preference shall be given to one who shall have most recently served either of the said Offices; and every Ex-Sheriff, Coroner, or Ex-Coroner shall have Power, if he think fit, to appoint a Deputy or Assessor.

Provisions applicable to Sheriff to apply to Coroner.

XL. Throughout the Enactments contained in this Act relating to the Reference of a Jury, where the Term "Sheriff" is used, the Provisions applicable thereto shall be held to apply to every Coroner or other Person lawfully acting in his Place, and in every Case in which any such Warrant shall have been directed to any other Person than the Sheriff, such Sheriff shall, immediately on receiving Notice of the Delivery of the Warrant, deliver over, on Application for that Purpose, to the Person to whom the same shall have been directed, or to any Person appointed by him to receive the same the Jurors Book and Special Jurors List belonging to the County where the Lands in question shall be situate. [Sect. 39 amended by Lands Clauses Consolidation Act, 1869 (32 & 33 Vict. c. 18, s. 3). High Bailiff or deputy to be deemed to be substituted for Sheriff, where Lands are in Westminster. As to taxation of costs, *see* Sect 1 of same Act.]

---

9 & 10 VICT. c. 62.

An Act to abolish Deodands. [18th August 1846.]

Whereas the Law respecting the Forfeiture of Chattels which have moved to or caused the Death of Man, and respecting Deodands, is unreasonable and inconvenient: Be it enacted by the Queen's most Excellent Majesty, by and with the Advice and Consent of the Lords Spiritual and Temporal, and Commons, in this present Parliament assembled, and by the Authority of the same, That from and after the First Day of *September* One thousand eight hundred and forty-six there shall be no Forfeiture of any Chattel for or in respect of the same having moved to or caused the Death of Man; and no Coroner's Jury sworn to inquire, upon the Sight of any dead Body, how the Deceased came by his Death, shall find any Forfeiture of any Chattel which may have moved to or caused the Death of the Deceased, or any Deodand whatsoever; and it shall not be necessary in any Indictment or Inquisition for Homicide to allege the Value of the Instrument which caused the Death of the Deceased, or to allege that the same was of no Value. [Repealed by Stat. Law Rev. Act, 1875 (38 & 39 Vict. c. 66).]

Marginal note: Deodands and Forfeiture of Chattels moving to or causing Death abolished from and after 1 Sept. 1846.

13 & 14 VICT. c. 100.

An Act for Inspection of Coal Mines in Great Britain.
[14th August 1850.]

Provision for giving Notice to Secretary of State of holding Inquests on Deaths from Accidents in Coal Mines.

VI. And be it enacted, That every Coroner holding an Inquest upon the Body of any Person whose Death may have been caused by any such Accident as aforesaid shall (unless some Person be present on behalf of One of Her Majesty's Principal Secretaries of State to watch the Proceedings at such Inquest, or Notice of such Accident shall have been sent, Two Days at the least previously thereto, through the Post Office, by Letter addressed to One of such Secretaries of State, and the sending of the same be proved to the Satisfaction of the Coroner,) adjourn such Inquest, and by Letter sent Two Days at the least before holding such adjourned Inquest, through the Post Office, addressed to One of such Secretaries of State give Notice to such Secretary of State of the Time and Place of holding the same. [Repealed (but re-enacted and extended) by Coal Mines Inspection Act, 1855 (18 & 19 Vict. c. 108, s. 1), *q.v.* p. 175.]

---

14 & 15 VICT. c. 55.

An Act to amend the Law relating to the Expenses of Prosecutions, and to make further Provision for the Apprehension and Trial of Offenders in certain Cases.
[1st August 1851.]

In certain Counties of Cities and Towns Prisoners may be committed, and tried at Assizes held for adjoining County.

XIX. Whenever any Justice or Justices of the Peace, or Coroner, acting for any County of a City or County of a Town Corporate within which Her Majesty has not been pleased for Five Years next before the passing of this Act to direct a Commission of Oyer and Terminer and Gaol Delivery to be executed, and until Her Majesty shall be pleased to direct a Commission of Oyer and Terminer and Gaol Delivery to be executed within the same, shall commit for safe Custody to the Gaol or House of Correction of such County of a City or Town any Person charged with any Offence committed within the Limits of such County of a City or Town not triable at the Court of Quarter Sessions of the said County of a City or County of a Town, the Commitment shall specify that such Person is committed pursuant to this Act, and the Recognizances to appear to prosecute and give Evidence taken by such Justice, Justices, or Coroner shall in all such Cases be conditioned for Appearance, Prosecution, and giving Evidence at the Court of Oyer and Terminer and Gaol Delivery for the next adjoining County; and whenever any such Person shall be so committed, the Keeper of such Gaol or House of Correction shall deliver to the Judges of Assize for such next adjoining County a Calendar of all Prisoners in his Custody so commited, in the same way that the Sheriff of the County would be by Law required to do if such Prisoners had been committed to the Common Gaol of such adjoining County; and the Justice, Justices, or Coroner by whom Persons charged as aforesaid many be committed, shall deliver or cause to be delivered to the proper Officer of the Court the several Examinations, Informations, Evidence, Recognizances, and Inquisitions relative to such Persons at the Time and in the Manner that would be required in case such Persons had been committed to the Gaol of such adjoining County by a Justice or Justices, or Coroner, having Authority so to commit, and the same Proceedings shall and may be had thereupon at the Sessions of Oyer and Terminer or General Gaol Delivery for such adjoining County as in the Case of Persons charged with Offences of the like Nature committed within such County.

XX. It shall be lawful for the Justices of the Peace, at their General or Quarter Sessions for any County, Riding, or Division, by Order made for that Purpose, to declare that any Gaol or House of Correction for such County, Riding, or Division is a fit Prison for Persons committed for Trial at the Assizes for such County, or for the County of such Riding or Division; and every such Order shall be signed by the Chairman of such Sessions, and trans- *Justices to declare when Gaols or Houses of Correction are fit Prisons for Persons committed for Trial.*

mitted to One of Her Majesty's Principal Secretaries of State; and in case such Secretary of State see fit to approve such Order, then, after the Approval thereof under the Hand of such Secretary of State, it shall be lawful for any Justice or Justices of the Peace, or Coroner, acting for such County, Riding, or Division, to commit for safe Custody for Trial at the next Assizes, to such Gaol or House of Correction, any Person charged with any Offence triable at the Assizes for such County or for the County of such Riding or Division; and the Commitment shall specify that such Person is committed under the Authority of this Act; and the Recognizances to appear to prosecute and give Evidence taken by such Justice, Justices, or Coroner shall in all such Cases be conditioned for Appearance, Prosecution, and giving Evidence at the Court of Oyer and Terminer and Gaol Delivery for the County; and the Keeper of such Gaol or House of Correction shall deliver to the Judges of Assize a Calendar of all Prisoners in Custody for Trial at such Assizes, in the same Way that the Sheriff of the County would be by Law required to do if such Prisoners had been committed to the Common Gaol of such County; and the Justice, Justices, or Coroner by whom Persons charged as aforesaid may be committed shall deliver or cause to be delivered to the proper Officer of the Court of Assize the several Examinations, Informations, Evidence, Recognizances, and Inquisitions relative to such Persons at the Time and in the Manner that would be required in case such Persons had been committed for Trial as aforesaid to such Common Gaol, and the same Proceedings shall and may be had thereupon at the Sessions of Oyer and Terminer or General Gaol Delivery for such County as in the Case of Persons so committed to such Common Gaol. [Sect. 19 in part (from "and whenever" to "Common Gaol of such adjoining County"), and 20 in part (from "and the Keeper" to "Gaol of such County") repealed by Stat. Law Rev. Act, 1875 (38 & 39 Vict. c. 66, s. 1, and Sch.).]

16 VICT. c. 80.

An Act for the better Prevention and Punishment of aggravated Assaults upon Women and Children, and for preventing Delay and Expense in the Admistration of certain Parts of the Criminal Law.
[14th June 1853.]

IX. It shall be lawful for One of Her Majesty's Principal Secretaries of State, or any Judge of the Court of Queen's Bench or Common Pleas, or any Baron of the Exchequer, in any Case where he may see fit to do so, upon Aplication by Affidavit, to issue a Warrant or Order under his Hand for bringing up any Prisoner or Person confined in any Gaol, Prison or Place, under any Sentence or under Commitment for Trial or otherwise, (except under Process in any Civil Action, Suit, or Proceeding,) before any Court, Judge, Justice, or other Judicature, to be examined as a Witness in any Cause or Matter, civil or criminal, depending or to be inquired of, or determined in or before such Court, Judge, Justice, or Judicature; and the Person required by any such Warrant or Order to be so brought before such Court, Judge, Justice, or other Judicature shall be so brought under the same Care and Custody, and be dealt with in like Manner in all respects, as a Prisoner required by any Writ of Habeas corpus awarded by any of Her Majesty's Superior Courts of Law at *Westminster* to be brought before such Court to be examined as a Witness in any Cause or Matter depending before such Court is now by Law required to be dealt with.

Secretary of State may issue his Warrant for bringing up a Prisoner (not in Custody under Civil Process) to give Evidence.

---

16 & 17 VICT. c. 96.

An Act to amend an Act passed in the Ninth Year of Her Majesty, "for the Regulation of the Care and Treatment of Lunatics."
[20th August 1853.]

XIX. The Superintendent or Proprietor of every registered Hospital and licensed House, and every Person

On Recovery of a Patient Notice to be

given to Friends, and in the Case of a Pauper to Guardians, etc., and in default of Discharge or Removal, to Commissioners and Visitors.

having the Care or Charge of any single Patient, shall forthwith, upon the Recovery of any Patient in such Hospital or House, or of such single Patient, transmit Notice of such Recovery in the Case of a Patient not a Pauper to the Person who signed the Order for his Reception, or by whom the last Payment on account of such Patient was made, and in the Case of a Pauper to the Guardians of his Union or Parish, or if there be no such Guardians to One of the Overseers of the Poor of his Parish, or if such Pauper be chargeable to any County to the Clerk of the Peace thereof, and in case such Patient be not discharged or removed within Fourteen Days from the giving of such Notice, such Superintendent, Proprietor, or Person as aforesaid shall immediately after the Expiration of such Period transmit Notice of the Recovery of such Patient to the Commissioners, and also, in the Case of a licensed House within the Jurisdiction of any Visitors, to the Clerk of such Visitors, with the Date of the Notice firstly in this Enactment mentioned, and where Notice is so given to the Clerk of any Visitors, he shall forthwith communicate the same to the Visitors, or Two of them, One of whom shall be a Physician, Surgeon, or Apothecary;

Provision in case of Death of Patient in any Hospital or licensed House.

and in case of the Death of any Patient in any Hospital or licensed House, a Statement setting forth the Time and Cause of the Death, and the Duration of the Disease of which such Patient died, shall be prepared and signed by the Medical Person or Persons who attended the Patient during the Illness which terminated in Death, and such Statement shall be entered in the "Case Book," and a Copy of such Statement, certified by the Superintendent or Proprietor, shall, within Two Days of the Date of the Death, be transmitted to the Coroner, for the County or Borough, and in case such Coroner, after receiving such Statement, shall think that any reasonable Suspicion attends the Cause and Circumstances of the Death of such Patient, he shall summon a Jury to inquire into the Cause of such Death. [This Act and 8 & 9 Vict. c. 100, to be construed as one, and read with Lunacy Law Amendment Act, 1862 (25 & 26 Vict. c. 111, s. 1). Whole Act repealed by Lunacy Act, 1890 (53 Vict. c. 5, s. 342, and Sch. 5.)]

THE STATUTES. 175

18 & 19 VICT. c. 108.

An Act to amend the Law for the Inspection of Coal Mines in Great Britain. [14th August 1855.]

X. Every Coroner holding an Inquest upon the Body of any Person whose Death may have been caused by any such Accident as aforesaid shall (unless some Person be present on behalf of One of Her Majesty's Principal Secretaries of State to watch the Proceedings at such Inquest, or Notice of such Accident shall have been sent, Four clear Days at the least previously thereto, through the Post Office, by Letter addressed to One of such Secretaries of State, and the sending of the same be proved to the Satisfaction of the Coroner,) adjourn such Inquest, and by Letter sent Two Days at the least before holding such adjourned Inquest, through the Post Office, addressed to One of such Secretaries of State, give Notice to such Secretary of State of the Time and Place of holding the same: Provided always, that it shall be lawful for such Coroner, before the Adjournment of any such Inquest, to take Evidence to identify the Body, and to order the Interment thereof. [Whole Act repealed by Mines Regulation and Inspection Act, 1860 (23 & 24 Vict. c. 151, s. 6).] *(Provision for giving Notice to Secretary of State of holding Inquests on Deaths from Accidents in Coal Mines.)*

---

19 VICT. c. 16.

An Act to empower the Court of Queen's Bench to order certain Offenders to be tried at the Central Criminal Court. [11th April 1856.]

II. Whenever any such Order shall have been made, the Queen's Coroner and Attorney, or other Officer having the Custody of the Records of the said Court of Queen's Bench, shall forthwith upon Notice of such Order transmit such Indictment or Inquisition so removed by Certiorari as in the preceeding Section mentioned, together with any Depositions, Examinations, or Informations relating to any Offence charged therein which shall be in his *(When any such Order has been made, the Indictment shall be transmitted to the Central Criminal Court.)*

Custody, to the proper Officer of the said Central Criminal Court, to be by him kept among the Records of the said Central Criminal Court.

The Court of Queen's Bench may order any Person charged with any Offence committed out of the Jurisdiction of the Central Criminal Court to be tried at that Court, and thereupon a Certiorari shall issue to remove the Indictment into the Central Criminal Court.

III. Whenever any Person shall have been committed or held to Bail for any Felony or Misdemeanor committed or supposed to have been committed at any Place out of the Jurisdiction of the said Central Criminal Court, and it shall appear to the said Court of Queen's Bench in Term Time, or to any Judge thereof in Vacation that it is expedient to the Ends of Justice that such Person should be tried for such Offence at the said Central Criminal Court, it shall be lawful for such Court of Queen's Bench in Term Time, or for such Judge thereof in Vacation, to order that such Person shall be tried for such Offence at the said Central Criminal Court, and thereupon a Writ of Certiorari shall be issued to the Justices of Oyer and Terminer or of Gaol Delivery, or of the Peace, before whom any Indictment or Inquisition charging such Person with such Offence shall then be pending, or before whom any such Indictment shall thereafter be found, or to the Coroner before whom any such Inquisition shall have been or shall thereafter be taken, commanding them or him to certify and return such Indictment or Inquisition into the said Central Criminal Court.

When any such Order has been made, the Depositions, etc., shall be returned to the Central Criminal Court.

IV. Whenever any such Order as is mentioned in any preceding Section of this Act shall have been made, the Justice before whom any Person charged with any Offence by such Indictment shall have been examined, the Coroner before whom such Inquisition shall have been taken, the Clerk of Assize, Clerk of the Peace, or any other Person having the Custody or Possession thereof, shall forthwith, upon the Delivery to him of an Office Copy of such Order, transmit any Recognizances, Depositions, Examinations, or Informations relating to the Offence charged in such Indictment or Inquisition which shall be in his Custody or Possession to the proper Officer of the said Central Criminal Court, to be by him kept among the Records of the said Central Criminal Court. [Should be read in conjunction with Central Criminal Court (Prisons) Act, 1881 (44 & 45 Vict. c. 64, s. 2, and Sch.)].

---

22 VICT. c. 33.

An Act to enable Coroners in England to admit to Bail Persons charged with Manslaughter.

[19th April 1859.]

Whereas in many Cases Inconvenience and Expense have been occasioned by the Inability of Coroners in *England* to admit to Bail Persons charged by the Verdict of a Coroner's Jury with the Offence of Manslaughter: Be it therefore enacted by the Queen's most Excellent Majesty, by and with the Advice and Consent of the Lords Spiritual and Temporal, and Commons, in this present Parliament assembled, and by the Authority of the same, as follows:

I. In every Case in which a Coroner's Jury shall have found a Verdict of Manslaughter against any Person or Persons it shall be lawful for the Coroner or Deputy Coroner before whom the Inquest was taken to accept Bail, if he shall think fit, with good and sufficient Sureties, for the Appearance of the Person so charged with the Offence of Manslaughter at the next Assize and General Gaol Delivery to be holden in and for the County within which the Inquest was taken; and thereupon such Person if in Custody of any Bailiff or other Officer of the Coroner's Court, or in any Gaol under a Warrant of Commitment issued by such Coroner, shall be discharged therefrom. *In cases of Manslaughter the Coroner may admit the Persons charged to Bail.*

II. In every Case in which any Coroner or Deputy Coroner shall admit any Person to Bail he shall cause Recognizances to be taken in the Form given in the Schedule to this Act, and give a Notice thereof to every Person so bound, and shall return such Recognizances to the then next ensuing Assizes, and such Coroner or Deputy Coroner shall be entitled to such Fees and *Recognizances to be taken.*

Charges as the Clerks of Justices of the Peace are by Law entitled to on admitting Persons charged to Bail.

<small>Persons against whom Coroner's Juries have found Verdicts of Manslaughter to be supplied with Depositions.</small>
III. At any Time after all the Depositions of Witnesses shall have been taken, every Person against whom any Coroner's Jury may have found a Verdict of Manslaughter shall be entitled to have from the Person having Custody thereof Copies of the Depositions on which such Verdict shall have been found, on Payment of a reasonable Sum for the same, not exceeding the Rate of Three Halfpence for every Folio of Ninety Words. [Repealed by Coroners Act, 1887 (50 & 51 Vict. c. 71, s. 45, Sch. 3).]

SCHEDULE.

Be it remembered, That on the   Day of in the Year of our Lord   A. B. of [Labourer], L. M. of , [Grocer], and N. O. of , [Butcher], personally came before me, One of Her Majesty's Coroners for the [County] of , and severally acknowledged themselves to owe to our Lady the Queen the several Sums following; that is to say, the said A. B. the Sum of and the said L. M. and N. O. the Sum of each, of good and lawful Money of Great Britain, to be made and levied of their Goods and Chattels, Lands and Tenements respectively, to the Use of our said Lady the Queen, Her Heirs and Successors, if he the said A. B. fail in the Condition endorsed.

Taken and acknowledged the Day and Year first above mentioned, at , before me,

      J. S.,
    Coroner for the [County] of

Condition endorsed.

The Condition of the within-written Recognizance is such, That whereas a Verdict of Manslaughter has been found against the said A. B. by a Jury empannelled to inquire how and by what Means came by [his] Death; if therefore the said A. B. shall appear at the next Court of Oyer and Terminer and General Gaol Delivery to be holden in and for the [County] of , and there surrender himself into the Custody of the Keeper of the Gaol there, and plead to such Inquisition, and take his Trial upon the same, and not depart the said Court without Leave, then the said Recognizance shall be void, or else the same shall stand in full force and virtue.

22 & 23 VICT. c. 21.

An Act to regulate the Office of Queen's Remembrancer, and to amend the Practice and Procedure on the Revenue Side of the Court of Exchequer. [13th August 1859.]

XL. Every Recognizance forfeited at any Inquest to be holden before the Coroner of any County, City, Town, Liberty, or place in *England*, shall be certified by such Coroner to the Clerk of the Peace for the County, Riding, Division, or Place in which the Person forfeiting such Recognizance shall reside, on or before the First Day of the Quarter Session of the Peace then next ensuing, and such Coroner shall cause a Copy of such Certificate to be served upon the Person liable to the Payment of such Forfeiture by leaving it at his Residence; and every such Clerk of the Peace shall proceed to act in respect of such Forfeiture as in the Case of Fines certified by Coroners pursuant to Section Seventeen of the Act passed in the Seventh and Eighth Years of Her Majesty, Chapter Ninety-two, and such Forfeiture shall be levied and applied in like Manner, and subject to the like Powers, Provisions and Penalties, as such Fines. [Sec. 40 repealed by Coroners Act, 1887 (50 & 51 Vict. c. 71, s. 45, Sch. 3.)]

Recognizances forfeited at Coroners Inquests to be returned to Clerks of the Peace, as in the Case of Fines imposed by Coroners.

---

23 & 24 VICT. c. 116.

An Act to amend the Law relating to the Election, Duties, and Payment of County Coroners. [28th August 1860.]

Whereas it is expedient to amend the Law with respect to the Election and Payment of Coroners for Counties, and to extend the Provisions of the Act Seven and Eight Victoria, Chapter Ninety-two, to all Counties, whether divided into Districts or not: Be it therefore enacted by the Queen's most Excellent Majesty, by and with the Advice and Consent of the Lords Spiritual and Temporal, and Commons, in this present Parliament assembled, and by the Authority of the same, as follows; that is to say,

Provisions of 7 & 8 Vict. c. 92, extended to all Counties, although not divided into Districts for the Purposes of such Act.

I. *From and after the passing of this Act, all the Provisions of the Act Seven and Eight* Victoria, *Chapter Ninety-two, shall, so far as the same may be applicable to the Election of Coroners, be extended and be construed to extend and apply to all Counties, notwithstanding the same may not have been divided into Two or more Districts for the Purposes of such Act; and every Election of a Coroner for a County not so divided as aforesaid which may have taken place previous to the passing of this Act, shall be and the same is hereby declared to be as legal and valid to all Intents and Purposes whatsoever as if such Election had taken place subsequent to the passing of this Act.*

Polling at Elections for Coroners to continue for One Day only.

II. *From and after the passing of this Act, so much of the Act Seven and Eight* Victoria, *Chapter Ninety-two, as authorizes the Polling at Elections for Coroners to continue for Two Days shall be and the same is hereby repealed, and thenceforth such Polling shall continue for One Day only.*

Provisions as to Remuneration of Coroners by Fees repealed.

III. *From and after the Thirty-first Day of* December *One thousand eight hundred and sixty, so much of any Act as provides for the Remuneration of County Coroners by Fees, Mileage, and allowances, shall be and the same is hereby repealed.* [Repealed by Coroners Act, 1887.]

County Coroners to be paid by Salary.

IV. On and after the First Day of *January* One thousand eight hundred and sixty-one, there shall be paid to every County Coroner, in lieu of the Fees, Mileage and Allowances which if this Act had not been passed he would have been entitled to receive, such an annual Salary as shall be agreed upon between him and the Justices in General or Quarter Sessions assembled for the County for which, or for some Portion of which, such Coroner shall act, such Salary in the case of any Person holding the Office of County Coroner at the Time of the passing of this Act not being less than the average Amount of the Fees, Mileage, and Allowances actually received by such

Coroner and his Predecessors, if any, for the Five Years immediately preceding the Thirty-first Day of *December* One thousand eight hundred and fifty-nine; and such Salary shall be paid quarterly to such Coroner by the Treasurer of the County out of the County Rate; and whenever from Death, Removal, or any other Cause whatever any County Coroner shall not be entitled to a Salary for the whole of a Quarter, a proportionate Part of the Salary shall be paid to him, or, in case of his Death, to his Personal Representatives: Provided always, that in case any such Justices and any such County Coroner as aforesaid shall be unable to agree as to the Amount of the Salary to be paid to such Coroner, it shall be lawful for Her Majesty's Principal Secretary of State for the Home Department, and he is required, upon the Application of such Coroner, to fix and determine the Amount of such Salary, having regard to such Average as aforesaid, also the Average Number of Inquests held by any such Coroner in the preceding Five Years as aforesaid, and also to the special Circumstances of each Case, and the general Scale of Salaries of County Coroners; provided also, that after the Lapse of every successive Period of Five years it shall be lawful for any such Justices and such Coroner as aforesaid to revise, and thereby increase or diminish, any such Salary, having regard to the average Number of Inquests held by any such Coroner in the Five Years immediately preceding, and subject in case of their Disagreement to such Appeal to the Home Secretary as before mentioned: Provided always, that nothing herein contained shall in any Manner take away, alter, or deprive any such Coroner of the Right to be repaid out of the County Rate the Expenses and Disbursements which may have been paid or made by him on the holding of any Inquest as provided by the Act First *Victoria*, Chapter Sixty-eight.[1]

V. If any Coroner shall refuse or neglect to hold an Inquest in any Case when such Inquest ought to be held, *If Coroner refuse to hold Inquest, Ap-*

---

[1] 7 Will. IV. and 1 Vict. c. 68 is repealed by the Coroners Act, 1887.

plication may be made to a Judge for a Rule to show Cause.

it shall be lawful for Her Majesty's Attorney General to apply to the Court of Queen's Bench, or during Vacation to a Judge of any One of Her Majesty's Superior Courts of Law at *Westminster*, for a Rule calling on such Coroner to show Cause why he should not hold such Inquest, and if after due Service of such Rule good Cause shall not be shown against it, it shall be lawful for the Judge to make such Rule absolute, with or without Payment of Costs as to such Judge shall seem meet, and the Coroner, upon being served with such Rule Absolute, shall obey the same, and hold such Inquest, upon pain of being liable to an Attachment in case of Refusal or Neglect.

Power to remove Coroner.

VI. It shall be lawful for the Lord Chancellor, if he shall think fit, to remove for Inability or Misbehaviour in his Office any such Coroner already elected or appointed, or hereafter to be elected or appointed.

County of Chester to be henceforth subject to the General Law.

VII. *From and after the passing of this Act so much of the Public General Act Seventh and Eighth* Victoria, *Chapter Ninety-two, as exempts the County of* Chester *from the Provisions of that Act, and also the Local and Personal Act, Three* Victoria, *Chapter Eighty-seven authorizing the Appointment of additional Coroners for the County Palatine of* Chester (*except the Twenty-first Section of that Act, so far as regards the Head Coroners now in Office for the Three Divisions into which that County is now divided*), *and also so much of the Act of the Thirty-third Year of King* Henry *the Eighth, Chapter Thirteen, as relates to Coroners for the Shire of Chester are hereby repealed, and* all the Provisions of this Act, and of the Public General Act, Seventh and Eighth *Victoria*, Chapter Ninety-two (except the said Exemption) and all other Public General Acts, Laws, Statutes, and Usages relating to Coroners for Counties, from Time to Time in force, shall, from and after the passing of this Act, extend and apply to the County of *Chester* and the Coroners for the Divisions into which that County is now or hereafrer may be divided: Provided always, that notwithstanding such Repeal the present Divisions of the County of *Chester* under the

Powers of the said Local and Personal Act, Three *Victoria*, Chapter Eighty-seven, shall continue, unless and until that County shall be divided into other Districts under the Powers of the said Public General Act, Seventh and Eighth *Victoria*, Chapter Ninety-two, and the said present Divisions shall be deemed to have been made under the last-mentioned Act, without Prejudice to the Provisions contained in the Twenty-first Section of the said Local and Personal Act so far as regards the present Head Coroners of the said County; provided also, that such Repeal shall not invalidate or affect the Election of the present Head Coroners for the said County, but (subject to any future Alteration or Division of their respective Divisions or Districts under the Public General Act, Seventh and Eighth *Victoria*, Chapter Ninety-two,) they shall continue in Office as if such Repeal had not taken place.

VIII. The Word "County" in and throughout this Act shall be deemed and taken to include all Counties, Ridings, Divisions, Hundreds, Wards, Liberties, and other Places the Coroners whereof are paid out of the County Rates. *Interpretation of "County."*

IX. *Nothing herein contained shall be construed to abridge or affect the Royal Prerogative, or any Right vested in any Person or Persons, to appoint by Patent or by Election, or otherwise, any Coroner for any City, Borough Liberty, Franchise, Manor, or Place, or the Authority of the Lord Chancellor, or to issue a Writ De coronatore eligendo.* Repealed by Coroners Act, 1887. *Saving Rights of the Crown, etc.*

X. The said Act of the Seventh and Eighth *Victoria* Chapter Ninety-two (as varied by this Act), and this Act shall extend only to that Part of the United Kingdom called *England* and *Wales*. [Sec. 1 in part repealed by Stat. Law Rev. Act. 1875 (38 & 39 Vict. c. 66, Secs. 1, 2, 3, 5, 6, 7 in part, (down to "hereby repealed, and,") and 9 repealed by Coroners Act, 1887 (50 & 51 Vict. c. 71, s. 45, Sch. 3.)] *Extent of Acts.*

23 & 24 VICT. c. 151.

An Act for the Regulation and Inspection of Mines.
[28th August 1860.]

<small>Provision for Adjournment of Inquests on Deaths from Accidents in Mines in certain Cases.</small>

XX. Every Coroner holding an Inquest upon the Body of any Person whose Death may have been caused by any such Accident as aforesaid shall, unless the Inspector of the District or some Person on behalf of the Secretary of State be present to watch the Proceedings at such Inquest, adjourn such Inquest, and by Letter sent through the Post Office, Four Days at the least before holding such adjourned Inquest, addressed to the Inspector of the District, give Notice to such Inspector of the Time and Place of holding the same; provided that such Coroner may before the Adjourment of any such Inquest take Evidence to identify the Body, and may order the Interment thereof; provided also, that if the Accident has not occasioned more than One Death, and Notice of the Inquest has been given by the Coroner to the Inspector of the District by Letter sent through the Post Office not less than Forty-eight Hours before the Time of holding the Inquest, it shall not be imperative on the Coroner to adjourn such Inquest as aforesaid, in case the Majority of the Jury think it unecessary so to adjourn; and the Inspector shall be at liberty to examine any Witness at any such Inquest, subject to the Order of the Coroner. [Repealed by Mines (Coal) Regulation Act, 1872 (35 & 36 Vict. c. 76, s. 76, and Sch. 3.)]

---

24 & 25 VICT. c. 100.

An Act to consolidate and amend the Statute Law of England *and* Ireland *relating to Offences against the Person.* [6th August 1861.]

<small>Indictment for Murder or Manslaughter.</small>

9. In any Indictment for Murder or Manslaughter, or for being an Accessory to any Murder or Manslaughter, it shall not be necessary to set forth the Manner in which

or the Means by which the Death of the Deceased was caused, but it shall be sufficient in any Indictment for Murder to charge that the Defendant did feloniously, wilfully, and of his Malice aforethought kill and murder the Deceased; and it shall be sufficient in any Indictment for Manslaughter to charge that the Defendant did feloniously kill and slay the Deceased; and it shall be sufficient in any Indictment against any Accessory to any Murder or Manslaughter to charge the Principal with the Murder or Manslaughter (as the Case may be) in the Manner herein-before specified, and then to charge the Defendant as an Accessory in the Manner heretofore used and accustomed.

---

25 & 26 VICT. c. 111.

An Act to amend the Law relating to Lunatics.
[7th August 1862.]

44. The Superintendent of every Asylum, and every Person having the Care or Charge of a single Patient, shall in the event of the Death of any Patient, transmit to the Coroner of the County or Borough the same Statement as is required by Law to be transmitted in the Case of the Death of any Patient in any Hospital or Licensed House, and if such Coroner, after receiving such Statement, thinks that any reasonable Suspicion attends the Cause and Circumstances of the Death of such Patient, he shall summon a Jury to inquire into the Circumstances of such Death. <small>Report to Coroner of Death of single Patient.</small>

Any Superintendent or Person in charge who makes default in complying with the Requisitions of this Section shall be guilty of a Misdemeanor. [Whole Act repealed by Lunacy Act, 1890 (53 Vict. c. 5, s. 342, and Sch. 5).]

28 & 29 VICT. c. 103.

An Act to provide for the Discontinuance of a separate Court of Quarter Sessions and a separate Gaol in the Borough of Falmouth. [5th July 1865.]

Falmouth to cease to have separate Court of Quarter Sessions. 3. From and after the Commencement of this Act no separate Court of Quarter Sessions shall be holden for the Borough of *Falmouth*, and there shall be no Recorder and no Coroner for the said Borough, and the said Borough, shall for all the Purposes of a County Rate, and of the Jurisdiction of the County Justices and of the County Coroner, and for all other Purposes, be deemed to be a Borough to which a separate Commission of the Peace, but no separate Court of Quarter Sessions, has been granted.

---

28 & 29 VICT. c. 126.

THE PRISON ACT, 1865.

An Act to consolidate and amend the Law relating to Prisons. [6th July 1865.]

Inquests on Prisoners. 48. It shall be the Duty of the Coroner having Jurisdiction in the Place to which the Prison belongs to hold an Inquest on the Body of every Prisoner who may die within the Prison. Where it is practicable, One clear Day shall intervene between the Day of the Death and the Day of the holding the Inquest; and in no Case shall any Officer of the Prison, or any Prisoner confined in the Prison, be a Juror on such Inquest.

---

29 & 30 VICT. c. 90.

An Act to amend the Law relating to the Public Health. [7th August 1866.]

Places for Reception of dead Bodies 28. Any Nuisance Authority may provide a proper Place (otherwise than at a Workhouse or at a Mortuary

House as lastly hereinbefore provided for) for the Reception of dead Bodies for and during the Time required to conduct any *Post-mortem* Examination ordered by the Coroner of the District or other constituted Authority, and may make such Regulations as they may deem fit for the Maintenance, Support, and Management of such Place; and where any such Place has been provided, any Coroner or other constituted Authority may order the Removal of the Body for carrying out such *Post-mortem* Examination and the Re-removal of such body, such Costs of Removal and Re-removal to be paid in the same Manner and out of the same Fund as the Cost and Fees for *Post-mortem* Examinations when ordered by the Coroner. [Repealed (except as regards the Metropolis) by Public Health Act, 1875 (38 & 39 Vic. c. 55, s. 343, Sch. 5.)]

during Time required for post-mortem Examination may be provided.

[Repealed in part (as to Coroners ordering removal of bodies) by Coroners' Act, 1887 (50 & 51 Vict. 71, s. 45, Sch. 3.)]

[Remainder repealed by Public Health (London) Act, 1891 (54 & 55 Vict. c. 76, s. 142, and Sch. 4.)]

---

30 & 31 VICT. c. 59.

An Act for further promoting the Revision of the Statute Law by repealing certain Enactments which have ceased to be in force or have become unnecessary.

[15 July 1867.]

Section 1 Repeals (*inter alia*) 25 Geo. II. c. 29, except the last two sections, viz. V. and VI. which are repealed by the Coroners Act, 1887 (50 & 51 Vict. c. 71 s. 45, sch. 3).

---

31 VICT. c. 24.

An Act to provide for carrying out of Capital Punishment within Prisons. [29th May 1868.]

4. As soon as may be after Judgment of Death has been executed on the Offender, the Surgeon of the Prison shall examine the Body of the Offender, and shall ascertain the

Surgeon to certify Death; and Declaration

to be signed by Sheriff, etc. Fact of Death, and shall sign a Certificate thereof, and deliver the same to the Sheriff.

The Sheriff and the Gaoler and Chaplain of the Prison, and such Justices and other Persons present (if any) as the Sheriff requires or allows, shall also sign a Declaration to the Effect that Judgment of Death has been executed on the Offender.

Coroner's Inquest on Body. 5. The Coroner of the Jurisdiction to which the Prison belongs wherein Judgment of Death is executed on any Offender shall within Twenty-four Hours after the Execution hold an Inquest on the Body of the Offender, and the Jury at the Inquest shall inquire into and ascertain the Identity of the Body, and whether Judgment of Death was duly executed on the Offender; and the Inquisition shall be in duplicate, and One of the Originals shall be delivered to the Sheriff.

No Officer of the Prison or Prisoner confined therein shall in any Case be a Juror on the Inquest. [Repealed in part ("no officer of the prison," to end of section), by Coroners Act, 1887 (50 & 51 Vict. c. 71, s. 45, Sch. 3.)]

---

33 & 34 VICT. c. 77.

THE JURIES ACT, 1870.

An Act to amend the Laws relating to the qualifications, summoning, attendance, and remuneration of Special and Common Juries. [9th August 1870.]

Persons exempt from serving on juries. 9. The inhabitants of the city and liberty of Westminster shall, as heretofore, be exempt from serving on any jury at the sessions of the peace for the county of Middlesex.

The persons described in the schedule[1] hereto shall be severally exempt as therein specified from being returned to serve and from serving upon any juries or inquests whatsoever, and their names shall not be inserted in the lists of the persons qualified and liable to serve on the same, but, save as aforesaid, no man otherwise qualified so

[1] For schedule, *vide* p. 284.

THE STATUTES.

to serve on such juries or inquests shall be exempt from serving thereon, any enactment, prescription, charter, grant, or writ to the contrary notwithstanding.

12. No person whose name shall be in the jury book as a juror shall be entitled to be excused from attendance on the ground of any disqualification or exemption other than illness not claimed by him at or before the revision of the list by the justices of the peace, and a notice to that effect shall be printed at the bottom of every jury list. *Disqualification or exemption to be pleaded before revision of list.*

---

34 & 35 VICT. c. 78.

An Act to amend the Law respecting the Inspection and Regulation of Railways. [14th August 1871.]

8. Where any coroner in England holds or is about to hold an inquest on the death of any person occasioned by an accident, of which notice for the time being is required by or in pursuance of this Act to be sent to the Board of Trade, and makes a written request to the Board of Trade in this behalf, the Board of Trade may appoint an inspector or some person possessing legal or special knowledge to assist in holding such inquest, and such appointee shall act as the assessor of the coroner, and shall make the like report to the Board of Trade, and the report shall be made public in like manner as in the case of a formal investigation of an accident under this Act. *Appointment of an assessor to coroner.*

---

35 & 36 VICT. c. 38.

THE INFANT LIFE PROTECTION ACT, 1872.

An Act for the better Protection of Infant Life.
[25th July 1872.]

8. The person registered as aforesaid shall within twenty-four hours after the death of every infant so retained or received cause notice thereof to be given to the coroner for *Inquest to be held on death of infant.*

the district within which the said infant died, and the said coroner shall hold an inquest on the body of every such infant unless a certificate under the hand of a registered medical practitioner shall be produced to him by the person so registered certifying that such registered medical practitioner has personally attended or examined such infant, and specifying the cause of its death, and the said coroner shall be satisfied by such certificate that there is no ground for holding such inquest. If the person so registered shall neglect to give notice as aforesaid he shall be guilty of an offence under this Act.

Act subject to certain provisions in its application to Scotland.

14. This Act shall, in its application to Scotland, be subject to the following provisions:

1. The expression "crime and offence" shall be equivalent to the expression "offence," and shall be substituted therefor:
2. For a coroner's inquest shall be substituted an inquiry by the procurator fiscal of the county into the cause of death:
3. The expenses of an inquiry by a procurator fiscal under this Act shall be defrayed out of the same funds as the expenses of an inquiry by him in a case of sudden death:
4. The court of summary jurisdiction, when hearing, trying, determining, and adjudicating, an information or complaint in respect of any offence or matter arising under this Act, shall be constituted of a sheriff or sheriff substitute. [Repealed by 60 & 61 Vict. c. 57, s. 18.]

---

85 & 86 VICT. c. 76.

THE COAL MINES REGULATION ACT, 1872.

An Act to consolidate and amend the Acts relating to the Regulation of Coal Mines and certain other Mines.

[10th August 1872.]

Provisions as to coroners inquests on

50. With respect to coroners inquests on the bodies of persons whose death may have been caused by explosions

THE STATUTES. 191

or accidents in mines to which this Act applies, the following provisions shall have effect: {deaths from accidents in mines.}

1. Where a coroner holds an inquest upon a body of any person whose death may have been caused by any explosion or accident, of which notice is required by this Act to be given to the inspector of the district, the coroner shall adjourn such inquest unless an inspector, or some person on behalf of a Secretary of State, is present to watch the proceedings:

2. The coroner, at least four days before holding the adjourned inquest, shall send to the inspector for the district notice in writing of the time and place of holding the adjourned inquest:

3. The coroner, before the adjournment, may take evidence to identify the body, and may order the interment thereof:

4. If an explosion or accident has not occasioned the death of more than one person, and the coroner has sent to the inspector of the district notice of the time and place of holding the inquest not less than forty-eight hours before the time of holding the same, it shall not be imperative on him to adjourn such inquest in pursuance of this section, if the majority of the jury think it unnecessary so to adjourn:

5. An inspector shall be at liberty at any such inquest to examine any witness, subject nevertheless to the order of the coroner:

6. Where evidence is given at an inquest at which an inspector is not present of any neglect as having caused or contributed to the explosion or accident, or of any defect in or about the mine appearing to the coroner or jury to require a remedy, the coroner shall send to the inspector of the district notice in writing of such neglect or default:

7. Any person having a personal interest in or employed in or in the management of the mine in which the explosion or accident occurred shall not be qualified to serve on the jury empanelled

on the inquest; and it shall be the duty of the constable or other officer not to summon any person disqualified under this provision, and it shall be the duty of the coroner not to allow any such person to be sworn or to sit on the jury.

Every person who fails to comply with the provisions of this section shall be guilty of an offence against this Act. [Whole Act repealed by Coal Mines Regulation Act, 1887 (50 & 51 Vict. c. 58, s. 84, Sch. 4), but substance of section 50 re-enacted by Metalliferous Mines Regulation Act, 1872 (35 & 36 Vict. c. 77, s. 22).]

---

35 & 36 VICT. c. 77.

THE METALLIFEROUS MINES REGULATION ACT, 1872.

An Act to consolidate and amend the Law relating to Metalliferous Mines. [10th August 1872.]

Provisions as to coroners inquests on deaths from accidents in mines.

22. With respect to coroners inquests on the bodies of persons whose death may have been caused by explosions or accidents in mines to which this Act applies, the following provisions shall have effect:

1. Where a coroner holds an inquest upon a body of any person whose death may have been caused by any explosion or accident, of which notice is required by this Act to be given to the inspector of the district, the coroner shall adjourn such inquest unless an inspector, or some person on behalf of a Secretary of State, is present to watch the proceedings:

2. The coroner, at least four days before holding the adjourned inquest, shall send to the inspector of the district notice in writing of the time and place of holding the adjourned inquest:

3. The coroner, before the adjournment, may take evidence to identify the body, and may order the interment thereof:

4. If an explosion or accident has not occasioned the

death of more than one person, and the coroner has sent to the inspector of the district notice of the time and place of holding the inquest not less than forty-eight hours before the time of holding the same, it shall not be imperative on him to adjourn such inquest in pursuance of this section, if the majority of the jury think it unnecessary so to adjourn:

5. An inspector shall be at liberty at any such inquest to examine any witness, subject nevertheless to the order of the coroner:

6. Where evidence is given at an inquest at which an inspector is not present of any neglect as having caused or contributed to the explosion or accident, or of any defect in or about the mine appearing to the coroner or jury to require a remedy, the coroner shall send to the inspector of the district notice in writing of such neglect or default:

7. Any person having a personal interest in or employed in or in the management of the mine in which the explosion or accident occurred shall not be qualified to serve on the jury empannelled on the inquest; and it shall be the duty of the constable or other officer not to summon any person disqualified under this provision, and it shall be the duty of the coroner not to allow any such person to be sworn or to sit on the jury.

Every person who fails to comply with the provisions of this section shall be guilty of an offence against this Act.

---

86 & 87 VICT. c. 76.

An Act to make further Provision for the Regulation of Railways. [5th August 1873.]

5. Every coroner in England and Ireland within seven days after holding an inquest on the body of any person who is proved to have been killed on a railway, or to have died in consequence of injuries received on a railway, and

Returns by coroners.

in Scotland every procurator fiscal within the like time and in like cases, shall make to one of Her Majesty's Principal Secretaries of State, in such form as he may require, a return of the death and the cause thereof.

---

36 & 87 VICT. c. 81.

An Act to authorise the division of the Wapentake of Langbaurgh in the county of York into districts for the purpose of Coroners jurisdiction, and the appointment of additional Coroners for the said Wapentake.

[5th August 1873.]

Whereas the wapentake of Langbaurgh in the county of York is a liberty having a separate coroner, and the right of appointing such coroner is vested in the chief bailiff for the time being of the wapentake:

And whereas the said wapentake is a large and populous district, and it is expedient that it be divided into separate districts for the purpose of coroners jurisdiction, that additional coroners be appointed for the wapentake, and that such provision as is hereinafter contained be made for the apportionment among the several coroners for the wapentake of the salary and functions of the existing coroner:

Be it enacted by the Queen's most Excellent Majesty, by and with the advice and consent of the Lords Spiritual and Temporal, and Commons, in this present Parliament assembled, and by the authority of the same, as follows:

Short title.
1. This Act may be cited as the Langbaurgh Coroners Act, 1873.

Scheme to be framed for the division of wapentake of Langbaurgh into districts.
2. The justices of the north riding of the county of York in quarter sessions assembled may, at the Michaelmas quarter sessions to be held next after the passing of this Act, settle a scheme for the division of the wapentake of Langbaurgh into three districts, to be assigned to separate coroners, and for the appointment among such coroners of the salary received by the existing coroner for the wapentake.

The said justices shall, before settling such scheme, consult the existing chief bailiff and the existing coroner of the wapentake with respect thereto.

The scheme shall set out the boundaries of the proposed districts, and shall give a name to each of such districts, and shall declare for which of the three districts the existing coroner for the wapentake is to act.

The scheme when settled shall be submitted for confirmation to one of Her Majesty's Principal Secretaries of State, and he may, after hearing such representations, if any, as the existing chief bailiff and coroner of the wapentake respectively may make with respect to the scheme, confirm the same with or without variations.

The scheme, when and as so confirmed, shall be published in the London Gazette.

3. Upon the publication of the scheme, the existing coroner for the wapentake shall become the coroner for such one of the three districts as may be assigned to him by the scheme. *Appointment of coroners.*

The chief bailiff for the time being of the wapentake shall, as soon as may be after the publication of the scheme, appoint a coroner for each of the other two districts.

Upon the occurrence of any vacancy in the office of coroner for any of the said three districts, the chief bailiff for the time being of the wapentake may appoint a successor to fill such vacancy.

4. Each of the coroners for the said districts shall, for all purposes whatsoever, except as in this Act mentioned, be considered as a coroner for the whole wapentake, and shall have the same jurisdiction, rights, powers, and authorities as if he had been appointed sole coroner for the wapentake. *Jurisdiction of coroners.*

5. Each of the said coroners shall reside within the district assigned to him, and shall, except during the illness or incapacity or unavoidable absence of any other coroner for the wapentake, or during a vacancy in the office of any such coroner, hold inquests only in such districts. *Each coroner to reside and act in his own district.*

o 2

When any of the said coroners holds by himself or deputy any inquest in any district save that which has been assigned to him, he shall in his inquisition to be returned on such inquest, certify the cause of his attendance and of his holding such inquest, and such certificate shall be conclusive evidence of the illness or incapacity or unavoidable absence of the coroner in whose stead he attends, or of there being a vacancy in the office of coroner for the district in which such inquest is holden.

Salaries.

6. Each of the said coroners shall, until the next quinquennial revision of his salary, receive such salary as may be assigned to him by the said scheme.

The next quinquennial revision of the salaries of all the coroners for the wapentake shall take place at the expiration of five years from the last revision of the salary of the existing coroner for the wapentake.

Definition of "existing."

7. In this Act the term "existing" means existing at the time of the passing of this Act. [Sect. 6 repealed by Stat. Law Rev. Act, 1883 (46 & 47 Vict. c. 39, s. 1 and Sch.]

---

37 & 38 VICT. c. 85.

An Act for further promoting the Revision of the Statute Law by repealing certain Enactments which have ceased to be in force or have become unnecessary.

[16th July 1874.]

SCHEDULE.

7 Will. 4 and 1 Vict. c. 64. in part.	An Act for regulating the Coroners of the County of Durham — in part; namely,— Section Three from "and so much" to the end of that Section.
c. 68. in part.	An Act to provide for Payment of the Expences of holding Coroners' Inquests — in part; namely,— Section Five.

37 & 38 VICT. c. 88.

An Act to amend the Law relating to the Registration of Births and Deaths in England, and to consolidate the Law respecting the Registration of Births and Deaths at Sea. [7th August 1874.]

Registration of Deaths.

16. Where an inquest is held on any dead body the jury shall inquire of the particulars required to be registered concerning the death, and the coroner shall send to the registrar, within five days after the finding of the jury is given, a certificate under his hand, giving information concerning the death and specifying the finding of the jury with respect to the said particulars, and to the cause of death, and specifying the time and place at which the inquest was held, and the registrar shall in the prescribed form and manner enter the death and particulars. If the death has been previously registered the said particulars shall be entered in the prescribed manner without any alteration of the original entry. *[Furnishing of information by coroner.]*

Where an inquest is held on any dead body no person shall, with respect to such dead body or death, be liable to attend upon a requisition of a registrar, or be subject to any penalty for failing to give information in pursuance of any other provision of this Act.

Burials.

17. A coroner, upon holding an inquest upon any body, may, if he thinks fit, by order under his hand authorise the body to be buried before registry of the death, and shall give such order to the relative of the deceased or other person who causes the body to be buried, or to the undertaker or other person having charge of the funeral; and, except upon holding an inquest, no order, warrant, or other document for the burial of any body shall be given by the coroner. *[Coroner's order and registrar's certificate for burial.]*

The registrar, upon registering any death or upon receiving a written requisition to attend at a house to register a death, or upon receiving such written notice of the occurrence of a death, accompanied by a medical certificate as is before provided by this Act, shall forthwith, or as soon after as he is required, give, without fee or reward, either to the person giving information concerning the death or sending the requisition or notice, or to the undertaker or other person having charge of the funeral of the deceased, a certificate under his hand that he has registered or received notice of the death, as the case may be.

Every such order of the coroner and certificate of the registrar shall be delivered to the person who buries or performs any funeral or religious service for the burial of the body of the deceased; and any person to whom such order or certificate was given by the coroner or registrar who fails so to deliver or cause to be delivered the same shall be liable to a penalty not exceeding forty shillings.

The person who buries or performs any funeral or religious service for the burial of any dead body, as to which no order or certificate under this section is delivered to him, shall, within seven days after the burial, give notice thereof in writing to the registrar, and if he fail so to do shall be liable to a penalty not exceeding ten pounds.

Burial of deceased children as still-born.

18. A person shall not wifully bury or procure to be buried the body of any deceased child as if it were still-born.

A person who has control over or ordinarily buries bodies in any burial ground shall not permit to be buried in such burial ground the body of any deceased child as if it were still-born, and shall not permit to be buried or bury in such burial ground any still-born child before there is delivered to him either,—

  (*a*) A written certificate that such child was not born alive, signed by a registered medical practitioner who was in attendance at the birth or has examined the body of such child; or

  (*b*) A declaration signed by some person who would, if the child had been born alive, have been required by this Act to give information concerning the birth, to the effect that no registered medical practitioner was present at the birth, or that his certificate cannot be obtained, and that the child was not born alive; or

(c) If there has been an inquest, an order of the coroner.

Any person who acts in contravention of this section shall be liable to a penalty not exceeding ten pounds.

Certificates of Cause of Death.

20. With respect to certificates of the cause of death, the following provisions shall have effect:

1. The Registrar General shall from time to time furnish to every registrar printed forms of certificates of cause of death by registered medical practitioners, and every registrar shall furnish such forms gratis to any registered medical practitioner residing or practicing in such registrar's sub-district: *Regulations as to certificates of cause of death.*

2. In case of the death of any person who has been attended during his last illness by a registered medical practitioner, that practitioner shall sign and give to some person required by this Act to give information concerning the death a certificate stating to the best of his knowledge and belief the cause of death, and such person shall, upon giving information concerning the death, or giving notice of the death, deliver that certificate to the registrar, and the cause of death as stated in that certificate shall be entered in the register, together with the name of the certifying medical practitioner:

3. Where an inquest is held on the body of any deceased person a medical certificate of the cause of death need not be given to the registrar, but the certificate of the finding of the jury furnished by the coroner shall be sufficient.

If any person to whom a medical certificate is given by

a registered medical practitioner in pursuance of this section fails to deliver that certificate to the registrar, he shall be liable to a penalty not exceeding forty shillings.

Correction of Errors.

<small>Correction of errors in registers.</small>

36. With regard to the correction of errors in registers of births and deaths, it shall be enacted as follows:

1. No alteration in any such register shall be made except as authorised by this Act:
2. Any clerical error which may from time to time be discovered in any such register may be corrected by any person authorised in that behalf by the Registrar General, subject to the prescribed rules:
3. An error of fact or substance in any such register may be corrected by entry in the margin (without any alteration of the original entry) by the officer having the custody of the register, upon payment of the appointed fee and upon production to him by the person requiring such error to be corrected of a statutory declaration setting forth the nature of the error and the true facts of the case, and made by two persons required by this Act to give information concerning the birth or death with reference to which the error has been made, or in default of such persons then by two credible persons having knowledge of the truth of the case:
4. Where an error of fact or substance (other than an error relating to the cause of death) occurs in the information given by a coroner's certificate concerning a dead body upon which he has held an inquest, the coroner, if satisfied by evidence on oath or statutory declaration that such error exists, may certify under his hand to the officer having the custody of the register in which such information is entered the nature of the error and the true facts of the case as ascertained by him on such evidence, and the error may there-

upon be corrected by such officer in the register by entering in the margin (without any alteration of the original entry) the facts as so certified by the coroner.

Miscellaneous.

38. An entry or certified copy of an entry of a birth or death in a register under the Births and Deaths Registration Acts, 1836 to 1874, or in a certified copy of such a register, shall not be evidence of such birth or death, unless such entry either purports to be signed by some person professing to be the informant and to be such a person as is required by law at the date of such entry to give to the registrar information concerning such birth or death, or purports to be made upon a certificate from a coroner, or in pursuance of the provisions of this Act with respect to the registration of births and deaths at sea.

Register when not evidence.

When more than three months have intervened between the day of the birth and the day of the registration of the birth of any child, the entry or certified copy of the entry made after the commencement of this Act of the birth of such child in a register under the Births and Deaths Registration Acts, 1836 to 1874, or in a certified copy of such a register, shall not be evidence of such birth, unless such entry purports:

(a) If it appear that not more than twelve months have so intervened, to be signed by the superintendent registrar as well as by the registrar; or,

(b) If more than twelve months have so intervened, to have been made with the authority of the Registrar General, and in accordance with the prescribed rules.

Where more than twelve months have intervened between the day of a death or the finding of a dead body and the day of the registration of the death or the finding of such body, the entry or certified copy of the entry made after the commencement of this Act of the death in a register under the Births and Deaths Registration Acts, 1836 to 1874, or in a certified copy of such register, shall not be evidence of such death, unless such entry purports to have been made with the authority of the Registrar General, and in accordance with the prescribed rules. [Sect. 17 amended by Burial Law Amendment Act, 1880 (43 & 44 Vict. c. 41, s. 11), and Burial and Registration Acts (Doubts Removal) Act, 1881 (44 & 45 Vict. c. 2, ss. 1 & 2).]

[Sects. 16 and 17 repealed in part by Coroners Act 1887 (50 & 51 Vict. c. 71, s. 45, and Sch. 3).]

37 & 38 VICT. c. 96.

An Act for further promoting the Revision of the Statute Law by repealing certain Enactments which have ceased to be in force or have become unnecessary.

[7th August 1874.]

SCHEDULE.

c. 12. in part.	An Act for the more convenient holding of Coroners' Inquests	in part; namely,— Section Five.
c. 88. in part.	An Act to amend the Law respecting the Duties of Coroners	in part; namely,— Section Four.
c. 92. in part.	An Act to amend the Law respecting the Office of County Coroner	in part; namely,— Sections One, Twenty-three and Thirty-one.

38 VICT. c. 17.

THE EXPLOSIVES ACT, 1875.

An Act to amend the Law with respect to manufacturing, keeping, selling, carrying, and importing Gunpowder, Nitro-glycerine, and other explosive substances.

[14th June 1875.]

Provisions as to coroners inquests on

65. With respect to coroners inquests on the bodies of persons whose death may have been caused by the

explosion of any explosive or by any accident in connexion with an explosive, the following provisions shall have effect: *deaths from accidents connected with explosives.*

(1.) Where a coroner holds an inquest upon a body of any person whose death may have been caused by any accident of which notice is required by this Act to be given to the Secretary of State, or by the explosion of any explosive, the coroner shall adjourn such inquest unless a Government inspector, or some person on behalf of the Secretary of State, is present to watch the proceedings:

(2.) The coroner, at least four days before holding the adjourned inquest, shall send to the Secretary of State notice in writing of the time and place of holding the adjourned inquest:

(3.) The coroner, before the adjournment, may take evidence to identify the body, and may order the interment thereof:

(4.) If an explosion or accident has not occasioned the death of more than one person, and the coroner has sent to the Secretary of State notice of the time and place of holding the inquest not less than forty-eight hours before the time of holding the same, it shall not be imperative on him to adjourn such inquest in pursuance of this section, if the majority of the jury think it unnecessary so to adjourn:

(5.) A Government inspector or person employed on behalf of the Secretary of State shall be at liberty at any such inquest to examine any witness, subject nevertheless to the order of the coroner on points of law:

(6.) Where evidence is given at an inquest at which no Government inspector or person employed on behalf of the Secretary of State is present, of any neglect as having caused or contributed to the explosion or accident, or of any defect in or about or in connexion with any factory, magazine, store, or registered premises, or any carriage, ship, or boat carrying an explosive, appearing to the coroner or jury to require a remedy, the coroner shall send to the Secretary of State notice in writing of such neglect or defect.

---

38 & 39 VICT. c. 55.

The Public Health Act, 1875.

An Act for consolidating and amending the Acts relating to Public Health in England. [11th August 1875.]

Be it enacted as follows:

Mortuaries,[1] &c.

Power of local authority to provide mortuaries.

141. Any local authority may, and if required by the Local Government Board shall, provide and fit up a

[1] This word is used in different significations. In the old ecclesiastical law it meant a payment to the church on the decease of one of its members (*Vide* Burn. Eccl. Law, vol. ii.). In modern usage it denotes a place for the reception of dead bodies before interment. *Mortuarium* is defined by Lord Coke as "a gift left by a man at his death pro recompensatione substractionis decimarum personalium et oblationum" (2 Inst. 491). Originally, however, a mortuary seems to have been merely an oblation to the parish church of the donor, and not a recompense for forgotten tithes. In Saxon times a funeral due was paid under the name of pecunia sepulchratis symbolumaminæ or saul-sceat (soul-shot), and its payment was enforced by the council of Aenham, and by the laws of Canute (Phill. Eccl. Law, 685). Dugdale, from whose writings later writers are indebted, and who in his turn owes his indebtedness to Master Thomas Barlow of Qu. Coll. Oxon., in his 'Antiquities of Warwickshire' (2nd ed. 729), gives examples of wills containing bequests both for mortuaries and for forgotten tithes. Amongst others he cites from a will of Henry VIII.'s reign: "I bequethe for my mortuaries or cors presente a black Geldyng Amblyng that Almighty God may the rather take my soul into His mercy and grace; I bequethe unto the high Aultar of Aston for tithes and offerings negligently forgotten iii s. iii d."

Whether there was any difference between mortuaries and corse-presents seems doubtful (1 Stillingfleet, Eccl. Cases, 245).

When the making of wills was entirely in ecclesiastical hands, some sufficient mortuary was considered essential to a will; they were distinguished into dead mortuaries, such as money, or in-proper place for the reception of dead bodies before interment (in this Act called a mortuary), and may make byelaws with respect to the management and charges for use of the same; and they may also provide for the decent and economical interment, at charges to be fixed by such byelaws, of any dead body which may be received into a mortuary.[1]

143. Any local authority may provide and maintain a proper place, (otherwise than at a workhouse or at a mortuary) for the reception of dead bodies during the time required to conduct any post-mortem examination ordered by a coroner or other constituted authority, and may make regulations with respect to the management of such place; (and where any such place has been provided, a coroner or other constituted authority may order the removal of the body to and from such place for carrying out such post-mortem examination, such costs of removal to be paid in the same manner and out of the same fund as the costs and fees for post-mortem examinations when ordered by the coroner). [Sect. 143 repealed in part (from "and where any such place has been provided" to end of section) by Coroners Act, 1887 (50 & 51 Vict. c. 71, s. 45. Sch. 3.)]

Power of local authority to provide places for post-mortem examinations.

---

animate goods, and mortuaria viva, the latter being live stock or "quick goods." It was apparently customary to bequeath the second best beast to the church, the first best being due to the Lord as a heriot. Two constitutions of Archbishop Winchelsie and a constitution of Simon Langham enjoin the gift of the second best beast. Horses given as mortuaries were frequently brought to the church at the burial, and this custom appears to be the origin of taking horses to funerals (Baker, 'Burial Laws,' p. 88).

[1] The provisions as to mortuaries are extended by the Public Health (Interments) Act, 1879 (42 & 43 Vict. c. 31), to cemeteries.

38 & 39 VICT. c. 66.

An Act for further promoting the Revision of the Statute Law by repealing certain Enactments which cease to be in force or have become unnecessary.

[11th August 1875.]

Be it therefore enacted as follows:

I. The enactments described in the schedule to this Act are hereby repealed, &c. &c.

SCHEDULE.

23 & 24 Vict. c. 116. in part.	An Act to amend the Law relating to the Election, Duties, and Payment of County Coroners. . . . . in part; namely,— Section One from "and every" to the end of that Section.

40 & 41 VICT. c. 21.

THE PRISON ACT, 1877.

An Act to amend the Law relating to Prisons in England.

[12th July 1877.]

As to Jurisdiction.

Jurisdiction of sheriff, coroner, and other officers. 30. The Secretary of State may from time to time, if he think it expedient so to do, for the purpose of any enactment, law, or custom, descriptive of or dependent on the circumstance of a prison being the prison of any county, riding, county of a city, county of a town, liberty, borough, or other place having a separate prison jurisdicton, by any general or special rule direct that for such purpose as aforesaid any prison locally situate within the county in which such riding, county of a city, county of a town, liberty, borough, or place is situate, or any prison which he may in pursuance of this Act have appointed as a prison to which prisoners may be committed, is to be considered to be the prison of such county, riding, county of a city, county of a town, liberty, borough, or other place, but subject to any such rule as in this section mentioned, and until the same be made the transfer under this Act of the prisons to which this Act applies, and of the powers and jurisdiction of prison authorities, and of justices in sessions assembled, and of visiting justices, shall not affect the jurisdiction of any sheriff or coroner, or, save as provided by this Act, of any justice of the peace or other officer having at the commencement of this Act, jurisdiction in, over, or in respect of such prison.

44. In no case, where an inquest is held on the body of a prisoner who dies within the prison, shall any person engaged in any sort of trade or dealing with the prison be a juror on such inquest. [Sect. 30, *vide* Spring Assizes Act, 1879 (42 Vict. c. 1, s. 3.) Sect. 44 repealed by Coroners Act, 1887 (50 & 51 Vict. c. 71, s. 45, and 3rd Sch.)] *As to inquests on the bodies of prisoners.*

---

42 VICT. c. 1.

THE SPRING ASSIZES ACT, 1879.

An Act to amend the Law respecting the holding of Assizes.
[14th March 1879.]

3. Notwithstanding anything in the Prison Act, 1877, or anything done in pursuance of that Act, where judgment of death has been passed upon a convict at any assizes held after the passing of this Act, the judgment may be carried into execution in any prison in which the convict was confined for the purpose of safe custody prior to his removal to the place where the assizes were held, and the sheriff of the county for which such assizes were held shall be charged with the execution of that judgment, and shall for that purpose have the same jurisdiction and powers, and be subject to the same duties in the prison in which the judgment is to be carried into execution, although such prison is not situate within his county, as he has by law with respect to the common gaol of his county, *Execution of sentence of death. 40 & 41 Vict. c. 21.*

28 & 29 Vict. c. 126.
40 & 41 Vict. c. 21.
or would have had if the Prison Act, 1865, and the Prison Act, 1877, had not passed.

The coroner, whose duty it is to hold an inquest on the bodies of prisoners dying in any prison shall hold an inquest in accordance with the Capital Punishment Amendment Act, 1868, on the body of any convict executed in that prison.[1]

31 Vict. c. 24.

39 & 40 Vict. c. 57.
Nothing in this section shall affect any power authorised to be exercised by Order in Council under the Winter Assizes Act, 1876, and this Act. [Sect. 3 amended (as to execution in cases tried at Central Criminal Court) by 44 & 45 Vict. c. 64, s. 2 (5), and repealed down to "had not passed," by Sheriffs Act, 1887 (50 & 51 Vict. c. 55, s. 39, and Sch. 3.)]

42 & 43 VICT. c. 19.

THE HABITUAL DRUNKARDS ACT, 1879.

An Act to facilitate the control and cure of Habitual Drunkards. [3rd July 1879.]

Proceedings on death of person detained.
27. In case of the death of any person detained in any retreat a statement of the cause of the death of such person, with the name of any person present at the death, shall be drawn up and signed by the principal medical attendant of such retreat, and copies thereof, duly certified in writing by the licensee of such retreat, shall be by him transmitted to the coroner and to the registrar of deaths for the district and to the clerk of the local authority, and to the person by whom the last payment was made for the deceased, or one at least of the persons who signed the statutory declaration under section ten of this Act.

Penalty for neglect or omission.
Every medical attendant who shall neglect or omit to draw up and sign such statement as aforesaid, and every licensee of a retreat who shall neglect or omit to certify and transmit such statement as aforesaid, shall be deemed guilty of an offence against this Act.

[1] *Vide* p. 187.

42 & 43 VICT. c. 22.

THE PROSECUTION OF OFFENCES ACT, 1879.

An Act for more effectually providing for the prosecution of Offences in England, and for other purposes.

[3rd July 1879.]

5. Where the Director of Public Prosecutions gives notice to any justice or coroner that he has instituted, or undertaken, or is carrying on any criminal proceeding, such justice and coroner shall at the time and in the manner prescribed by the regulations under this Act, or directed in any special case by an order of the Attorney General, transmit to the said Director every recognizance, information, certificate, inquisition, deposition, document, and thing which is connected with the said proceeding, and which the justice or coroner is required by law to deliver to the proper officer of the court in which the trial is to be had, and the said Director shall, subject to the regulations under this Act, cause the same to be delivered to the said proper officer of the court, and shall be under the same obligation, on the same payment, to deliver to an applicant copies thereof as the said justice, coroner or officer. *[Delivery of recognizances, inquisitions, &c. to Director of Public Prosecutions.]*

It shall be the duty of every clerk to a justice or to a police court to transmit, in accordance with the regulations under this Act, to the Director of Public Prosecutions, a copy of the information and of all depositions and other documents relating to any case in which a prosecution for an offence instituted before such justice or court is withdrawn or is not proceeded with within a reasonable time.

A failure on the part of any justice or coroner to comply with this section shall be deemed to be a failure to comply with the said requirement to deliver to the proper officer of the court, and any clerk to a justice or to a police court failing to comply with this section shall be liable to the same penalty to which a justice or coroner is liable for such failure as aforesaid.

43 & 44 VICT. c. 41.

BURIAL LAWS AMENDMENT ACT, 1880.

An Act to amend the Burial Laws. [7th September 1880.]

<small>Order of coroner or certificate of registrar to be delivered to relative, &c., instead of to person who buries.</small>

11. Every order of a coroner or certificate of a registrar given under the provisions of section seventeen of the Births and Deaths Registration Act, 1874, shall, in the case of a burial under that Act, be delivered to the relative, friend, or legal representative of the deceased, having the charge of or being responsible for the burial, instead of being delivered to the person who buries or performs any funeral or religious service for the burial of the body of the deceased; and any person to whom such order or certificate shall have been given by the coroner or registrar who fails so to deliver or cause to be delivered the same shall be liable to a penalty not exceeding forty shillings, and any such relative, friend, or legal representative so having charge of or being responsible for the burial of the body of any person buried under this Act as aforesaid, as to which no order or certificate under the same section of the said Act shall have been delivered to him, shall, within seven days after the burial, give notice thereof in writing to the registrar, and if he fail so to do shall be liable to a penalty not exceeding ten pounds. [Amended by Burial and Registration Acts (Doubts Removal) Act, 1881 (44 Vict. c. 2)].

---

44 & 45 VICT. c. 58.

THE ARMY ACT, 1881.

An Act to consolidate the Army Discipline and Regulation Act, 1879, and the subsequent Acts amending the same.

[27th August 1881.]

Be it enacted as follows:

Military Prisons.

<small>Establishment and regulation of military prisons.</small>

133.—(2.) It shall be lawful for a Secretary of State, and in India for the Governor-General, from time to time to make, alter, and repeal rules for the government, management and regulation of Military prisons, and for the appointment and removal and powers of inspectors, visitors, governors, and officials thereof, and for the labour of Military prisoners therein, and for the safe custody of such prisoners, and for the maintenance of discipline among them, and for the punishment by personal correction, not exceeding twenty-five lashes in the case of corporal punishment, restraint, or otherwise of offences committed by such prisoners, so, however, that such rules shall not authorise corporal punishment to be inflicted for any offence in addition to the offences for which such punishment can be inflicted in pursuance of the Prison Act, 1865, and the Prison Act, 1877, nor render the imprisonment more severe than it is under the law in force for the time being in any public prison in England, subject to the Prison Act, 1877, and provided that all the regulations in the Prison Act, 1865, and in the Prison Act, 1877, as to the duties or gaolers, medical officers, and coroners shall be contained in such rules, so far as the same can be made applicable. 28 & 29 Vict. c. 126; 40 & 41 Vict. c. 21.

(3.) On all occasions of death by violence or attended with suspicious circumstances in any military prison in India an inquest is to be held, to make inquiry into the cause of death. The commanding officer shall cause notice to be given to the nearest magistrate, duly authorised to hold inquests, and such magistrate shall hold an inquest into the cause of any such death, in the manner and with the powers provided in the case of similar inquiries held under the law for the time being in force in India for regulating criminal procedure.

(4.) Where from any cause there is no competent civil authority available, the commanding officer shall convene a court of inquest. Such court shall be convened and shall hold the inquest in such manner as may be prescribed.

Exemptions of Officers and Soldiers.

147. Every soldier in Her Majesty's regular forces shall be exempt from serving on any jury. Exemption from jury.

44 & 45 VICT. c. 64.

CENTRAL CRIMINAL COURT (PRISONS) ACT, 1881.

An Act to remove certain doubts as to the application of section twenty-four of the Prison Act, 1877, and enactments amending the same, to the Central Criminal Court district. [27th August 1881.]

2.—(3.) Any justice of the peace or coroner who commits any person charged with an offence cognisable by the Central Criminal Court may commit such person to the gaol of Newgate or to any prison so for the time being appointed as aforesaid.

(5.) Where judgment of death is passed at the Central Criminal Court upon a person convicted of any offence, the judgment may be carried into execution in any prison in the Central Criminal Court district or in the county, if any, where the offence was committed or is supposed to have been committed, which the justice or judge of the said court passing sentence or any other justice or judge of the court subsequently may order, and if no order is made, then in the prison in which the convict is for the time being confined; and such sheriff as is ordered by any justice or judge of the said court, or if no order is made, the sheriff of the county in which the offence was committed or is supposed to have been committed, or if the offence was committed or is supposed to have been committed on the high seas, or if the county in which the offence was committed does not clearly appear, the sheriff of Middlesex, shall be charged with the execution of the judgment; and the sheriff charged with the execution of the judgment shall for that purpose have the same jurisdiction and powers and be subject to the same duties in the prison in which the judgment is to be carried into execution, although such prison is not situate within his county as he has by law with respect to the common gaol of his county or would have had if the Prison Act, 1865, and the Prison Act, 1877, had not passed.

The coroner whose duty it is to hold an inquest on the

bodies of persons dying in any prison, shall hold an inquest in accordance with the Capital Punishment Amendment Act, 1868, on the body of any convict executed in that prison. *31 & 32 Vict. c. 24.*

So much of section nine of the Central Criminal Court Act, 1834, as relates to a prisoner who has been convicted or attainted, and also section nineteen of the Act of the nineteenth and twentieth years of the reign of Her present Majesty, chapter sixteen, and section eight of the Jurisdiction in Homicides Act, 1862, are hereby repealed without prejudice to anything done under those sections. *25 & 26 Vict. c. 65.*

---

45 & 46 VICT. c. 19.

INTERMENTS (*felo de se*) ACT, 1882.

An Act to amend the law relating to the interment of any person found felo de se. [3rd July 1882.]

Be it therefore enacted as follows:

2. From and after the passing of this Act it shall not be lawful for any coroner or other officer having authority to hold inquests to issue any warrant or other process directing the interment of the remains of persons against whom a finding of felo de se shall be had in any public highway, or with any stake being driven through the body of such person, but such coroner or other officer shall give directions for the interment of the remains of such person felo de se in the churchyard or other burial ground of the parish or place in which the remains of such person might by the laws or custom of England be interred if the verdict of felo de se had not been found against such person. *Coroner to give directions for interment.*

5. This Act shall extend to the Channel Islands, but shall not apply to Scotland or to Ireland. *Extent of Act.*

6. This Act may be cited as the Interments (felo de se) Act, 1882. *Short title.*

45 & 46 VICT. c. 50.

THE MUNICIPAL CORPORATIONS ACT, 1882.

An Act for consolidating, with Amendments, enactments relating to Municipal Corporations in England and Wales [18th August 1882.]

Coroner.

Appointment, fees, etc., of borough coroner in boroughs having a separate quarter sessions.

171.[1]—(1.) The Council of a borough having a separate court of quarter sessions shall, within ten days next after receipt of the grant thereof by the Council, and thenceforward from time to time, appoint a fit person, not an alderman or councillor of the borough to be coroner of the borough; *and thereafter no person other than the coroner so appointed shall take in the borough any inquisition belonging to the office of coroner.*[2]

(2.) The coroner shall hold office during good behaviour.

(3.) A vacancy in the office shall be filled up within ten days after it occurs.

(4.) The Coroner shall have, by order of the recorder, remuneration as appearing in the Fourth and Fifth Schedules.

Power of borough coroner to appoint a deputy.

172.—(1.) In case of illness or unavoidable absence, the coroner shall appoint by writing signed by him a fit person, being a barrister or solicitor, and not an alderman or Councillor of the borough, to act for him as deputy coroner during his illness or unavoidable absence, but not longer or otherwise.

(2.) The mayor or two justices for the borough shall on each occasion certify by writing signed by him or them the necessity for the appointment of a deputy coroner. This certificate shall state the cause of absence of the coroner, and shall be openly read to every inquest jury summoned by the deputy coroner.

Returns by borough coroners.

173. On or before the first of February in every year the coroner shall send to the Secretary of State a return

---

[1] A substantial reproduction of s. 62 of the Municipal Corporations Act of 1835.

[2] Words in italics repealed by Coroners Act, 1887.

in writing, in such form as the Secretary of State directs, of the particulars of each case in which the coroner or his deputy was called upon to hold an inquest during the year ending on the then last thirty-first of December.

174.—(1.) Where a borough has not a separate court of quarter sessions no person other than the coroner for the county or district in which the borough is situate shall take in the borough any inquisition belonging to the office of coroner. Acting of county coroner in borough.

(2.) That coroner shall, for every inquisition duly taken by him within the borough be entitled to such ratable fees and salary as would be allowed and due to him, and to be allowed and paid in like manner, as for any other inquisition taken by him within the county or district.

Cinque Ports.

248.—(1.) The boroughs of Hastings, Sandwich, Dover, Hythe, being four of the Cinque Ports, and the borough of Rye, are in this section referred to as the five boroughs. Special provisions as to certain of the Cinque Ports.

(2.) The jurisdiction, powers, and authorities of the court of quarter sessions, recorder, coroner, and clerk of the peace for each of the five boroughs shall extend to the non-corporate members and liberties thereof, and to such corporate members thereof as have not a separate court of quarter sessions.

(7.) Nothing in this section shall affect the Cinque Ports Act, 1869, or the Acts therein recited. 32 & 33 Vict. c. 53.

THE FOURTH SCHEDULE

Fees and Remuneration.

The following fees and remuneration shall be payable:

Coroner.

To the borough coroner (subject to the provisions of any other Act relating to Coroners)—

For every inquisition which he duly takes in the borough . . . . twenty shillings.

and

For every mile exceeding two miles which he is compelled to travel from his usual place of abode to such inquisition . . . . ninepence.

THE FIFTH SCHEDULE.

PAYMENTS OUT OF THE BOROUGH FUND.

PART II.

Payments which may not be made without order.

(4.) The fees payable to the clerk of the peace, if not paid by salary, and under this Act to the borough coroner.

[Sect. 171 in part (from "and thereafter" down to "office of coroner"); sects. 173 and 174 repealed by Coroners Act, 1887 (50 & 51 Vict. c. 71, s. 45, sch. 3); sect. 172 repealed by Coroners Act, 1892 (55 & 56 Vict. c. 56, s. 2, and sch.).]

---

46 & 47 VICT. c. 18.

MUNICIPAL CORPORATIONS ACT, 1883.

An Act to make provision respecting certain Municipal Corporations and other Local Authorities not subject to the Municipal Corporation Act. [29th June 1883.]

15.—(2.) Any mayor, jurat, recorder, justice of the peace, coroner, bailiff, sergeant, inspector, or constable, or any other officer by whatever name called, having or claiming the authority of any judge or officer above named, shall be deemed to be included in this Act in the expression judge or officer, as the case may be.

(3.) Where in any report of the Commissioners of 1834, or in any report of the Commissioners of 1876, any corporation, court, sessions, judge, recorder, justice, coroner, constable, inspector, authority, or officer, or any franchise, privilege, right, or exemption, or any property, is mentioned in connection with any place mentioned in the schedules to this Act, that mention shall be evidence that the same is subject to this Act.

THE STATUTES. 217

46 & 47 VICT. c. 39.

STATUTE LAW REVISION ACT, 1883.

An Act for further promoting the Revision of the Statute Law by repealing certain Enactments which have ceased to be in force or have become unnecessary.

[25th August 1883.]

36 & 37 Vict. c. 81. in part.	An Act to authorise the division of the Wapentake of Langbaurgh in the county of York into Districts for the purpose of Coroners jurisdiction, and the appointment of additional Coroners for the said Wapentake . . . . . Section Six. — in part; namely,—

50 & 51 VICT. c. 55.

SHERIFFS ACT, 1887.

An Act to consolidate the Law relating to the office of Sheriff in England, and to repeal certain enactments relating to Sheriffs which have ceased to be in force or have become unnecessary. [16th September 1887.]

40.—(1.) Notwithstanding the repeal of any enactment by this Act every court leet, court baron, law day, view of frankpledge, or other like court which is held at the passing of this Act shall continue to be held on the days and in the places heretofore accustomed, but shall not have any larger powers, nor shall any larger fees be taken thereat than heretofore, and any indictment or presentment found at such court shall be dealt with in like manner as heretofore. *Saving for courts leet, etc.*

(2.) Where any enactment repealed by this Act applied to any coroner, escheator, or other officer, he shall continue to be governed by such enactment in like manner as if it had not been repealed: Provided that any enactment of this Act which is substituted as regards a sheriff or sheriff's officer for the enactment so repealed, shall apply to such coroner, escheator, or officer, in lieu of the enactment so repealed.

THE THIRD SCHEDULE.

Acts Repealed.

Session and Chapter.	Title or Abbreviated Title.	Extent of Repeal.
3 Edw. 1. (*Stat. Westm. prim.*) c. 9.	Pursuit of felons. Punishment for neglect or corruption in officers.	The whole chapter, except from "and if the sheriffs' coroners" to the end of the chapter, so far as that portion relates to coroners.
27 Hen. 8, c. 26.	An Acte for Lawe and Justice to be ministred in Wales in like fourme as it is in this Realme.	Section three, from "and that the sheriff of the said countie" to the end of the section, except so far as relates to escheators and coroners.

---

50 & 51 VICT. c. 58.

Coal Mines Regulation Act, 1887.

An Act to consolidate with amendments the Coal Mines Acts, 1872 and 1886, and the Stratified Ironstone Mines (Gunpowder) Act, 1881.

[16th September 1887.]

Coroners.

Provisions as to coroners' inquests on deaths from accidents in mines.

48. With respect to coroners' inquests on the bodies of persons whose death may have been caused by explosions or accidents in or about mines, the following provisions shall have effect:

(1.) Where a coroner holds an inquest on the body of any person whose death may have been caused by any explosion or accident, of which notice is required by this Act to be given to the inspector of the district, the coroner shall adjourn the inquest unless an inspector, or some person on behalf of a Secretary of State, is present to watch the proceedings:

(2.) The coroner, at least four days before holding the adjourned inquest, shall send to the inspector for the district notice in writing of the time and place of holding the adjourned inquest:

(3.) The coroner, before the adjournment, may take evidence to identify the body, and may order the interment thereof:

(4.) If an explosion or accident has not occasioned the death of more than one person, and the coroner has sent to the inspector of the district notice of the time and place of holding the inquest at such time as to reach the inspector not less than twenty-four hours before the time of holding the same, it shall not be imperative on him to adjourn the inquest in pursuance of this section, if the majority of the jury think it unnecessary so to adjourn:

(5.) An inspector shall be at liberty at any such inquest to examine any witness, subject nevertheless to the order of the coroner:

(6.) Where evidence is given at an inquest at which an inspector is not present of any neglect as having caused or contributed to the explosion or accident, or of any defect in or about the mine appearing to the coroner or jury to require a remedy, the coroner shall send to the inspector of the district notice in writing of such neglect or defect:

(7.) Any person having a personal interest in or employed in or in the management of the mine in which the explosion or accident occurred shall not be qualified to serve on the jury empannelled on the inquest; and it shall be the duty of the constable or other officer not to summon any person disqualified under this provision, and it shall be the duty of the coroner not to allow any such person to be sworn or to sit on the jury:

(8.) Any relative of any person whose death may have been caused by the explosion or accident with respect to which the inquest is being held, and the owner agent or manager of the mine in which the explosion or accident occurred, and any person appointed by the order in writing of the majority of the workmen employed at the said mine, shall be at liberty to attend and examine any witness, either in person or by his counsel, solicitor, or agent, subject nevertheless to the order of the coroner.

Every person who fails to comply with the provisions of this section shall be guilty of an offence against this Act.

---

50 & 51 VICT. c. 71.

An Act to consolidate the Law relating to Coroners.

[16th September 1887.]

Be it enacted as follows:

Preliminary.

Short title. 1. This Act may be cited as the Coroners Act, 1887.

Extent of Act. 2. This Act shall not apply to Scotland or Ireland.

PART I.

LAW OF CORONERS.

Inquest.

Summoning and swearing of jury by coroner. 3.—(1.) Where a coroner is informed that the dead body of a person is lying within his jurisdiction, and

THE STATUTES. 221

there is reasonable cause to suspect[1] that such person has died either a violent or an unnatural death, or has died a sudden death of which the cause is unknown, or that such person has died in prison, or in such place or under such circumstances as to require an inquest in pursuance of any Act, the coroner, whether the cause of death arose within his jurisdiction or not, shall, as soon as practicable, issue his warrant for summoning not less than twelve nor more than twenty-three good and lawful men[2] to appear before him at a specified time and place, there to inquire as jurors touching the death of such person as aforesaid.

(2.) Where an inquest is held on the body of a prisoner who dies within a prison, an officer of the prison or a prisoner therein or a person engaged in any sort of trade or dealing with the prison shall not be a juror on such inquest.

(3.) When not less than twelve jurors are assembled they shall be sworn[3] by or before the coroner diligently to inquire touching the death of the person on whose body the inquest is about to be held, and a true verdict to give according to the evidence.

4.—(1.) The coroner and jury shall, at the first sitting[4] of the inquest, view the body,[5] and the coroner shall examine on oath[6] touching the death all persons[7] who tender their evidence respecting the facts and all persons

Proceedings at inquest— evidence and inquisition.

---

[1] *Vide* 11 East, 229; 10 Q.B. 796; 1 East, P.C. 382; and *Reg.* v. *Stephenson* (1884), 13 Q.B.D. 331.

[2] *Reg.* v. *Dutton* (1892), 1 Q.B. 486; 61 L.J. Q.B. 190; 66 L.T. 324; 40 W.R. 270; 56 J.P. 455.

[3] Or make affirmation. *Vide* Oaths Act, 1888.

[4] As to adjournment, *vide* Jervis, 6th ed. p. 80. *Reg.* v. *Payn*, 34 L.J. Q.B. 59.

[5] Without view inquisition is void. *Reg.* v. *Ferrand*, 3 B. & Ald. 260.

[6] Or affirmation. *Vide* Oaths Act, 1888. An inquisition cannot be quashed on the ground that unsworn evidence was received. *Reg.* v. *Ingham*, 5 B. & S. 267, which case would apply to affirmations.

[7] Including jurors, 1 Salk. 405; and witnesses for defence, *R.* v. *Scorey*, 1 Leach, 43.

having knowledge of the facts whom he thinks it expedient to examine.[1]

(2.) It shall be the duty of the coroner in a case of murder or manslaughter to put into writing the statement on oath of those who know the facts and circumstances of the case, or so much of such statement as is material, and any such deposition shall be signed by the witness and also by the coroner.

(3.) After viewing the body and hearing the evidence the jury shall give their verdict, and certify it by an inquisition in writing, setting forth, so far as such particulars have been proved to them, who the deceased was, and how, when, and where the deceased came by his death, and if he came by his death by murder or manslaughter, the persons, if any, whom the jury find to have been guilty of such murder or manslaughter, or of being accessories before the fact to such murder.

(4.) They shall also inquire of and find the particulars for the time being required by the Registration Acts to be registered concerning the death.[2]

(5.) In case twelve at least of the jury do not agree[3] on a verdict, the coroner may adjourn the inquest to the next sessions of oyer and terminer or gaol delivery held for the county or place in which the inquest is held, and if after the jury have heard the charge of the judge or commissioner holding such sessions, twelve of them fail to agree on a verdict, the jury may be discharged by such judge or commissioner without giving a verdict.

Proceedings upon inquisition charging person with murder or manslaughte

5.—(1.) Where a coroner's inquisition charges a person with the offence of murder or of manslaughter, or of being accessory before the fact to a murder (which latter offence

[1] As to criminating evidence, the proper course is for the coroner to tell the witness that he is not bound to criminate himself, and to allow him to make any statement he may wish: *Wakley* v. *Cooke*, 4 Ex. 511; 19 L.J. Ex. 91.

[2] This is taken from sect. 16 of the Births and Deaths Registration Act, 1874.

[3] It is said (Jervis, 6th ed. p. 44) that a disagreeing jury may be kept without refreshment, but it is submitted that sect. 28 of the Jurors Act, 1870, applies to a coroner's jury.

is in this Act included in the expression "murder"), the coroner shall issue his warrant for arresting or detaining such person (if such warrant has not previously been issued) and shall bind by recognizance all such persons, examined before him as know or declare anything material touching the said offence to appear at the next court of oyer and terminer or gaol delivery at which the trial is to be, then and there to prosecute or give evidence against the person so charged.[1]

(2.) Where the offence is manslaughter, the coroner may, if he thinks fit, accept bail[2] by recognizance with sufficient sureties for the appearance of the person charged at the next court of oyer and terminer or gaol delivery at which the trial is to be, and thereupon such person if in the custody of an officer of the coroner's court or under a warrant of commitment issued by such coroner shall be discharged therefrom.[3]

(3.) The coroner shall deliver the inquisition, deposition, and recognizances, with a certificate under his hand that the same have been taken before him, to the proper officer of the court in which the trial is to be, before or at the opening of the court.

6.—(1.) Where Her Majesty's High Court of Justice, upon application made by or under the authority of the Attorney General, is satisfied either—

Ordering of coroner to hold inquest.

    (a) that a coroner refuses or neglects to hold an inquest which ought to be held;[4] or

    (b) where an inquest has been held by a coroner that by reason of fraud, rejection of evidence, irregularity of proceedings, insufficiency of inquiry,[5]

---

[1] This is taken from 7 Geo. IV. c. 64, s. 4. As to fine for neglect, *vide* sect. 9.

[2] This is clearly a discretionary power, but if bail be refused there would seem to be a remedy by *habeas corpus*, or in some cases in *certiorari* without *habeas corpus*: *R.* v. *Jones*, 1 B. & Ald. 209.

[3] This is taken from 22 Vict. c. 33.

[4] This is taken from 23 & 24 Vict. c. 116, s. 5.

[5] *Vide Reg.* v. *Coulson*, 55 J.P. 262, in which a second inquest was held unnecessary.

or otherwise, it is necesssry or desirable, in the interests of justice, that another inquest should be held,[1]

the court may order an inquest to be held touching the said death, and may, if the court think it just, order the said coroner to pay such costs of and incidental to the application as to the court may seem just, and where an inquest has been already held may quash the inquisition on that inquest.

(2.) The court may order that such inquest shall be held either by the said coroner, or if the said coroner is a coroner for a county, by any other coroner for the county, or if he is a coroner of a borough or for a franchise then by a coroner for the county in which such borough or franchise is situate, or for a county to which it adjourns, and the coroner ordered to hold the inquest shall for that purpose have the same powers and jurisdiction as, and be deemed to be, the said coroner.

(3.) Upon any such inquest, if the case be one of death, it shall not be necessary, unless the court otherwise order, to view the body,[2] but save as aforesaid the inquest shall be held in like manner in all respects as any other inquest under this Act.

(4.) Any power vested by this section in Her Majesty's High Court of Justice may, subject to any rules of court made in pursuance of the Supreme Court of Judicature Act, 1875,[3] and the Acts amending the same,[4] be exercised by any judge of that court.

38 & 39 Vict. c. 77.

Local jurisdiction of coroner.

7.—(1.) The coroner only within whose jurisdiction the body of a person upon whose death an inquest ought to be holden is lying shall hold the inquest, and where a body is found dead in the sea, or any creek, river, or navigable canal within the flowing of the sea where there

---

[1] As to this case which was not previously provided for by statute, vide Reg. v. Carter, 45 L.J. Q.B. 711.

[2] Vide R. v. Bunney, 1 Salk. 190; Reg. v. Carter, ubi sup., per Cockburn, C.J.

[3] 38 & 39 Vict. c. 17, s. 17.

[4] Vide Judicature Act, 1881, s. 19.

is no deputy coroner for the jurisdiction of the Admiralty of England the inquest shall be held only by the coroner having jurisdiction in the place where the body is first brought to land.[1]

(2.) In a borough with a separate court of quarter sessions, no coroner, save as is otherwise provided by this Act, shall hold an inquest belonging to the office of coroner, except the coroner of the borough, or a coroner or deputy coroner for the jurisdiction of the Admiralty of England.[2]

(3.) In a borough which has not a separate court of quarter sessions no coroner, save as is otherwise provided by this Act, shall hold an inquest belonging to the office of coroner except a coroner for the county, or a coroner or a deputy coroner for the jurisdiction of the Admiralty of England.[3]

Liabilities of Coroner.

8.—(1.) The Lord Chancellor may, if he thinks fit, remove any coroner from his office for inability or misbehaviour in the discharge of his duty.[4]

Removal and punishment of coroner.

(2.) A coroner who is guilty of extortion or of corruption or of wilful neglect of his duty or of misbehaviour in the discharge of his duty shall be guilty of a misdemeanour, and in addition to any other punishment may, unless his office of coroner is annexed to any other office, be adjudged by the court before whom he is so convicted to be removed from his office, and to be disqualified for acting as coroner, and if he is a coroner for a county, a writ shall issue for an election of another coroner, and if, he is a coroner of a borough, the council of the borough, and if he is a coroner for a franchise the lord or other person or persons entitled to the appointment of the coroner, shall forthwith proceed

---

[1] Taken from 6 Vict. c. 12, s. 1.

[2] Taken from s. 171, sub-s. 1 of the Municipal Corporations Act, 1882.

[3] Taken from s. 174, sub-s. 1 of the Municipal Corporations Act, 1882.

[4] Taken from 23 & 24 Vict. c. 116, s. 6; *vide* also s. 85 of this Act and Jervis, 6th ed. p. 59 *et seq.*

to appoint another coroner as in the case of any other vacancy,[1]

Fine on coroner for neglect as to inquisition, depositions, and recognizances, etc.

9. If a coroner fails to comply with the provisions of this Act with respect to the delivery of the inquisition, or to the taking and delivery of the depositions and recognizances, in the case of murder or manslaughter, the court to whose officer the inquisition, depositions, and recognizances ought to have been delivered may, upon proof of the said non-compliance, in a summary manner, impose such fine upon the coroner as to the court seems meet.[2]

Coroner not to act as solicitor and as coroner in same case.

10.—(1.) A coroner shall not by himself or his partner, directly or indirectly, act as solicitor, in the prosecution or defence of a person for an offence for which such person is charged by an inquisition taken before him as coroner whether such person is tried on that inquisition or on any bill of any indictment found by a grand jury.

(2.) If a coroner acts in contravention of this section, he shall be deemed guilty of misbehaviour in the discharge of his duty.

(3.) Moreover, the court before whom such person is tried may impose on a coroner appearing to the court to act in contravention of this section such fine not exceeding fifty pounds as to the court seems fit.[3]

Appointment and Payment[4] of County Coroner and Deputy.

Election of county coroner.

11.—(1.) *A coroner for a county shall continue to be elected, until Parliament otherwise directs, by the freeholders of that county, and in the case of a county divided into districts, by the persons residing within that district who are at the time of election qualified to vote at an election for coroners for the county.*

(2.) *A writ de coronatore eligendo for the election of a*

---

[1] Taken from 25 Geo. II. c. 29, s. 6.
[2] Taken from 7 Geo. IV. c. 64, s. 5.
[3] This section is taken from 7 & 8 Vict. c. 92, s. 18.
[4] As to salary of county coroner, *vide* s. 43 and note, *infra*.

coroner for a county shall be issued as heretofore directed to the sheriff of the county, and shall be in such form as the Lord Chancellor from time to time determines.

(3.) The sheriff shall, not less than seven nor more than fourteen days after the receipt of the writ, hold an election of a coroner in pursuance thereof and shall make a return to the writ, naming the person elected coroner.[1] [Repealed and replaced by sect. 5 of the Local Government Act, 1888 (51 & 52 Vict. c. 41), which gives the appointment to the County Council.]

12. Every coroner for a county shall be a fit person[2] *having land in fee sufficient in the same county whereof he may answer to all manner of people.*[3]

Qualification of county coroner.

13.—(1.) A coroner for a county shall from time to time appoint by writing under his hand a fit person approved by the Lord Chancellor to be his deputy, and may at any time revoke such appointment.

Appointment of deputy coroner in county.

(2.) A deputy shall not act for a coroner except during the illness of such coroner or during his absence from any lawful or reasonable cause, or except on any inquest which he is disqualified, under this Act, for holding.

(3.) A duplicate of every appointment of a deputy shall be sent to the clerk of the peace of the county and kept by him amongst the records thereof.[4]

(4.) For the purpose of an inquest or other act which a deputy coroner is authorised to hold or do the deputy coroner

---

[1] This section was taken from 7 & 8 Vict. c. 92, ss. 9, 10.

[2] The vexed question whether a member of the legal or medical profession is the more "fit person" was decided in favour of the legal profession by a Government Bill of 1879, which failed to pass.

[3] This (with which compare Sheriffs Act, 1887, s. 4) is taken from 14 Edw. III. st. 1, c. 8. Insufficiency of estate is said to be no disqualification or ground for removal: Jervis, 6th ed. p. 78; 2 Hale, P.C. 74; 2 Inst. 174; but see *ibid.* p. 78 for a contrary view. A borough coroner need only be a "fit person," not being an alderman or councillor, Municipal Corporations Act, 1882, s. 171.

[4] The first three paragraphs were taken from 6 & 7 Vict. c. 88, s. 1.

shall be deemed to be the coroner whose deputy he is, and have the same jurisdiction, and powers, and be subject to the same obligations, liabilities, and disqualifications as that coroner, and he shall generally be subject to the provisions of this Act and to the law relating to coroners, in like manner as that coroner.[1] [Repealed and replaced by Coroners Act, 1892.]

Proceedings for election of county coroner.

14.—(1.) *The sheriff, in accordance with the rules contained in the First Schedule to this Act, shall hold a court for the election of a coroner for a county, and in case of a poll being demanded, adjourn the court and take a poll, and for that purpose may appoint such officers and erect such booths as are authorised by the said rules, and the said rules shall be duly observed.*

(2.) *Any such poll shall be taken at the place at which the court for the election is held, and at such other places as are for the time being appointed by the local authority of the county.*

(3.) *All reasonable costs, charges, and expenses which the sheriff or his deputy expends or is liable to in and about the providing of poll-books, booths, and clerks (such clerks to be paid not more than one guinea each) for the purpose of taking the poll at any such election shall be paid by the several candidates at such election in equal proportions.*

(4.) *Any person who wilfully and falsely takes any oath or affirmation appointed by the rules in the schedule to this Act to be taken shall be guilty of perjury.* [All sect. 14 repealed by sect. 5 of the Local Government Act, 1888.]

Payment of coroners when they act for sheriffs.

15. Where any writ, process, or extent whatsoever is directed to and executed by a coroner for a county in the place of a sheriff,[2] the coroner shall, in addition to any salary[3] to which he is entitled, receive the same poundage fees or other compensation or reward for executing the

---

[1] New statute law in 1887.

[2] As, for instance, where the sheriff is a party, or where for any other cause any just exception is taken to the sheriff: Jervis, 6th ed. p. 76; and see Land Clauses Act, 1845, s. 40.

[3] As to salary, see s. 43 and note.

THE STATUTES.

writ, process, or extent, and have the same right to retain, and all other remedies for the recovery of the fees, compensation, or reward as the sheriff would have been entitled to and had in whose place such coroner was substituted; and if the fees or compensation payable to the sheriffs are at any time after the passing of this Act increased by Act of Parliament or otherwise, the coroner shall be entitled to such increased fees or compensation.[1]

16. Where a coroner admits a person charged with manslaughter to bail, he shall be entitled to the like fee as a clerk to a justice of the peace is entitled to on the admission to bail of a person so charged.[2]

Fees on recognizances.

17. Save as is authorised by this or any other Act,[3] a coroner shall not take any fee or remuneration in respect of anything done by him in the execution of his office.[4]

Prohibition on coroner taking fee.

PART II.

SUPPLEMENTAL.

Procedure.

18. The following enactments shall be made with respect to procedure at coroner's inquests :

Enactments with respect to procedure at inquests.

(1.) The inquisition shall be under the hands, and in the case of murder or manslaughter also under the seals, of the jurors who concur in the verdict, and of the coroner;

(2.) An inquisition need not, except in the case of murder or manslaughter, be on parchment,[5] and

---

[1] This is taken from 7 & 8 Vict. c. 92, s. 22.

[2] This is taken from 22 Vict. c. 33, s. 2. As to fees of clerk to justice, see Justices' Clerks Act, 1877 (40 & 41 Vict. c. 43) from which it appears that such clerk is ordinarily paid by salary in lieu of fees.

[3] As to salary of county coroner, see s. 43 and 23 & 24 Vict. c. 116, s. 4.

[4] Anciently the office was purely gratuitous: Stat. West. 1, c. 10. Remuneration was first given by 3 Hen. VII. c. 1, s. 4.

[5] This is taken from 6 & 7 Vict. c. 83, s. 2. As to quashing, see *Reg.* v. *Whalley*, 7 D. & L. 817.

may be written or printed, or partly written, and partly printed, and may be in the form contained in the Second Schedule to this Act, or to the like effect or in such other form as the Lord Chancellor from time to time prescribes, or to the like effect, and the statements therein may be made in concise and ordinary language.

(3.) The coroner after the termination of an inquest on any death shall send to the registrar of deaths whose duty it is by law to register the death such certificate of the finding of the jury and within such time as is required by the Registration Acts.[1]

(4.) The coroner shall cause recognizances taken before him from a person charged by an inquisition with manslaughter to be taken, so far as circumstances admit, in one of the forms contained in the Second Schedule to this Act or in such other forms as the Lord Chancellor from time to time prescribes, and shall give notice of the recognizance to every person bound thereby.[2]

(5.) A person charged by an inquisition with murder or manslaughter shall be entitled to have from the person having for the time being the custody of the inquisition or of the depositions of the witnesses at the inquest, copies thereof on payment of a reasonable sum for the same, not exceeding the rate of three halfpence for every folio of ninety words.

(6.) A coroner, upon holding an inquest upon any body, may, if he thinks fit after view of the body, by order under his hand, authorise the body to be buried before verdict and before registry of the death, and shall deliver such order to the relative or other person to whom the same is required by the Registration Acts, to be delivered; but,

---

[1] *Vide* s. 16 of the Births and Deaths Registration Act, 1874, which requires the certificate to be sent within five days after the finding of the jury.

[2] This and sub-s. (5) are taken from 22 Vict. c. 33, ss. 2, 3.

THE STATUTES.

except upon holding an inquest, no order, warrant, or other document for the burial of a body shall be given by the coroner.[1]

19.—(1.) Where a person duly summoned as a juror at an inquest does not, after being openly called three times, appear to such summons, or appearing, refuses without reasonable excuse to serve as a juror, the coroner may impose on such person a fine not exceeding five pounds.[2]

Attendance of witnesses and jurors.

(2.) Where a person duly summoned to give evidence at an inquest does not, after being openly called three times, appear to such summons, or appearing, refuses without lawful excuse to answer a question put to him, the coroner may impose on such person a fine not exceeding forty shillings.[3]

(3.) Any power by this Act vested in a coroner of imposing a fine on a juror or witness, shall be deemed to be in addition to and not in derogation of any power the coroner may possess independently of this Act, for compelling any person to appear and give evidence before him on any inquest or other proceeding,[4] or for punishing any person for contempt of court in not so appearing and giving evidence with this qualification, that a person shall not be fined by the coroner under this Act, and also be punished under the power of a coroner independently of this Act.[5]

(4.) Where a coroner imposes a fine upon a person, he shall sign a certificate describing such person and stating the amount of the fine imposed and the cause of the fine, and shall send such certificate to the clerk of the peace for the county or place in which such person resides on or before the first day of the quarter sessions then next ensuing, and shall, twenty-four hours at the least before

---

[1] This is taken from s. 17 of the Births and Deaths Registration Act, 1874.

[2] This is taken from s. 58 of 6 Geo. IV. c. 50, repealed, as to coroners, by this Act.

[3] This is taken from 7 & 8 Vict. c. 92, s. 17, which applies to jurors as well as witnesses.

[4] As to summons and warrant to witness, *vide* Jervis, 6th ed. pp. 29 and 288, and as to contempt, *vide ibid.* p. 29.

[5] This is taken from 7 & 8 Vict. c. 92, s. 17.

that day, cause a copy of such certificate to be served upon the person fined by leaving it at his residence, and the clerk of the peace shall copy every fine so certified on the roll on which fines and forfeitures imposed at the said quarter sessions are copied, and the same shall be estreated, levied, and applied in like manner and subject to the like powers, provisions, and penalties in all respects as if such fine had been part of the fines imposed at the said quarter sessions.[1]

(5.) Where a recognizance is forfeited at an inquest held before a coroner, the coroner shall proceed in like manner under this section as if he had imposed a fine under this section upon the person forfeiting that recognizance, and the provisions of this section shall apply accordingly.

Inquisition to be amended and not quashed for defects.

20.—(1.) If in the opinion of the court having cognizance of the case an inquisition finds sufficiently the matters required to be found thereby, and where it charges a person with murder or manslaughter sufficiently designates that person and the offence charged, the inquisition shall not be quashed for any defects, and the court may order the proper officer of the court to amend any defect in the inquisition, and any variance occurring between the inquisition and the evidence offered in proof thereof, if the court are of opinion that such defect or variance is not material to the merits of the case, and that the defendant or person traversing the inquisition cannot be prejudiced by the amendment in his defence or traverse on the merits, and the court may order the amendment on such terms as to postponing the trial to be had before the same or another jury as to the court may seem reasonable, and after the amendment the trial shall proceed in like manner, and the inquisition, verdict, and judgment, shall be of the same effect, and the record shall be drawn up in the same form, in all respects as if the inquisition had originally been in the form in which it stands when so amended.[2]

[1] Taken from 7 & 8 Vict. c. 92, s. 17.

[2] This is founded upon 6 & 7 Vict. c. 83, s. 2, but goes considerably beyond it, as that enactment merely allowed amendment of specific defects. As to amendment of indictments, which include coroners' inquisitions, *vide* 14 & 15 Vict. c. 100, ss. 1, 24, 30. In

(2.) For the purpose of any such amendment, the court may respite any of the recognizances taken before the coroner, and the persons bound by such recognizances shall be bound without entering into any fresh recognizances to appear and prosecute, give evidence, or be tried at the time and place to which the trial is postponed, as if they were originally bound by their recognizances to appear and prosecute, give evidence, or be tried at that time and place.

Medical Witnesses and Post-mortem Examinations.[1]

21.—(1.) Where it appears to the coroner that the deceased was attended at his death or during his last illness by any legally qualified medical practitioner, the coroner may summon such practitioner as a witness; but if it appears to the coroner that the deceased person was not attended at his death or during his last illness by any legally qualified medical practitioner, the coroner may summon any legally qualified medical practitioner who is at the time in actual practice in or near the place where the death happened, and any such medical witness as is summoned in pursuance of this section, may be asked to give evidence as to how, in his opinion, the deceased came to his death. {Power of coroner to summon medical witnesses and to direct performance of post-mortem examination.}

(2.) The coroner may, either in his summons for the attendance of such medical witness or at any time between the issuing of that summons and the end of the inquest, direct such medical witness to make a post-mortem examination of the body of the deceased, with or without an analysis of the contents of the stomach or intestines.

Provided that where a person states upon oath before the

Reg. v. *Great Western Rail. Co.*, 20 Q.B.D. 410; 57 L.J. M.C. 31; 58 L.J. 765; 36 W.R. 506; the inquisition charged that "the directors" of the company did feloniously kill. It was held that this could not be amended by naming the directors, by the Q.B.D. because the power of amendment was limited by s. 20 to the court of trial, but that the jurisdiction of the Q.B.D. to quash for irregularity was left untouched by that section, and the inquisition was quashed accordingly.

[1] Sects. 21 and 22 are taken from 6 & 7 Will. IV. c. 89.

coroner that in his belief the death of the deceased was caused partly or entirely by the improper or negligent treatment of a medical practitioner or other person, such medical practitioner or other person shall not be allowed to perform or assist at the post-mortem examination of the deceased.

(3.) If a majority of the jury sitting at an inquest are of opinion that the cause of death has not been satisfactorily explained by the evidence of the medical practitioner or other witnessess brought before them, they may require the coroner in writing to summon as a witness some other legally qualified medical practitioner named by them, and further to direct a post-mortem examination of the deceased, with or without an analysis of the contents of the stomach or intestines, to be made by such last-mentioned practitioner, and that whether such examination has been previously made or not, and the coroner shall comply with such requisition, and in default shall be guilty of a misdemeanor.[1]

Fees to medical witnesses.

22. A legally qualified medical practioner who has attended at a coroner's inquest in obedience to a summons of the coroner under this Act shall be entitled to receive such remuneration as follows; that is to say,

(a) For attending to give evidence at any inquest whereat no post-mortem examination has been made by such practitioner, one guinea: and
(b) For making a post-mortem examination of the body of the deceased, with or without an analysis of the contents of the stomach or intestines, and for attending to give evidence thereon, two guineas:

Provided that—

(1.) Any fee or remuneration shall not be paid to a medical practitioner for the performance of a

---

[1] And liable upon conviction on indictment, but not otherwise, to fine or imprisonment or both, at the discretion of the court trying the indictment.

post-mortem examination instituted without the previous direction of the coroner:

(2.) Where an inquest is held on the body of a person who has died in a county or other lunatic asylum, or in a public hospital, infirmary or other medical institution, or in a building or place belonging thereto, or used for the reception of the patients thereof, whether the same be supported by endowments or by voluntary subscriptions, the medical officer, whose duty it may have been to attend the deceased person as a medical officer of such institution as aforesaid, shall not be entitled to such fee or remuneration.

23. Where a medical practitioner fails to obey a summons of a coroner issued in pursuance of this Act, he shall, unless he shows a good and sufficient cause for not having obeyed the same, be liable on summary conviction on the prosecution of the coroner or of any two of the jury, to a fine not exceeding five pounds.[1] *Penalty on medical practitioner for neglecting to attend.*

24. Where a place has been provided by a sanitary authority or nuisance authority for the reception of dead bodies during the time required to conduct a post-mortem examination, the coroner may order the removal of a dead body to and from such place for carrying out such examination, and the cost of such removal shall be deemed to be part of the expenses incurred in and about the holding of an inquest.[2] *Removal of body for post-mortem examination.*

Expenses and Returns of Inquests.

25. The local authority[3] for a county or borough from time to time may make, and when made may alter and vary a schedule of fees, allowances, and disbursements which on the holding of an inquest may lawfully be paid *Schedule of fees and disbursements payable on holding inquest.*

[1] This is taken from 6 & 7 Will. IV. c. 89, s. 6. As to procedure to obtain conviction, *vide* the Summary Jurisdiction Acts.
[2] This is taken from s. 148 of the Public Health Act, 1875 (88 & 89 Vict. c. 55).
[3] *Vide* s. 41 for definition of "local authority."

and made by the coroner holding such inquest (other than the fees payable to medical witnesses in pursuance of this Act), and the local authority shall cause a copy of every such schedule to be deposited with the clerk of the peace of the county or with the town clerk of the borough, and one other copy thereof to be delivered to every coroner concerned.[1]

Payment of expenses by coroner.

26. A coroner holding an inquest shall immediately after the termination of the proceedings pay the fees of every medical witness not exceeding the fees fixed by this Act, and all expenses reasonably incurred in and about the holding thereof[2] not exceeding the sums set forth in the schedule of fees for the time being in force under this Act, and the sums so paid shall be repaid to the coroner in manner provided by this Act.[3]

Coroners to lay their accounts before the local authority.

27.—(1.) Every coroner shall, within four months after holding an inquest, cause a full and true account of all sums paid by him under this Act to be laid before the local authority of the county or borough by whom the sums are to be reimbursed to him.

(2.) Every account shall be accompanied by such vouchers as under the circumstances may to the local authority seem reasonable, and the local authority may, if they think fit, examine the said coroner on oath as to the account, and on being satisfied of the correctness thereof, the local authority shall order their treasurer to pay to the coroner the sum due to him on such account, with the addition, in the case of a coroner of a borough, of six shillings and eight pence for each inquest; and the treasurer shall pay the same out of the local rate, without any abatement or deduction whatever, and shall be allowed the same on passing his accounts.[4]

28. Every coroner of a borough shall on or before the

---

[1] Taken from 7 Will. IV. and 1 Vict. c. 68, s. 1.
[2] Jurors are not entitled by law to any remuneration, but in many places the authorities have allowed a fee to be paid to them.
[3] Taken from 7 Will. IV. and 1 Vict. c. 68, s. 2.
[4] Taken from 7 Will. IV. and 1 Vict. c. 68, s. 3.

first day of February in every year make and transmit to a Secretary of State a return in writing, in such form and containing such particulars as the Secretary of State from time to time directs, of all cases in which an inquest has been held by him, or by some person in lieu of him, during the year ending on the thirty-first day of December immediately preceding.[1]

Coroners to make yearly returns to Secretary of State.

Coroner of the Queen's Household.

29.—(1.) The coroner of Her Majesty the Queen's household, shall continue to be appointed by the Lord Steward for the time being of the Queen's household.

Appointment and jurisdiction of the coroner of the Queen's household.

(2.) The coroner of the Queen's household shall have exclusive jurisdiction in respect of inquests on persons whose bodies are lying within the limits of any of the Queen's palaces or within the limits of any other house where Her Majesty is then demurrant and abiding in her own royal person, notwithstanding the subsequent removal of Her Majesty from such palace or house.

(3.) The jurors on an inquest held by the coroner of the Queen's household, shall consist of officers of the Queen's household, to be returned by such officer of the Queen's household as may be directed to summon the same by the warrant of the said coroner.

(4.) The limits of the said palace or house shall be deemed to extend to any courts, gardens, or other places within the curtilage of such palace or house but not further, and where a body is lying dead in any place beyond those limits, the coroner of the Queen's household shall not have jurisdiction to hold an inquest on such body, and the coroner of the county or borough shall have jurisdiction to hold that inquest in the same manner as if that place were not within the verge.

(5.) Where the inquisition charges a person with murder or manslaughter, the coroner of the Queen's household shall deliver the inquisition, depositions, and recognizances to the Lord Steward of the Queen's household, or in his absence, to the treasurer and controller of

[1] Taken from Municipal Corporations Act, 1882, s. 178.

the Queen's household, and the recognizances shall be taken for the appearance of the persons bound by them before the said Lord Steward, or in his absence before the said treasurer and comptroller.

(6.) All other inquisitions, depositions, and recognizances shall be delivered to the Lord Steward of the Queen's household to be filed among the records of his office.

(7.) The coroner of the Queen's household shall make his declaration of office before the Lord Steward of the Queen's household, and shall reside in one of the Queen's palaces, or in such other convenient place as may from time to time be allowed by the Lord Steward of the Queen's household.

(8.) Save as is in this section specially provided, the coroner of the Queen's household shall, within the said limits have the same jurisdiction and powers, be subject to the same obligations liabilities, and disqualifications, and generally to the provisions of this Act and to the law relating to coroners in like manner as any other franchise coroner.

(9.) The Lord Steward of the Queen's household or the treasurer and comptroller of the Queen's household shall not have any jurisdiction to inquire of, try, hear, or determine, any offence committed beyond the limits aforesaid, or to array, try, or give judgment upon any person charged by any inquisition found before a coroner for any place beyond the limits aforesaid, and every such offence shall be inquired of, tried, heard, and determined and every such person shall be arraigned, tried, and have judgment according to the ordinary course of law.

Franchise Coroners.

Saving for remuneration of franchise coroners.

30.—(1.) Where a franchise coroner[1] is, at the passing of this Act, paid a salary out of the local rate, the provisions of this Act with respect to the expenses of inquests, shall apply as if such coroner were a coroner for a county.

[1] For definition, *vide* s. 42.

(2.) Nothing in this Act shall affect the remuneration to which a franchise coroner who is not at the passing of this Act paid a salary out of the local rate is entitled at the passing of this Act, and every such coroner shall continue to be entitled to receive the same fees, allowances, and remuneration as he would have been entitled to if this Act had not passed.

(3.) Nothing in this Act shall affect the mode in which a franchise coroner is appointed, or is, otherwise than is provided by this Act, removed.

(4.) Subject as aforesaid, the provisions of this Act shall apply to a franchise coroner, except those provisions in which a coroner for a county or a coroner of a borough is expressly named.[1]

31. The provisions of this Act with respect to the expenses of inquests, shall apply to the City of London and the Borough of Southwark. *Provisions as to expenses of inquests to extend to City of London.*

32. Where a coroner appointed and acting for the jurisdiction of the Cinque Ports who is not paid a salary out of the local rate in lieu of allowances deems it unnecessary to hold and declines to hold an inquest, and shows to the justices in general or quarter sessions assembled that he had nevertheless been compelled in the discharge of his office to travel from his usual place of abode for the purpose of taking that inquest, such justices may order the payment to that coroner of the same allowances for travelling as might be allowed in any other case. *Payment of travelling expenses of coroner in Cinque Ports where inquisition is not taken.*

Savings and Miscellaneous.

33. Nothing in this Act shall affect the application to coroners of a borough of the provisions of the Municipal Corporations Act, 1882,[2] with respect to the appointment, *Saving as borough coroners. 45 & 46 Vict. c. 50.*

---

[1] The appointment of franchise coroners is not transferred to county councils by the Local Government Act, 1888 (*London County Council*, Ex parte, 1892, 1 Q.B. 83; 61 L.J. Q.B. 27).

[2] 45 & 46 Vict. c. 50. By s. 271 of that Act the council of a borough having a separate court of quarter sessions appoints as coroner a fit person, not being an alderman or councillor, who holds office during good behaviour.

qualification, tenure of office, and payment of a coroner of a borough, *and the appointment of a deputy by such coroner.*[1]

Saving clause as to official coroners.

34. Nothing in this Act shall prejudice the jurisdiction of a judge exercising the jurisdiction of a coroner by virtue of his office, and such judge may, notwithstanding the passing of this Act, exercise any jurisdiction, statutable or otherwise, previously exerciseable by him in the same manner as if this Act had not passed.[2]

Saving of jurisdiction as to removal of coroner, or otherwise in relation to a coroner.

35. Nothing in this Act shall prejudice the jurisdiction of the Lord Chancellor or the High Court of Justice in relation to moving a coroner otherwise than in manner provided by this Act, or in any manner prejudice or affect the jurisdiction of the High Court of Justice or of any judge thereof in relation to or over a coroner or his duties.[3]

Inquest on treasure trove.

36. A coroner shall continue as heretofore to have jurisdiction to inquire of treasure that is found, who were the finders, and who is suspected thereof,[4] and the provisions of this Act shall, so far as is consistent with the tenor thereof, apply to every such inquest.[5]

---

[1] The words in italics are repealed by the Coroners Act, 1892.

[2] The Lord Chief Justice of England is supreme coroner over all England and the judges of the High Court are also sovereign coroners. *Vide* p. 24 of this work; also 4 Rep. 57 b, and 4 Inst. 78 a.

[3] As to jurisdiction under this Act to remove, *vide* s. 8. As to general jurisdiction, *vide* Ex parte *Parnell*, 1 J. & W. 455.

[4] But he has no jurisdiction to inquire into any question of title to the treasure as between the Crown and any other claimant (*Attorney-General* v. *Moore*, 1893, 1 Ch. 676, per Stirling, J.).

[5] Treasure that is found, or "treasure trove," is where coin, or plate, or bullion is found *concealed*, and the owner is unknown, in which case the king or the lord of the manor, if he have grant of treasure trove, becomes entitled to it. If the owner casually lost the treasure, the first finder is entitled to it as against every one but the owner, it being concealment and not abandonment that entitles the king or lord of the manor to it. Every person finding treasure is bound to acquaint the coroner on pain of fine and imprisonment, *vide R.* v. *Thomas*, 9 Cox, C.C. 376, and the repealed 4 Edw. I. st. 2.

37. The Schedules to this Act shall be construed and have effect as part of this Act, and the forms given in any of those schedules, or such other forms as the Lord Chancellor from time to time directs, may be used in all matters to which they apply, and when so used shall be sufficient in law.

Effect of Schedules.

Definitions.

38. In this Act the expression "county," unless there is something inconsistent in the context, does not include a county of a city or a county of a town, but includes any division or liberty of a county which has a separate court of quarter sessions for which a separate coroner has customarily been elected, but the whole of Yorkshire and the whole of Lincolnshire shall respectively be a county for the purposes of this Act.

Construction of Act with respect to counties.

The counties in Wales, and the counties of Durham and Chester, and the liberty of the Isle of Ely shall, save as is otherwise expressly provided by this Act, be, for the purposes of this Act and any other Act relating to coroners, subject to the same provisions as the other counties of England, and the coroners thereof shall have the same jurisdiction as other coroners in England; and for the purpose of the provisions of any Act with respect to coroners districts a ward in the county of Durham shall be deemed to be a coroner's district in that county.

39. This Act and any other Act relating to coroners shall apply to the county of Lancaster in like manner as it applies to the other counties of England, subject as follows:

Provision for application of Act to county of Lancaster.

(1.) The provisions of this Act with respect to the Lord Chancellor shall be construed in the case of the said county to mean the Chancellor of the Duchy and county palatine of Lancaster, and all writs relating to coroners issued by that Chancellor, shall be issued by such persons and in such manner as the Chancellor and the council of the Duchy of Lancaster from time to time direct:

(2.) An Order in Council with respect to coroners districts in the county of Lancaster shall be made on the recommendation of the Chancellor and council of the Duchy of Lancaster.

<small>Provisions as to detached parts of counties.</small>

40.—(1.) For the purpose of holding coroners inquests every detached part of a county shall be deemed to be within the county by which it is wholly surrounded, or where it is partly surrounded by two or more counties within the county with which it has the longest common boundary.[1]

(2.) The treasurer of every county shall keep an account of all expenses occasioned to such county by any inquest in or in respect to any such detached part of any other county, and shall twice in every year, send a copy of such account to the treasurer of the other county to which such detached part belongs, and the last-mentioned shall, out of the moneys in his hand as such treasurer, pay to the treasurer sending the account the sum appearing thereby to be due, together with all reasonable charges for making and sending the account.

(3.) Any difference which may arise concerning the said account, if not adjusted by agreement, shall be determined by an arbitrator, who shall be a barrister-at-law nominated on the application of either party by one of the justices of assize of the last preceding circuit or of the next succeeding circuit. Such arbitrator may adjourn the hearing from time to time, and require all such information from either party as appears to him necessary, and his award shall be final. He shall also assess the costs of the arbitration and direct by whom and out of what funds the same shall be paid.

<small>Definition of "local authority" and "local rate."</small>

41. For the purposes of this Act—

(a.) The local authority of a county shall be the court of quarter sessions of the county; and

(b.) The local authority of a borough shall be the mayor, aldermen, and burgesses of the borough acting by the council; and

---

[1] Taken from 6 Vict. c. 12, s. 12, and 7 & 8 Vict. c. 92, s. 8.

(c.) The local rate shall be, in the case of a county, the county rate, or rate in the nature of a county rate, and, in the case of a borough, the borough fund or borough rate; and

(d.) In Lincolnshire and Yorkshire respectively the justices in gaol sessions shall be the local authority, and the clerk to such justices shall act as clerk of the peace, and the rate in the nature of a county rate levied by those sessions shall be the local rate.

42. In this Act, if not inconsistent with the context, the following terms and expressions have the meanings herein-after respectively assigned to them: *Definitions.*

> The expression "quarter sessions" includes general sessions. *"Quarter sessions."*
>
> The expression "borough" means any place for the time being subject to the Municipal Corporations Act, 1882, and the Acts amending the same. *"Borough." 45 & 46 Vict. c. 50.*
>
> The expression "franchise coroner" means any of the following coroners, that is to say, the coroner of the Queen's household, a coroner or deputy coroner for the jurisdiction of the Admiralty, a coroner appointed by Her Majesty the Queen in right of Her Duchy of Lancaster, and a coroner appointed for a town corporate, liberty, lordship, manor, university, or other place, the coroner for which has heretofore been appointed by any lord, or otherwise that by election of the freeholders of a county, or of any part of a county, or by the council of a borough, and the expression "franchise" means the area within which the franchise coroner exercises jurisdiction. *"Franchise coroner."*
>
> The expression "Secretary of State" means one of Her Majesty's Principal Secretaries of State. *"Secretary of State."*
>
> The expression "murder" includes the offence of being an accessory before the fact to a murder. *"Murder."*
>
> The expression "parish" means a parish, township, or place for which a separate poor rate is or can be *"Parish."*

made, or for which a separate overseer is or can be appointed.

The expression "the Lord Chancellor" means the Lord High Chancellor of Great Britain.

The expression "Registration Acts" means the Acts for the time being in force relating to the registration of deaths, inclusive of any enactment amending the same.

Temporary Provisions and Repeal.

<small>Saving as to coroners' salaries and districts.</small>

43. Nothing in this Act shall affect the law respecting the salaries of coroners for counties[1], or the division of a county into coroners' districts, or the rights and duties of coroners as respects such districts.[2]

<small>Abolition of certain jurisdictions of the coroner.</small>

44. A coroner shall not take pleas of the Crown nor hold inquests of royal fish nor of wreck nor of felonies except felonies on inquisitions of death[3]; and he shall not inquire of the goods of such as by the inquest are found guilty of murder or manslaughter, nor cause them to be valued and delivered to the township.

<small>Repeal of Acts in schedule.</small>

45. The Acts specified in the Third Schedule to this Act are hereby repealed, from and after the passing of this Act, to the extent specified in the third column of that schedule.

Provided that—

(1.) A coroner elected before the passing of this Act, shall continue to hold office in like manner as if he had been elected under this Act, and

(2.) Any schedule of fees, allowances, and disbursements made by a local authority for a county or borough before the passing of this Act shall,

---

[1] *Vide* 23 & 24 Vict. c. 116, s. 4, which provides for payment by salary in lieu of fees.

[2] *Vide* 7 & 8 Vict. c. 92.

[3] This, as to felonies, affirms the law, previously doubtful, as laid down in *Reg. v. Herford*, 29 L.J. Q.B. 249, where it was held that the coroner could not hold inquisitions in case of fire.

until a schedule had been made in pursuance of this Act, and

(3.) This repeal shall not affect—

(*a.*) The past operation of any enactment hereby repealed, nor anything duly done or suffered under any enactment hereby repealed; or

(*b.*) Any right, privilege, obligation, or liability acquired, accrued, or incurred under any enactment hereby repealed; or

(*c.*) Any penalty, forfeiture, or punishment incurred in respect of any offence committed against any enactment hereby repealed; or

(*d.*) Any inquest on any death which occurred before the commencement of this Act or an inquisition found thereon, or any investigation, legal proceeding, or remedy in respect of any such right, privilege, obligation, liability, penalty, forfeiture, or punishment as aforesaid; and any such inquest, investigation, legal proceeding, and remedy, and the trial of any such inquisition may be carried on as if this Act had not passed.

(4.) This repeal shall not revive any jurisdiction, office, duty, fee, franchise, liberty, custom, right, title, privilege, restriction, exemption, usage, practice, procedure, or other matter or thing not in force or existing at the passing of this Act.

(5.) Save in so far as is inconsistent with this Act, any principle or rule of law, or established jurisdiction, practice, or procedure, or existing usage, franchise, liberty, or custom, shall, notwithstanding the repeal of any enactment by this Act, remain in full force.

[Ss. 11, 14, Sch. 1, repealed by Local Government (England and Wales) Act, 1888 (51 & 52 Vict. c. 41, s. 5 (6)). Ss. 13 and 33 in part, repealed by Coroners Act, 1892 (55 & 56 Vict. c. 56, s. 2 and Sch.)]

SCHEDULES.

FIRST SCHEDULE.

Sections 14, 37.

Rules for Election of Coroner.

(1.) The sheriff shall hold a court for the election at some convenient place appointed by him within the county, or, in a county divided into districts, within the district for which the election is to take place, on such day not less than seven nor more than fourteen days after the receipt of the writ as he appoints.

(2.) If a poll is demanded the sheriff shall adjourn the court to eight o'clock in the morning of the next day but one, unless such next day but one is Saturday or Sunday, and then of the Monday following.

(3.) The sheriff with such others as are deputed by him shall then and there proceed to take a poll in some public place or places, which shall be the place appointed for holding the court for the election, or such other places within the same county or district (as the case may be) as may be from time to time appointed by the quarter sessions, and such poll shall continue for one day only for eight hours, and no poll shall be kept open later than four o'clock in the afternoon.

(4.) The sheriff or sheriff's deputy may, if required by or on behalf of any candidate on or before the day fixed for the election, or if he deem it expedient, cause booths to be erected for taking the poll at the several polling places, and shall cause to be affixed on the most conspicuous part of the booth the names of the parishes to which such booth is allotted.

(5.) Where a booth is allotted to any parish a person shall not be admitted to vote in respect of any property situate in that parish except at that booth.

(6.) Where there is no booth allotted to any parish, a person entitled to vote in respect of property situate therein shall vote at the place at which the court for the election is held.

(7.) The sheriff or such person as he deputes shall appoint such number of clerks as to him may seem meet and convenient for taking the poll, and those clerks shall take the poll in the presence of the sheriff or such person as he deputes, and before they begin to take the poll each clerk shall by the sheriff or such person as he deputes as aforesaid be sworn truly and indifferently to take the poll, and to set down the names of each elector, the place of his residence, and the person for whom he polls, and to poll no elector who is not sworn, if required to be sworn by either of the candidates, which oath the said sheriff or such person as he deputes may administer.

(8.) The sheriff shall appoint for each candidate such one person *as is nominated to him by each candidate to be an inspector of every clerk who is appointed for taking the poll.*

(9.) *Every elector before he is admitted to poll at an election, shall if required by or on behalf of any candidate, first take the oath following, which the sheriff or any such sworn clerk as aforesaid may administer, that is to say:*—I swear [or solemnly declare, as the case may be] *that I am a freeholder of the county of   , and have a freehold estate consisting of   , lying at   , in the parish of   , within the said county, and that such freehold estate has not been granted to me fraudulently or colourably on purpose to qualify me to give my vote at this election, and that the place of my abode is at   ,* [and if it be a place consisting of more streets or places than one, specifying what street or place,] *that I am twenty-one years of age, as I believe, and that I have not voted before at this election.*

(10.) *The poll clerks shall at the close of the poll, enclose and seal their several books, and deliver them so enclosed and sealed to the sheriff or sheriff's deputy presiding at the poll, who shall give a receipt for the same.*

(11.) *Where the deputy receives them, he shall forthwith deliver or transmit them so enclosed and sealed to the sheriff.*

(12.) *The sheriff shall receive and keep all the poll books unopened until the re-assembling of the court on the day next but one after the close of the poll, unless that day be Sunday, and then on the Monday following, and on that day he shall openly break the seals thereon, and count the votes appearing in the said books, and openly delare the said poll, and make proclamation of the person chosen not later than two o'clock in the afternoon of the said day.*

(13.) *In these rules the expression " sheriff " includes "under-sheriff."* [Repealed by sect. 5 of the Local Government Act, 1888.]

SECOND SCHEDULE.

FORMS.[1]

[Form of Declaration of Office of Coroner.]

I solemnly, sincerely, and truly declare and affirm that I will well and truly serve our Sovereign Lady the Queen and her liege people in the office of coroner for this county [or borough *or as the case may be*] of   , and that I will diligently and truly do everything appertaining to my office after the best of my power for the doing of right, and for the good of the inhabitants within the said county [or borough *or as the case may be*]. Sections 18, 37.

---

[1] These forms were not in the repealed Acts.

Form of Oath of Jury.

You shall diligently inquire and a true presentment make of all such matters and things as are here given you in charge on behalf of our Sovereign Lady the Queen, touching the death of *C.D.*, now lying dead, of whose body you shall have the view and shall without fear or favour, affection, or illwill, a true verdict give according to the evidence and to the best of your skill and knowledge.[1] So help you God.

FORM OF INQUISITION.

Middlesex to wit. } An inquisition taken for our Sovereign lady the Queen at , in the parish of , in the county [*or as the case may be*] of , on the day of , 18 . [and by adjournment on the day of , *or as the case may require*] before *A.B.*, one of the coroners of our Lady the Queen for the said [county, *or, as the case may be*] upon the oath [*or and affirmation*] of [*in the case of murder or manslaughter here insert the names of the jurors,* L.M., N.O., &c. *being*] good and lawful men of the said [county, *or, as the case may be*] duly sworn to inquire for our Lady the Queen, on view of the body of *C.D.* [*or of a person to the jurors unknown*] as to his death; and those of the said jurors whose names are hereunto subscribed upon their oaths do say:—

Here set out the circumstances of the death, as, for example:

(*a.*) That the said *C.D.* was found dead on the day of in the year aforesaid at in the county of , [*or set out other place of death*] and

(*b.*) That the cause of his death was that he was thrown by *E.F.* against the ground, whereby the said *C.D.* had a violent concussion of the brain and instantly died [*or set other cause of death*].

Conclusion. — *Here set out the conclusion of the jury as to the death, as, for example:*

Manslaughter or murder. — (*c.*) and so do further say, that the said *E.F.* did feloniously kill [*or* feloniously, wilfully, and of malice aforethought murder] the said *C.D.*

By misadventure. — Or, do further say that the said *E.F.* by misfortune and against his will did kill the said *C.D.*

---

[1] The words "to the best of your skill and knowledge" are not in the oath of jurors sworn at an ordinary criminal trial, whence it seems that a coroner's jury have a more independent authority.

Or, do further say that *E.F.* in the defence of himself [and property] did kill the said *C.D.* *Justifiable homicide.*

In case of there being an accessory before the fact add: *Addition for accessory before the fact.*
And do further say that *K.L.*, before the said murder was committed, did feloniously incite [*or* procure, aid, counsel, and command, *or as the case may be*] the said *E.F.* to commit the said murder.

At end add:
In witness whereof as well the said coroner as the jurors have hereunto subscribed their hands and seals the day and year first above written.

Another example is:
That the said *C.D.*, did on the   day of   fall into a pond of water situate at   , by means whereof he died.

Here set out the conclusion of the jury as to the death, as for example:

And so do further say that the said *C.D.*, not being of sound mind, did kill himself. *Unsound mind.*

Or do further say that the said *C.D.* did feloniously kill himself.[1] *For felo de se.*

Or do further say that by the neglect of *E.F.* to fence the said pond *C.D.* fell therein, and that therefore *E.F.* did feloniously kill the said *C.D.* *Manslaughter by neglect.*

Or do further say that the said *C.D.* by misadventure fell into the said pond and was killed. *By misadventure.*

FORM OF RECOGNIZANCE.

          to wit } Be it remembered that   on the   day of   , 18   , each of the following persons, namely, *J.K.* of   and *R.S.* of   [*insert the names of all bound over*] personally came before me, *A.B.*, one of the coroners of our Lady the Queen for the county [*or, as the case may be*] of   , and acknowledged to owe to our Sovereign Lady the Queen the sum of   pounds to be levied on his goods and lands by way of recognizance to Her Majesty's use if default is made on his part [*or* on the part of *I.K.*] in the conditions following:—

In case of recognisance to appear and give evidence before the coroner, add:

He shall appear personally at the court of the said coroner to be held on the   day of   next, at   in the said county [or, *as the case may be*], for holding an inquest on the view of the body of *C.D.*, there to give evidence of anything he

---

[1] As to interments of *felo de se*, Vide Interments (*Felo de se*) Act, 1882 (45 & 46 Vict. c. 19).

qualification, tenure of office, and payment of a coroner of a borough, *and the appointment of a deputy by such coroner*.[1]

Saving clause as to official coroners.
34. Nothing in this Act shall prejudice the jurisdiction of a judge exercising the jurisdiction of a coroner by virtue of his office, and such judge may, notwithstanding the passing of this Act, exercise any jurisdiction, statutable or otherwise, previously exerciseable by him in the same manner as if this Act had not passed.[2]

Saving of jurisdiction as to removal of coroner, or otherwise in relation to a coroner.
35. Nothing in this Act shall prejudice the jurisdiction of the Lord Chancellor or the High Court of Justice in relation to moving a coroner otherwise than in manner provided by this Act, or in any manner prejudice or affect the jurisdiction of the High Court of Justice or of any judge thereof in relation to or over a coroner or his duties.[3]

Inquest on treasure trove.
36. A coroner shall continue as heretofore to have jurisdiction to inquire of treasure that is found, who were the finders, and who is suspected thereof,[4] and the provisions of this Act shall, so far as is consistent with the tenor thereof, apply to every such inquest.[5]

---

[1] The words in italics are repealed by the Coroners Act, 1892.

[2] The Lord Chief Justice of England is supreme coroner over all England and the judges of the High Court are also sovereign coroners. *Vide* p. 24 of this work; also 4 Rep. 57 b, and 4 Inst. 78 a.

[3] As to jurisdiction under this Act to remove, *vide* s. 8. As to general jurisdiction, *vide* Ex parte *Parnell*, 1 J. & W. 455.

[4] But he has no jurisdiction to inquire into any question of title to the treasure as between the Crown and any other claimant (*Attorney-General* v. *Moore*, 1893, 1 Ch. 676, per Stirling, J.).

[5] Treasure that is found, or "treasure trove," is where coin, or plate, or bullion is found *concealed*, and the owner is unknown, in which case the king or the lord of the manor, if he have grant of treasure trove, becomes entitled to it. If the owner casually lost the treasure, the first finder is entitled to it as against every one but the owner, it being concealment and not abandonment that entitles the king or lord of the manor to it. Every person finding treasure is bound to acquaint the coroner on pain of fine and imprisonment, *vide* R. v. *Thomas*, 9 Cox, C.C. 376, and the repealed 4 Edw. I. st. 2.

37. The Schedules to this Act shall be construed and have effect as part of this Act, and the forms given in any of those schedules, or such other forms as the Lord Chancellor from time to time directs, may be used in all matters to which they apply, and when so used shall be sufficient in law. *Effect of Schedules.*

Definitions.

38. In this Act the expression "county," unless there is something inconsistent in the context, does not include a county of a city or a county of a town, but includes any division or liberty of a county which has a separate court of quarter sessions for which a separate coroner has customarily been elected, but the whole of Yorkshire and the whole of Lincolnshire shall respectively be a county for the purposes of this Act. *Construction of Act with respect to counties.*

The counties in Wales, and the counties of Durham and Chester, and the liberty of the Isle of Ely shall, save as is otherwise expressly provided by this Act, be, for the purposes of this Act and any other Act relating to coroners, subject to the same provisions as the other counties of England, and the coroners thereof shall have the same jurisdiction as other coroners in England; and for the purpose of the provisions of any Act with respect to coroners districts a ward in the county of Durham shall be deemed to be a coroner's district in that county.

39. This Act and any other Act relating to coroners shall apply to the county of Lancaster in like manner as it applies to the other counties of England, subject as follows: *Provision for application of Act to county of Lancaster.*

(1.) The provisions of this Act with respect to the Lord Chancellor shall be construed in the case of the said county to mean the Chancellor of the Duchy and county palatine of Lancaster, and all writs relating to coroners issued by that Chancellor, shall be issued by such persons and in such manner as the Chancellor and the council of the Duchy of Lancaster from time to time direct:

R

Session and Chapter.	Title.	Extent of Repeal.
1 Edw. III. stat. 2, c. 17.	Statutes made at Westminster. Statute the first. Indictments shall be taken by Indenture.	The whole chapter so far as it relates to coroners.
14 Edw. III. stat. 1, c. 8.	Statute the first. Chapter eight; escheators; their number, appointment, continuance in office. Coroners; their sufficiency.	The whole chapter.
28 Edw. III. c. 6.	Coroners shall be chosen by the commons of the counties.	The whole chapter.
23 Hen. VI. c. 9.	No sheriff shall let his county to ferm.	The whole chapter so far as it relates to coroners.
3 Hen. VII. c. 2.	An Acte agaynst murderers.	The whole Act, except from "And also be "yt ordyned by the "authority afore- "said," to the end of the chapter.
1 Hen. VIII. c. 7	An Acte concerning coroners.	The whole Act.
33 Hen. VIII. c. 12	An Acte for murther and malicious bloudshed within the Courte.	Section one from "And "that all inquiscons "upon the viewe "of psons slayne" down to the end of the section, section eight, section nine, section ten from " or "within two hun- "dred" to the end of the section, and section eleven.
34 & 35 Hen. VIII. c. 26.	An Acte for certaine ordinaunces in the Kinges Majesties dominion and principalitie of Waless.	Section twenty-five.

THE STATUTES. 241

37. The Schedules to this Act shall be construed and have effect as part of this Act, and the forms given in any of those schedules, or such other forms as the Lord Chancellor from time to time directs, may be used in all matters to which they apply, and when so used shall be sufficient in law.

Effect of Schedules.

Definitions.

38. In this Act the expression "county," unless there is something inconsistent in the context, does not include a county of a city or a county of a town, but includes any division or liberty of a county which has a separate court of quarter sessions for which a separate coroner has customarily been elected, but the whole of Yorkshire and the whole of Lincolnshire shall respectively be a county for the purposes of this Act.

Construction of Act with respect to counties.

The counties in Wales, and the counties of Durham and Chester, and the liberty of the Isle of Ely shall, save as is otherwise expressly provided by this Act, be, for the purposes of this Act and any other Act relating to coroners, subject to the same provisions as the other counties of England, and the coroners thereof shall have the same jurisdiction as other coroners in England; and for the purpose of the provisions of any Act with respect to coroners districts a ward in the county of Durham shall be deemed to be a coroner's district in that county.

39. This Act and any other Act relating to coroners shall apply to the county of Lancaster in like manner as it applies to the other counties of England, subject as follows:

Provision for application of Act to county of Lancaster.

> (1.) The provisions of this Act with respect to the Lord Chancellor shall be construed in the case of the said county to mean the Chancellor of the Duchy and county palatine of Lancaster, and all writs relating to coroners issued by that Chancellor, shall be issued by such persons and in such manner as the Chancellor and the council of the Duchy of Lancaster from time to time direct:

R

(2.) An Order in Council with respect to coroners districts in the county of Lancaster shall be made on the recommendation of the Chancellor and council of the Duchy of Lancaster.

<small>Provisions as to detached parts of counties.</small>

40.—(1.) For the purpose of holding coroners inquests every detached part of a county shall be deemed to be within the county by which it is wholly surrounded, or where it is partly surrounded by two or more counties within the county with which it has the longest common boundary.[1]

(2.) The treasurer of every county shall keep an account of all expenses occasioned to such county by any inquest in or in respect to any such detached part of any other county, and shall twice in every year, send a copy of such account to the treasurer of the other county to which such detached part belongs, and the last-mentioned shall, out of the moneys in his hand as such treasurer, pay to the treasurer sending the account the sum appearing thereby to be due, together with all reasonable charges for making and sending the account.

(3.) Any difference which may arise concerning the said account, if not adjusted by agreement, shall be determined by an arbitrator, who shall be a barrister-at-law nominated on the application of either party by one of the justices of assize of the last preceding circuit or of the next succeeding circuit. Such arbitrator may adjourn the hearing from time to time, and require all such information from either party as appears to him necessary, and his award shall be final. He shall also assess the costs of the arbitration and direct by whom and out of what fund the same shall be paid.

<small>Definition of "local authority" and "local rate."</small>

41. For the purposes of this Act—

    (*a*.) The local authority of a county shall be the court of quarter sessions of the county; and

    (*b*.) The local authority of a borough shall be the mayor, aldermen, and burgesses of the borough acting by the council; and

---

[1] Taken from 6 Vict. c. 12, s. 12, and 7 & 8 Vict. c. 92, s. 8.

(c.) The local rate shall be, in the case of a county, the county rate, or rate in the nature of a county rate, and, in the case of a borough, the borough fund or borough rate; and

(d.) In Lincolnshire and Yorkshire respectively the justices in gaol sessions shall be the local authority, and the clerk to such justices shall act as clerk of the peace, and the rate in the nature of a county rate levied by those sessions shall be the local rate.

42. In this Act, if not inconsistent with the context, the following terms and expressions have the meanings herein-after respectively assigned to them: — *Definitions.*

The expression "quarter sessions" includes general sessions. *"Quarter sessions."*

The expression "borough" means any place for the time being subject to the Municipal Corporations Act, 1882, and the Acts amending the same. *"Borough." 45 & 46 Vict. c. 50.*

The expression "franchise coroner" means any of the following coroners, that is to say, the coroner of the Queen's household, a coroner or deputy coroner for the jurisdiction of the Admiralty, a coroner appointed by Her Majesty the Queen in right of Her Duchy of Lancaster, and a coroner appointed for a town corporate, liberty, lordship, manor, university, or other place, the coroner for which has heretofore been appointed by any lord, or otherwise that by election of the freeholders of a county, or of any part of a county, or by the council of a borough, and the expression "franchise" means the area within which the franchise coroner exercises jurisdiction. *"Franchise coroner."*

The expression "Secretary of State" means one of Her Majesty's Principal Secretaries of State. *"Secretary of State."*

The expression "murder" includes the offence of being an accessory before the fact to a murder. *"Murder."*

The expression "parish" means a parish, township, or place for which a separate poor rate is or can be *"Parish."*

made, or for which a separate overseer is or can be appointed.

The expression "the Lord Chancellor" means the Lord High Chancellor of Great Britain.

The expression "Registration Acts" means the Acts for the time being in force relating to the registration of deaths, inclusive of any enactment amending the same.

Temporary Provisions and Repeal.

Saving as to coroners' salaries and districts.

43. Nothing in this Act shall affect the law respecting the salaries of coroners for counties[1], or the division of a county into coroners' districts, or the rights and duties of coroners as respects such districts.[2]

Abolition of certain jurisdictions of the coroner.

44. A coroner shall not take pleas of the Crown nor hold inquests of royal fish nor of wreck nor of felonies except felonies on inquisitions of death[3]; and he shall not inquire of the goods of such as by the inquest are found guilty of murder or manslaughter, nor cause them to be valued and delivered to the township.

Repeal of Acts in schedule.

45. The Acts specified in the Third Schedule to this Act are hereby repealed, from and after the passing of this Act, to the extent specified in the third column of that schedule.

Provided that—

(1.) A coroner elected before the passing of this Act, shall continue to hold office in like manner as if he had been elected under this Act, and

(2.) Any schedule of fees, allowances, and disbursements made by a local authority for a county or borough before the passing of this Act shall,

---

[1] *Vide* 23 & 24 Vict. c. 116, s. 4, which provides for payment by salary in lieu of fees.

[2] *Vide* 7 & 8 Vict. c. 92.

[3] This, as to felonies, affirms the law, previously doubtful, as laid down in *Reg.* v. *Herford*, 29 L.J. Q.B. 249, where it was held that the coroner could not hold inquisitions in case of fire.

until a schedule had been made in pursuance of this Act, and

(3.) This repeal shall not affect—

- (*a.*) The past operation of any enactment hereby repealed, nor anything duly done or suffered under any enactment hereby repealed; or
- (*b.*) Any right, privilege, obligation, or liability acquired, accrued, or incurred under any enactment hereby repealed; or
- (*c.*) Any penalty, forfeiture, or punishment incurred in respect of any offence committed against any enactment hereby repealed; or
- (*d.*) Any inquest on any death which occurred before the commencement of this Act or an inquisition found thereon, or any investigation, legal proceeding, or remedy in respect of any such right, privilege, obligation, liability, penalty, forfeiture, or punishment as aforesaid; and any such inquest, investigation, legal proceeding, and remedy, and the trial of any such inquisition may be carried on as if this Act had not passed.

(4.) This repeal shall not revive any jurisdiction, office, duty, fee, franchise, liberty, custom, right, title, privilege, restriction, exemption, usage, practice, procedure, or other matter or thing not in force or existing at the passing of this Act.

(5.) Save in so far as is inconsistent with this Act, any principle or rule of law, or established jurisdiction, practice, or procedure, or existing usage, franchise, liberty, or custom, shall, notwithstanding the repeal of any enactment by this Act, remain in full force.

[Ss. 11, 14, Sch. 1, repealed by Local Government (England and Wales) Act, 1888 (51 & 52 Vict. c. 41, s. 5 (6)). Ss. 13 and 33 in part, repealed by Coroners Act, 1892 (55 & 56 Vict. c. 56, s. 2 and Sch.)]

made, or for which a separate overseer is or can be appointed.

The expression "the Lord Chancellor" means the Lord High Chancellor of Great Britain.

The expression "Registration Acts" means the Acts for the time being in force relating to the registration of deaths, inclusive of any enactment amending the same.

Temporary Provisions and Repeal.

Saving as to coroners' salaries and districts.

43. Nothing in this Act shall affect the law respecting the salaries of coroners for counties[1], or the division of a county into coroners' districts, or the rights and duties of coroners as respects such districts.[2]

Abolition of certain jurisdictions of the coroner.

44. A coroner shall not take pleas of the Crown nor hold inquests of royal fish nor of wreck nor of felonies except felonies on inquisitions of death[3]; and he shall not inquire of the goods of such as by the inquest are found guilty of murder or manslaughter, nor cause them to be valued and delivered to the township.

Repeal of Acts in schedule.

45. The Acts specified in the Third Schedule to this Act are hereby repealed, from and after the passing of this Act, to the extent specified in the third column of that schedule.

Provided that—

(1.) A coroner elected before the passing of this Act, shall continue to hold office in like manner as if he had been elected under this Act, and

(2.) Any schedule of fees, allowances, and disbursements made by a local authority for a county or borough before the passing of this Act shall,

---

[1] *Vide* 23 & 24 Vict. c. 116, s. 4, which provides for payment by salary in lieu of fees.

[2] *Vide* 7 & 8 Vict. c. 92.

[3] This, as to felonies, affirms the law, previously doubtful, as laid down in *Reg.* v. *Herford*, 29 L.J. Q.B. 249, where it was held that the coroner could not hold inquisitions in case of fire.

until a schedule had been made in pursuance of this Act, and

(3.) This repeal shall not affect—

- (*a.*) The past operation of any enactment hereby repealed, nor anything duly done or suffered under any enactment hereby repealed; or
- (*b.*) Any right, privilege, obligation, or liability acquired, accrued, or incurred under any enactment hereby repealed; or
- (*c.*) Any penalty, forfeiture, or punishment incurred in respect of any offence committed against any enactment hereby repealed; or
- (*d.*) Any inquest on any death which occurred before the commencement of this Act or an inquisition found thereon, or any investigation, legal proceeding, or remedy in respect of any such right, privilege, obligation, liability, penalty, forfeiture, or punishment as aforesaid; and any such inquest, investigation, legal proceeding, and remedy, and the trial of any such inquisition may be carried on as if this Act had not passed.

(4.) This repeal shall not revive any jurisdiction, office, duty, fee, franchise, liberty, custom, right, title, privilege, restriction, exemption, usage, practice, procedure, or other matter or thing not in force or existing at the passing of this Act.

(5.) Save in so far as is inconsistent with this Act, any principle or rule of law, or established jurisdiction, practice, or procedure, or existing usage, franchise, liberty, or custom, shall, notwithstanding the repeal of any enactment by this Act, remain in full force.

[Ss. 11, 14, Sch. 1, repealed by Local Government (England and Wales) Act, 1888 (51 & 52 Vict. c. 41, s. 5 (6)). Ss. 13 and 33 in part, repealed by Coroners Act, 1892 (55 & 56 Vict. c. 56, s. 2 and Sch.)]

SCHEDULES.

FIRST SCHEDULE.

Sections 14, 37.

Rules for Election of Coroner.

(1.) The sheriff shall hold a court for the election at some convenient place appointed by him within the county, or, in a county divided into districts, within the district for which the election is to take place, on such day not less than seven nor more than fourteen days after the receipt of the writ as he appoints.

(2.) If a poll is demanded the sheriff shall adjourn the court to eight o'clock in the morning of the next day but one, unless such next day but one is Saturday or Sunday, and then of the Monday following.

(3.) The sheriff with such others as are deputed by him shall then and there proceed to take a poll in some public place or places, which shall be the place appointed for holding the court for the election, or such other places within the same county or district (as the case may be) as may be from time to time appointed by the quarter sessions, and such poll shall continue for one day only for eight hours, and no poll shall be kept open later than four o'clock in the afternoon.

(4.) The sheriff or sheriff's deputy may, if required by or on behalf of any candidate on or before the day fixed for the election, or if he deem it expedient, cause booths to be erected for taking the poll at the several polling places, and shall cause to be affixed on the most conspicuous part of the booth the names of the parishes to which such booth is allotted.

(5.) Where a booth is allotted to any parish a person shall not be admitted to vote in respect of any property situate in that parish except at that booth.

(6.) Where there is no booth allotted to any parish, a person entitled to vote in respect of property situate therein shall vote at the place at which the court for the election is held.

(7.) The sheriff or such person as he deputes shall appoint such number of clerks as to him may seem meet and convenient for taking the poll, and those clerks shall take the poll in the presence of the sheriff or such person as he deputes, and before they begin to take the poll each clerk shall by the sheriff or such person as he deputes as aforesaid be sworn truly and indifferently to take the poll, and to set down the names of each elector, the place of his residence, and the person for whom he polls, and to poll no elector who is not sworn, if required to be sworn by either of the candidates, which oath the said sheriff or such person as he deputes may administer.

(8.) The sheriff shall appoint for each candidate such one person

THE STATUTES. 247

as is nominated to him by each candidate to be an inspector of every clerk who is appointed for taking the poll.

(9.) *Every elector before he is admitted to poll at an election, shall if required by or on behalf of any candidate, first take the oath following, which the sheriff or any such sworn clerk as aforesaid may administer, that is to say:—I swear* [or *solemnly declare,* as the case may be] *that I am a freeholder of the county of   , and have a freehold estate consisting of   , lying at   , in the parish of   , within the said county, and that such freehold estate has not been granted to me fraudulently or colourably on purpose to qualify me to give my vote at this election, and that the place of my abode is at   ,* [and if it be a place consisting of more streets or places than one, specifying what street or place,] *that I am twenty-one years of age, as I believe, and that I have not voted before at this election.*

(10.) *The poll clerks shall at the close of the poll, enclose and seal their several books, and deliver them so enclosed and sealed to the sheriff or sheriff's deputy presiding at the poll, who shall give a receipt for the same.*

(11.) *Where the deputy receives them, he shall forthwith deliver or transmit them so enclosed and sealed to the sheriff.*

(12.) *The sheriff shall receive and keep all the poll books unopened until the re-assembling of the court on the day next but one after the close of the poll, unless that day be Sunday, and then on the Monday following, and on that day he shall openly break the seals thereon, and count the votes appearing in the said books, and openly delare the said poll, and make proclamation of the person chosen not later than two o'clock in the afternoon of the said day.*

(13.) *In these rules the expression " sheriff " includes " undersheriff."* [Repealed by sect. 5 of the Local Government Act, 1888.]

SECOND SCHEDULE.

FORMS.[1]

[*Form of Declaration of Office of Coroner.*]

Sections 18, 37.

I solemnly, sincerely, and truly declare and affirm that I will well and truly serve our Sovereign Lady the Queen and her liege people in the office of coroner for this county [*or* borough *or as the case may be*] of   , and that I will diligently and truly do everything appertaining to my office after the best of my power for the doing of right, and for the good of the inhabitants within the said county [*or* borough *or as the case may be*].

---

[1] These forms were not in the repealed Acts.

the district is partly within and partly without the county of London, shall be apportioned between the counties in which such district is situate.

(2.) In the case of any coroner's district being situate partly within and partly without the county of London, the county councils of the counties in which such district is situate shall arrange for the alteration in manner provided by law of the district, so that on the next avoidance of the office of coroner, or any earlier date fixed when the alteration is made, the coroners districts shall not be situate in more than one county.

(3.) For the purposes of this Act respecting compensation, the coroners shall be deemed to be officers of the quarter sessions of the county for which they are coroners.

---

51 & 52 VICT. c. 46.

OATHS ACT, 1888.

An Act to amend the Law as to Oaths.

[24th December 1888.]

Be it enacted by the Queen's most Excellent Majesty, by and with the advice and consent of the Lords Spiritual and Temporal, and Commons, in this present Parliament assembled, and by the authority of the same, as follows:

When affirmation may be made instead of oath.

1. Every person upon objecting to being sworn, and stating, as the ground of such objection, either that he has no religious belief, or that the taking of an oath is contrary to his religious belief, shall be permitted to make his solemn affirmation instead of taking an oath in all places and for all purposes where an oath is or shall be required by law, which affirmation shall be of the same force and effect as if he had taken the oath; and if any person making such affirmation shall wilfully, falsely, and corruptly affirm any matter or thing which, if deposed on oath, would have amounted to wilful and corrupt perjury, he shall be liable to prosecution, indictment, sentence, and punishment in all

respects as if he had committed wilful and corrupt perjury.

2. Every such affirmation shall be as follows: *Form of affirmation.*

"I, A.B., do solemnly sincerely, and truly declare and affirm," and then proceed with the words of the oath prescribed by law, omitting any words of imprecation or calling to witness.

3. Where an oath has been duly administered and taken, the fact that the person to whom the same was administered had, at the time of taking such oath, no religious belief, shall not for any purpose affect the validity of such oath. *Validity of oath not affected by absence of religious belief.*

4. Every affirmation in writing shall commence "I,   , of   , do solemnly and sincerely affirm," and the form in lieu of jurat shall be "Affirmed at   this   day of   , 18 , Before me." *Form of affirmation in writing.*

5. If any person to whom an oath is administered desires to swear with uplifted hand, in the form and manner in which an oath is usually administered in Scotland, he shall be permitted so to do, and the oath shall be administered to him in such form and manner without further question. *Swearing with uplifted hand.*

6. The Acts mentioned in the schedule to this Act are hereby repealed to the extent in the third column of the schedule mentioned. *Repeal.*

7. This Act may be cited as the Oaths Act, 1888. *Short title.*

SCHEDULE.

Session and Chapter.	Title.	Extent of Repeal.
17 & 18 Vict. c. 125	The Common Law Procedure Act, 1854.	Section twenty.
19 & 20 Vict. c. 102	The Common Law Procedure Amendment Act (Ireland), 1856.	Sections twenty-three and twenty-four.
24 & 25 Vict. c. 66	An Act to give relief to persons who may refuse or be unwilling, from alleged conscientious motives, to be sworn in criminal proceedings.	The entire Act.
28 & 29 Vict. c. 9	The Affirmation (Scotland) Act, 1865.	The entire Act.
30 & 31 Vict. c. 35	An Act to remove some defects in the administration of the Criminal Law.	Section eight.
31 & 32 Vict. c. 39	The Jurors Affirmation (Scotland) Act, 1868.	The entire Act.
31 & 32 Vict. c. 75	The Juries Act (Ireland), 1868.	Section three.
32 & 33 Vict. c. 68	The Evidence Further Amendment Act, 1869.	Section four.
33 & 34 Vict. c. 49	The Evidence Amendment Act, 1870.	The entire Act.

---

53 VICT. c. 5.

LUNACY ACT, 1890.

An Act to consolidate certain of the Enactments respecting Lunatics. [29th March 1890.]

Inquiry into Cause of Death.

Coroner to inquire into death, if necessary.

84. Every coroner shall upon receiving notice of the death of a lunatic within his district, if he considers that

any reasonable suspicion attends the cause and circumstances of the death, summon a jury to inquire into the same.

319. If the manager of an institution for lunatics, or the person having charge of a single patient, omits to send to the coroner notice of the death of a lunatic within the prescribed time, he shall be guilty of a misdemeanor. *Notice to coroner of death.*

---

53 & 54 VICT. c. 248.

LONDON COUNCIL (GENERAL POWERS) ACT, 1890.

An Act to confer further powers on the London County Council for the acquisition and maintenance of Parks and Open Spaces and as to local management and procedure and to make various provisions with regard to Buildings and Streets in the Administrative County of London. [18th August 1890.]

Mortuary for Unidentified Bodies.

22. It shall be lawful for the Council to provide and fit up within the administrative county of London one or two suitable place or places to which dead bodies found within the administrative county and not identified together with any clothing articles and other things found with or on such dead bodies may on the order of a coroner be removed and in which they may be retained and preserved with a view to the ultimate identification of such dead bodies Her Majesty's Secretary of State for the Home Department may from time to time make regulations as to— *Mortuary.*

> The manner in which and conditions subject to which any such bodies shall be removed to any such place and the payments to be made at such place to persons bringing any unidentified dead body for reception;
> The fees and charges to be paid upon the removal or

interment of any such dead body which shall have been identified after its reception and the persons by whom such fees and payments shall be made and the manner and the method of recovering the same;

The disposal and interment of any such bodies;

And the Council may provide at such place or places all such appliances as they may think expedient for the reception and preservation of bodies and may make such regulations as they think fit subject to the provisions aforesaid as to the management of the said places and bodies therein and as to the conduct of persons employed therein or resorting thereto for the purpose of identifying any body and any expenses of the Council arising under any of the provisions of this section shall be defrayed as a payment for general county purposes out of the county fund.

Subject to and in accordance with such regulations as may be made by Her Majesty's Secretary of State for the Home Department any such body found within the administrative county may (on the order in writing of the coroner holding or having jurisdiction to hold the inquest on the same) be removed to any place provided under this section and subject as aforesaid the inquest on any such body shall be held by the same coroner and in the same manner as if no order for its removal had been made except that it may be had either in the district in which the body was found or at the place to which it has been removed or partly in such district and partly at such place. [Repealed by Public Health (London) Act, 1891 (54 & 55 Vict. c. 76, s. 142, and Sch. 4.).]

54 & 55 VICT. c. 75.

FACTORY AND WORKSHOP ACT, 1891.

An Act to amend the Law relating to Factories and Workshops. [5th August 1891.]

22.—(3.) Where a death has occurred by accident in any factory or workshop, the coroner shall forthwith advise the district inspector under this Act of the time and place of the holding of the inquest, and at such inquest any relative of any person whose death may have been caused by the accident with respect to which the inquest it being held, and any inspector under the principal Act, and the occupier of the factory or workshop in which the accident occurred, and any person appointed by the order in writing of the majority of the workpeople employed in the said factory or workshop shall be at liberty to attend and examine any witness either in person or by his counsel, solicitor, or agent, subject nevertheless to the order of the coroner.

Amendment of 41 & 42 Vict. c. 16, s. 81, as to notice of accidents.

---

54 & 55 VICT. c. 76.

PUBLIC HEALTH (LONDON) ACT, 1891.

An Act to consolidate and amend the Laws relating to Public Health in London. [5th August 1891.]

Mortuaries, &c.

88. Every sanitary authority shall provide and fit up a proper place for the reception of dead bodies before interment (in this Act called a mortuary), and may make byelaws with respect to the management and charges for the use of the same; they may also provide for the decent and economical interment, at charges to be fixed by such byelaws, of any dead body received into a mortuary.

Power of local authority to provide mortuaries.

89.—(1.) Where either—
   (a.) the body of a person who has died of any

Power of justice in certain cases

to order removal of dead body to mortuary.

infectious disease is retained in a room in which persons live or sleep; or

(b.) the body of a person who has died of any dangerous infectious disease is retained without the sanction of the medical officer of health or any legally qualified medical practitioner for more than forty-eight hours, elsewhere than in a room not used at the time as a dwelling-place, sleeping-place, or work-room; or

(c.) any dead body is retained in any house or room, so as to endanger the health of the inmates thereof, or of any adjoining or neighbouring house or building,

a justice may, on a certificate signed by a medical officer of health or other legally qualified medical practitioner, direct that the body be removed, at the cost of the sanitary authority, to any available mortuary, and be buried within the time limited by the justice; and may if it is the body of a person who has died of an infectious disease, or if he considers immediate burial necessary, direct that the body be buried immediately, without removal to the mortuary.

(2.) Unless the friends or relations of the deceased undertake to bury and do bury the body within the time so limited, it shall be the duty of the relieving officer to bury such body, and any expense so incurred shall be paid (in the first instance) by the board of guardians of the poor law union, but may be recovered by them in a summary manner from any person legally liable to pay the expense of such burial.

(3.) If any person obstructs the execution of any direction given by a justice under this section, he shall be liable to a fine not exceeding five pounds.

Power of sanitary authority to provide places for post-mortem examinations.

90.—(1.) Any sanitary authority may, and if required by the county council shall, provide and maintain a proper building (otherwise than at a workhouse) for the reception of dead bodies during the time required to conduct any post-mortem examination ordered by a coroner or other constituted authority, and may make regulations with respect to the management of such building.

(2.) Any such building may be provided in connexion with a mortuary, but this enactment shall not authorise the conducting of any post-mortem examination in a mortuary.

91. Any sanitary authorities may, with the approval of the county council, execute their duty under this Act with respect to mortuaries and buildings for post-mortem examinations by combining for the purpose thereof, or by contracting for the use by one of the contracting authorities of any such mortuary or building provided by another of such contracting authorities, and may so combine or contract upon such terms as may be agreed upon. *Power to sanitary authorities to unite for providing mortuary.*

92. The county council shall provide and maintain proper accommodation for the holding of inquests, and may by agreement with a sanitary authority provide and maintain the same in connexion with a mortuary or a building for post-mortem examinations provided by that authority, or with any building belonging to that authority, and may do so on such terms as may be agreed on with the authority. *Place for holding inquests.*

93.—(1.) The county council may provide and fit up in London one or two suitable buildings to which dead bodies found in London and not identified, together with any clothing, articles, and other things found with or on such dead bodies, may on the order of a coroner be removed, and in which they may be retained and preserved with a view to the ultimate identification of such dead bodies. *Mortuary for unidentified bodies.*

(2.) A Secretary of State may make regulations as to—

(a.) the manner in which and conditions subject to which any such bodies shall be removed to any such building, and the payments to be made at such building to persons bringing any unidentified dead body for reception; and

(b.) the fees and charges to be paid upon the removal or interment of any such dead body which has been identified after its reception and the persons by whom such fees and payments are to be made, and the manner and method of recovering the same; and

(c.) the disposal and interment of any such bodies.

(3.) The county council may provide at the said buildings all such appliances as they think expedient for the reception and preservation of bodies, and make regulations (subject to the provisions aforesaid) as to the management of the said buildings and the bodies therein, and as to the conduct of persons employed therein or resorting thereto for the purpose of identifying any body.

(4.) Subject to and in accordance with such regulations as may be made by a Secretary of State, any such body found in London may (on the order in writing of a coroner holding or having jurisdiction to hold the inquest on the same) be removed to any building provided under this section, and subject as aforesaid the inquest on any such body shall be held by the same coroner and in the same manner as if the said building were within the district of such coroner.

---

55 & 56 VICT. c. 56.

CORONERS ACT, 1892.

An Act to amend the Law in relation to the Appointment of Coroners and Deputy Coroners in Counties and Boroughs. [28th June 1892.]

Be it enacted by the Queen's most Excellent Majesty, by and with the advice and consent of the Lords Spiritual and Temporal, and Commons, in this present Parliament assembled, and by the authority of the same, as follows:

Appointment and powers of a deputy coroner of both a county and a borough.

1.—(1.) Every coroner, whether for a county or a borough, shall appoint[1] by writing under his hand, a fit

[1] It seems that by these words an immediate obligation is imposed on every coroner to appoint a deputy, as was the case with county coroners under section 13 of the Act of 1887, whereas borough coroners, under section 172 of the Municipal Corporations Act, 1882, were bound only to appoint deputies in case of sickness, etc.

person approved by the chairman[1] or mayor, as the case may be, of the council who appointed the coroner, not being an alderman or councillor of such council,[2] to be his deputy, and may revoke such appointment, but such revocation shall not take effect until the appointment of another deputy has been approved as aforesaid.

(2.) A duplicate of every appointment shall be sent to the said council and be kept among the records of the county or borough, as the case may be.

(3.) A deputy may act for the coroner during his illness or during his absence for any lawful or reasonable cause, or at any inquest which the coroner is disqualified for holding, but not otherwise. In the case of a borough coroner the necessity of his so acting shall be certified on each occasion by a justice of the peace, and such certificate shall state the cause of absence of the coroner, be openly read to every inquest jury summoned by the deputy coroner, and be conclusive evidence of the jurisdiction of the deputy to act.[3]

(4.) The deputy of a coroner shall, notwithstanding the coroner vacates his office by death or otherwise, continue in office until a new deputy is appointed, and shall act as the coroner while the office is so vacant in like manner as during the illness of the coroner, and one certificate may extend to the period of the vacancy, and he shall be entitled to receive in respect of the period of the vacancy the like remuneration as the vacating coroner.[4]

(5.) For the purpose of an inquest or act which a deputy of a coroner is authorised to hold or do, he shall be deemed to be that coroner, and have the same jurisdiction and powers and be subject to the same obligations, liabilities, and disqualifications as that coroner, and he

---

[1] Under the Act of 1887, section 18, the deputy, in the case of a county, had to be approved by the Lord Chancellor.

[2] This repeals the law before the Act, except that by section 172 of the Act of 1882, the deputy, in a borough, had to be either a barrister or solicitor.

[3] Sub-section 3 is taken from section 13 of the Act of 1887, and section 172 of the Act of 1882.

[4] Sub-section 4 is apparently new.

shall generally be subject to the provisions of the Coroners Act, 1887,[1] and to the law relating to coroners in like manner as that coroner.

(6.) A council may postpone the appointment of a coroner to fill a vacancy, either generally or in any particular case, for a period not exceeding three months from the date at which that vacancy occurs.

(7.) For the purposes of this section the council who appointed a coroner shall—

    (a) where the coroner was, in pursuance of any section of the Local Government Act, 1888,[2] appointed by or on the recommendation of a joint committee, be deemed to be any of the councils who appointed any members of that committee; and,

    (b) where a coroner for a district of a county is, in pursuance of sub-section four of section thirty-four of the Local Government Act, 1888, appointed by the council of any county boroug be deemed to be that council.

(8,) In the case of a county coroner who has been elected before the date on which the provisions of the Local Government Act, 1888, as to the appointment of coroners came into force, the council of any county or county borough in which the district of the coroner is wholly or partially situated, shall for the purposes of this section be deemed to be the council who appointed the coroner.

Repeal. 2. The Acts specified in the schedule to this Act are hereby repealed to the extent in the third column of that schedule mentioned.

Construction of Act and short title. 3. This Act shall be construed as one with the Coroners Act, 1887, and this Act and that Act may be cited together as the Coroners Act, 1887 and 1892, and this Act may be cited separately as the Coroners Act, 1892.

[1] 50 & 51 Vict. c. 71.   [2] 51 & 52 Vict. c. 41.

SCHEDULE.

Session and Chapter.	Short Title.	Extent of Repeal.
45 & 46 Vict. c. 50[1]	The Municipal Corporations Act, 1882.	Section one hundred and seventy-two.
50 & 51 Vict. c. 71[2]	The Coroners Act, 1887.	Section thirteen, and in section thirty-three the words "and the appointment of a deputy by such coroner."

---

60 & 61 VICT. c. 89.

YORKSHIRE CORONERS ACT, 1897.

An Act to constitute the Ridings of Yorkshire separate Counties for all the purposes of the Coroners Acts.

[6th August 1897.]

Be it enacted by the Queen's most Excellent Majesty, by and with the advice and consent of the Lords Spiritual and Temporal, and Commons, in this present Parliament assembled, and by the authority of the same, as follows:—

1. For all the purposes of the Coroners Acts, 1844, 1860, 1887, and 1892, the ridings of Yorkshire shall respectively be separate counties, and the county council of each riding shall, to the exclusion of any other authority, be the county authority for all the purposes of those Acts:

Ridings of Yorkshire to be separate counties in respect of the Coroners Acts.

Provided that nothing in this section shall affect the

---

[1] By section 172 the coroner for a borough was directed to appoint as deputy in case of illness, etc., a fit person being a barrister or solicitor, and not an alderman, etc.

[2] By section 18 a coroner for a county was directed to appoint from time to time as deputy a fit person approved by the Lord Chancellor.

alteration in manner provided by section five, subsection three, of the Local Government Act, 1888, of the district of any coroner which is at the commencement of this Act situate partly in one and partly in another of the ridings.

51 & 52 Vict. c. 41.

Rights of existing county coroners.

2. Nothing herein contained shall affect the rights, duties, powers, or liabilities of any county coroner holding office at the commencement of this Act, and if the district of any such coroner is divided into two or more districts, residence in any one of such districts shall be deemed to comply with section five of the Coroners Act, 1844.

7 & 8 Vict. c. 92.

Commencement of Act.

3. This Act shall come into operation on the first day of April, one thousand eight hundred and ninety-eight.

Short title.

4. This Act may be cited as the Yorkshire Coroners Act, 1897.

---

60 & 61 VICT. c. 57.

INFANT LIFE PROTECTION ACT, 1897.

An Act to amend the Law for the better Protection of Infant Life. [6th August 1897.]

Be it enacted as follows:

Notice to coroner.

8. In case of the death of any infant respecting whom notice is required under this Act, the person having the care of such infant shall, within twenty-four hours of such death, cause notice thereof to be given to the coroner of the district within which the body of such infant lies, and the coroner shall hold an inquest thereon, unless a certificate under the hand of a registered medical practitioner shall be produced to him, certifying that such registered medical practitioner has personally attended or examined such infant, and specifying the cause of its death, and the coroner shall be satisfied by such certificate that there is no ground for holding such inquest. If the person having the care of such infant shall neglect to give the notice in this section mentioned he shall be guilty of an offence against this Act.

62 & 63 VICT. c. 48.

LINCOLNSHIRE CORONERS ACT, 1899.

An Act to constitute the Divisions of Lincolnshire separate Counties for all the purposes of the Coroners Acts.

[9th August 1899.]

Be it enacted by the Queen's most Excellent Majesty, by and with the advice and consent of the Lords Spiritual and Temporal, and Commons in this present Parliament assembled, and by the authority of the same, as follows:—

1. For all the purposes of the Coroners Acts, 1844, 1860, 1887, and 1892, the divisions of Lincolnshire shall respectively be separate counties, and the County Council of each division shall, to the exclusion of any other authority, be the local authority for all the purposes of those Acts. *Divisions of Lincolnshire to be separate counties in respect of Coroners Acts.*

Provided that nothing in this section shall affect the alteration in manner provided by section five subsection three of the Local Government Act, 1888, of the district of any coroner which is at the commencement of this Act, situate partly in one and partly in another of the divisions. *51 & 52 Vict. c. 41.*

2. Nothing herein contained shall affect the rights, duties, powers, or liabilities of any county coroner in Lincolnshire holding office at the commencement of this Act. *Saving rights of existing coroners.*

3. This Act shall come into operation on the first day of January one thousand nine hundred. *Commencement of Act.*

4. This Act may be cited as the Lincolnshire Coroners Act, 1899. *Short title.*

1 EDW. VII. c. 22.

FACTORY AND WORKSHOP ACT, 1901.

An Act to consolidate with Amendments the Factory and Workshop Acts. [17th August 1901.]

Be it enacted as follows :—

Inquest in case of death by accident in factory or workshop.

21.—(1.) Where a death has occurred by accident in a factory or workshop, the coroner shall forthwith advise the district inspector of the time and place of holding the inquest, and, unless an inspector or some person on behalf of the Secretary of State is present to watch the proceedings, the coroner shall adjourn the inquest, and shall, at least four days before holding the adjourned inquest, send to the inspector notice in writing of the time and place of holding the adjourned inquest.

Provided that, if the accident has not occasioned the death of more than one person, and the coroner has sent to the inspector notice of the time and place of holding the inquest at such time as to reach the inspector not less than twenty-four hours before the time of holding the inquest, it shall not be imperative on him to adjourn the inquest in pursuance of this section, if the majority of the jury think it unnecessary so to adjourn.

(2.) Any relative of any person whose death may have been caused by the accident with respect to which the inquest is being held, and any inspector, and the occupier of the factory or workshop in which the accident occurred, and any person appointed by the order in writing of the majority of the workpeople employed in the factory or workshop, shall be at liberty to attend at the inquest, and, either in person or by his counsel, solicitor, or agent, to examine any witness, subject nevertheless to the order of the coroner.

SUPPLEMENTARY.

(i.) *Application and Definitions.*

Factories and workshops to which Act applies.

149.—(1.) Subject to the provisions of this section, the following expressions have in this Act the meanings hereby assigned to them; that is to say :—

The expression "textile factory" means any premises wherein or within the close or curtilage of which steam, water, or other mechanical power, is used to move or work any machinery employed in preparing, manufacturing, or finishing, or in any process incident to the manufacture of cotton, wool, hair, silk, flax, hemp, jute, tow, china-grass, cocoa-nut fibre, or other like material, either separately or mixed together, or mixed with any other material, or any fabric made thereof:

Provided that print works, bleaching and dyeing works, lace warehouses, paper mills, flax scutch mills, rope works, and hat works shall not be deemed to be textile factories:

The expression "non-textile factory" means—

(a) any works, warehouses, furnaces, mills, foundries, or places named in Part One of the Sixth Schedule to this Act; and

(b) any premises or places named in Part Two of the said schedule wherein or within the close or curtilage or precincts of which steam, water, or other mechanical power, is used in aid of the manufacturing process carried on there; and

(c) any premises wherein or within the close or curtilage or precincts of which any manual labour is exercised by way of trade or for purposes of gain in or incidental to any of the following purposes, namely—

(i.) the making of any article or of part of any article; or

(ii.) the altering, reparing, ornamenting, or finishing of any article; or

(iii.) the adapting for sale of any article,

and wherein or within the close or curtilage or precincts of which steam, water, or other mechanical power is used in aid of the manufacturing process carried on there:

The expression "factory" means textile factory and non-textile factory, or either of those descriptions of factories:

The expression "tenement factory" means a factory where mechanical power is supplied to different parts of the same building occupied by different persons for the purpose of any manufacturing process or handicraft, in such manner that those parts constitute in law separate factories, and for the purpose of the provisions of this Act with respect to tenement factories all buildings situate within the same close or curtilage shall be treated as one building:

The expression "workshop" means—

(a) any premises or places named in Part Two of the Sixth Schedule to this Act, which are not a factory; and

(b) any premises, room, or place, not being a factory, in which premises, room, or place, or within the close or curtilage or precincts of which premises, any manual labour is exercised by way of trade or for purposes of gain in or incidental to any of the following purposes, namely—

(i.) the making of any article or of part of any article, or

(ii.) the altering, repairing, ornamenting, or finishing of any article; or

(iii.) the adapting for sale of any article,

and to or over which premises, room, or place the employer of the persons working therein has the right of access or control:

The expression "workshop" includes a tenement workshop:

The expression "tenement workshop" means any workplace in which, with the permission of or under agreement with the owner or occupier, two or more persons carry on any work which would constitute the workplace a workshop if the persons working therein were in the employment of the owner or occupier.

(2.) A part of a factory or workshop may, with the approval in writing of the chief inspector, be taken for the purposes of this Act, to be a separate factory or workshop.

(3.) A room solely used for the purpose of sleeping therein shall not be deemed to form part of the factory or workshop for the purposes of this Act.

(4.) Where a place situate within the close, curtilage, or precincts forming a factory or workshop is solely used for some purpose other than the manufacturing process or handicraft carried on in the factory or workshop, that place shall not be deemed to form part of the factory or workshop for the purposes of this Act, but shall, if otherwise it would be a factory or workshop, be deemed to be a separate factory or workshop, and be regulated accordingly.

(5.) A place or premises shall not be excluded from the definition of a factory or workshop by reason only that the place or premises is or are in the open air.

(6.) The exercise by any young person or child in any recognised efficient school, during a portion of the school hours, of any manual labour for the purpose of instructing the young person or child in any art or handicraft shall not be deemed to be an exercise of manual labour for the purpose of gain within the meaning of this Act.

SIXTH SCHEDULE.

LIST OF FACTORIES AND WORKSHOPS.   Sections 54, 149, 156.

PART I.

Non-Textile Factories.

(1.) "Print works," that is to say, any premises in which any persons are employed to print figures, patterns, or designs upon any cotton, linen, woollen, worsted, or silken yarn, or upon any woven or felted fabric not being paper;   "Print works."

(2.) "Bleaching and dyeing works," that is to say, any premises in which the processes of bleaching, beetling, dyeing, calendering, finishing, hooking, lapping, and making up and packing any yarn or cloth of any material, or the dressing or finishing of lace, or any one or more of such processes, or any process incidental thereto, are or is carried on;   "Bleaching and dyeing works."

(3.) "Earthenware works," that is to say, any place in which persons work for hire in making or assisting in making, finishing,   "Earthenware works."

or assisting in finishing, earthenware or china of any description, except bricks and tiles not being ornamental tiles;

"Lucifer-match works." (4.) "Lucifer-match works," that is to say, any place in which persons work for hire in making lucifer matches, or in mixing the chemical materials for making them, or in any process incidental to making lucifer matches, except the cutting of the wood;

"Percussion-cap works." (5.) "Percussion-cap works," that is to say, any place in which persons work for hire in making percussion caps, or in mixing or storing the chemical materials for making them, or in any process incidental to making percussion caps;

"Cartridge works." (6.) "Cartridge works," that is to say, any place in which persons work for hire in making cartridges, or in any process incidental to making cartridges, except the manufacture of the paper or other material that is used in making the cases of the cartridges;

"Paper-staining works." (7.) "Paper-staining works," that is to say, any place in which persons work for hire in printing a pattern in colours upon sheets of paper, either by blocks applied by hand, or by rollers worked by steam, water, or other mechanical power;

"Fustian-cutting works." (8.) "Fustian-cutting works," that is to say, any place in which persons work for hire in fustian cutting;

"Blast furnaces." (9.) "Blast furnaces," that is to say, any blast furnace or other furnace or premises in or on which the process of smelting or otherwise obtaining any metal from the ores is carried on;

"Copper mills." (10.) "Copper mills";

"Iron mills." (11.) "Iron mills," that is to say, any mill, forge, or other premises, in or on which any process is carried on for converting iron into malleable iron, steel, or tin plate, or for otherwise making or converting steel;

"Foundries." (12.) "Foundries," that is to say, iron foundries, copper foundries, brass foundries, and other premises or places in which the process of founding or casting any metal is carried on; except any premises or places in which such process is carried on by not more than five persons and as subsidiary to the repair or completion of some other work;

"Metal and india-rubber works." (13.) "Metal and india-rubber works," that is to say, any premises in which steam, water, or other mechanical power is used for moving machinery employed in the manufacture of machinery, or in the manufacture of any article of metal not being machinery, or in the manufacture of india-rubber or gutta-percha, or of articles made wholly or partially of india-rubber or gutta-percha;

"Paper mills." (14.) "Paper mills," that is to say, any premises in which the manufacture of paper is carried on;

"Glass works." (15.) "Glass works," that is to say, any premises in which the manufacture of glass is carried on;

"Tobacco factories." (16.) "Tobacco factories," that is to say, any premises in which the manufacture of tobacco is carried on;

(17.) "Letter-press printing works," that is to say, any premises in which the process of letter-press printing is carried on;

(18.) "Bookbinding works," that is to say, any premises in which the process of bookbinding is carried on;

(19.) "Flax scutch mills";

(20.) "Electrical stations," that is to say, any premises or that part of any premises in which electrical energy is generated or transformed for the purpose of supply by way of trade, or for the lighting of any street, public place, or public building, or of any hotel, or of any railway, mine, or other industrial undertaking.

Part II.

Non-Textile Factories and Workshops.

(21.) "Hat works," that is to say, any premises in which the manufacture of hats or any process incidental to their manufacture is carried on;

(22.) "Rope works," that is to say, any premises being a ropery, ropewalk, or rope work, in which is carried on the laying or twisting or other process of preparing or finishing the lines, twines, cords, or ropes, and in which machinery moved by steam, water, or other mechanical power is not used for drawing or spinning the fibres of flax, hemp, jute, or tow, and which has no internal communication with any buildings or premises joining or forming part of a textile factory, except such communication as is necessary for the transmission of power;

(23.) "Bakehouses," that is to say, any places in which are baked bread, biscuits, or confectionery from the baking or selling of which a profit is derived;

(24.) "Lace warehouses," that is to say, any premises, room, or place not included in bleaching and dyeing works as hereinbefore defined, in which persons are employed upon any manufacturing process or handicraft in relation to lace, subsequent to the making of lace upon a lace machine moved by steam, water, or other mechanical power;

(25.) "Shipbuilding yards," that is to say, any premises in which any ships, boats, or vessels used in navigation, are made, finished or repaired;

(26.) "Quarries," that is to say, any place not being a mine, in which persons work in getting slate, stone, coprolites or other minerals;

(27.) "Pit-banks," that is to say, any place above ground adjacent to a shaft of a mine, in which place the employment of women is not regulated by the Coal Mines Regulation Act, 1887, or the Metalliferous Mines Regulation Act, 1872, whether such place does or does not form part of the mine within the meaning of those Acts.

(28.) Dry cleaning, carpet beating, and bottle washing works.

2 EDW. VII. c. 8.

THE CREMATION ACT, 1902.

An Act for the regulation of the burning of Human Remains, and to enable Burial Authorities to establish Crematoria. [22nd July 1902.]

Be it enacted as follows:—

Regulations as to burning. 7. The Secretary of State shall make regulations as to the maintenance and inspection of crematoria and prescribing in what cases and under what conditions the burning of any human remains may take place, and directing the disposition or interment of the ashes, and prescribing the forms of the notices, certificates and declarations to be given or made before any such burning is permitted to take place, such declarations to be made under and by virtue of the Statutory Declarations Act, 5 & 6 Will. 4, 1835, and also regulations as to the registration of such c. 62. burnings as have taken place, &c.

Saving for coroners. 10. Nothing in this Act shall interfere with the juris-50 & 51 Vict. diction of any coroner under the Coroners Act, 1887, or c. 71. any Act amending the same, and nothing in this Act shall authorise the burial authority or any person to create or permit a nuisance.

Extent of Act. 16. This Act shall not apply to Ireland.

STATUTORY RULES AND ORDERS, 1903.
No. 286.

CREMATION, ENGLAND AND WALES.

Regulations made by the Secretary of State for the Home Department, dated March 31, 1903, under Section 7 of the Cremation Act, 1902.

I hereby, in pursuance of Section 7 of the Cremation Act, 1902, make the following regulations:—

Definitions.

"Cremation authority" means any burial authority or any company or person by whom a crematorium has been established.

8. No cremation shall be allowed to take place unless
- (a.) A certificate in Form B be given by a registered medical practitioner who has attended the deceased during his last illness and who can certify definitely as to the cause of death, and a confirmatory medical certificate in Form C be given by another medical practitioner, who must be qualified as prescribed in Regulation 9; *or*
- (b.) A post-mortem examination has been made by a medical practitioner expert in pathology, appointed by the Cremation Authority (or in case of emergency appointed by the Medical Referee), and a certificate given by him in Form D; *or*
- (c.) An inquest has been held and a certificate has been given by the coroner in Form E.

SCHEDULE.

Form E.

Coroner's Certificate.

I certify that I held an inquest on the body of
and that the verdict of the Jury was as follows:—
Medical evidence was given by
I am satisfied from the evidence that the cause of death was
and that no circumstance exists which could render necessary any further examination of the remains or any analysis of any part of the body.

(*Date*)

Coroner.

2 EDW. VII. c. 28.

LICENSING ACT, 1902.

An Act to amend the Law relating to the Sale of Intoxicating Liquors and to Drunkenness, and to provide for the Registration of Clubs. [8th August 1902.]

Be it enacted as follows :—

Sessions not to be held in licensed premises.

21. From and after the thirty-first day of March one thousand nine hundred and seven, no meeting of justices in petty or special sessions shall be held in premises licensed for the sale of intoxicating liquors, or in any room, whether licensed or not, in any building licensed for the sale of intoxicating liquors; nor shall any coroner's inquest be held on such licensed premises where other suitable premises have been provided for such inquest.

THE JURIES ACT, 1870.

SCHEDULE.
(*Vide p.* 188.)

PERSONS EXEMPT FROM SERVING ON JURIES.

Peers.
Members of Parliament.
Judges.
Clergymen.
Roman Catholic priests.
Ministers of any congregation of Protestant dissenters and of Jews whose place of meeting is duly registered, provided they follow no secular occupation except that of a schoolmaster.
Serjeants, barristers-at-law, certificated conveyancers, and special pleaders, if actually practising.
Members of the Society of Doctors of Law and advocates of the civil law, if actually practising.
Attornies, solicitors, and proctors, if actually practising and having taken out their annual certificates, and their managing clerks, and notaries public in actual practice.

Officers of the courts of law and equity, and of the Admiralty and Ecclesiastical Courts, including therein the Courts of Probate and Divorce, and the clerks of the peace or their deputies, if actually exercising the duties of their respective offices.

Coroners.

Gaolers and keepers of houses of correction, and all subordinate officers of the same.

Keepers in public lunatic asylums.

Members and licentiates of the Royal College of Physicians in London, if actually practising as physicians.

Members of the Royal Colleges of Surgeons in London, Edinburgh, and Dublin, if actually practising as surgeons.

Apothecaries certificated by the Court of Examiners of the Apothecaries Company, and all registered medical practitioners and registered pharmaceutical chemists, if actually practising as apothecaries, medical practitioners, or pharmaceutical chemists respectively.

Officers of the navy, army, militia, and yeomanry while on full pay.[1]

The members of the Mersey Docks and Harbour Board.

The master, wardens, and brethren of the Corporation of Trinity House of Deptford Strond.

Pilots licensed by the Trinity House of Deptford Strond, Kingston-upon-Hull, or Newcastle-upon-Tyne, and all masters of vessels in the buoy and light service employed by either of those corporations, and all pilots licensed under any Act of Parliament or charter for the regulation of pilots.

The household servants of Her Majesty, Her heirs and successors.

Officers of the Post Office, Commissioners of Customs, and officers, clerks, or other persons acting in the management or collection of the Customs, Commissioners of Inland Revenue, and officers or persons appointed by the Commissioners of Inland Revenue or employed by them or under their authority or direction in any way relating to the duties of Inland Revenue.

Sheriffs officers.

Officers of the rural and metropolitan police.

Magistrates of the metropolitan police courts, their clerks, ushers, doorkeepers, and messengers.

Members of the council of the municipal corporation of any borough, and every justice of the peace assigned to keep the peace therein, and the town clerk and treasurer for the time being of every such borough, so far as relates to any jury summoned to serve in the county where such borough is situate.

---

[1] Also every soldier in His Majesty's regular forces. (*Vide* p. 211.)

Burgesses of every borough in and for which a separate court of quarter sessions shall be holden so far as relates to any jury summoned for the trial of issues joined in any court of general or quarter sessions of the peace in the county wherein such borough is situate.

Justices of the peace so far as relates to any jury summoned to serve at any sessions of the peace for the jurisdiction of which he is a justice.

Officers of the Houses of Lords and Commons.

INDEX.

	PAGE
ABJURING the realm. *See* Sanctuary.	
Accounts before Local Authority. Coroners to lay	286
Act 1887. Coroners	220–225
,, 1892. ,,	270–278
Admiralty	28
Affirmation. Form of	263
Antiquity of the office	1
Appointment of Coroner by County Council	259
Assessor to Coroner. Appointment of	189
Authority and duty	3
BAIL	82, 177, 228
Births. Registration of	117
Body. Burial of	118
Borough Coroner	29, 31, 124
Boroughs. Application of L. G. Act 1888 to County	260
Brightlingsea. Parish of	98, 99
Burial before registration of death	197
Burial order, or certificate, to whom to be delivered	210
CAPITAL punishment	187, 207
Certificates of cause of death	199
Chaucer	3
Chester. Coroners for	79, 133, 148
,, subject to general law	182
Cinque Ports. The	98, 125, 215
Coal mines. Inquests on deaths from accidents in	170–175
Committal to Central Criminal Court	212
Company." Meaning of words " Railway.	148
Coroner, a conservator of the peace	4
,, a justice of the peace	4
,, Authority of	3
,, Borough	30, 115, 116
,, County	30, 116

288 INDEX.

		PAGE
Coroner.	Duties of the	3, 6, 111, 150, 153
,,	,, ,, ,, County	179
,,	to act in other boroughs	116
,,	Election of	102, 154, 179
,,	in Wales. Election of	46
,,	Fees due to. *See* Payment.	
,,	not to act in prosecution or defence	226
,,	Office of (*de officio Coronatoris*)	89
,,	to hold inquest. Ordering of	223
,,	Payment of County	179
,,	Penalty for neglect	61, 71
,,	Qualification of	31, 59, 227
,,	Removal of	93
,,	Various names for	1
Coroners Act, 1887		220–255
,, ,, 1892		270–273
,, Kinds of		24
,, Rolls		18
,, Who shall be		38, 59
Correction of errors in registers		200
Corpse—present		204
County Coroner		29
,, Definition of		241
Cremation Act, 1902 (and Regulations)		282
Crown. Demise of the		5
" Pleas of the		1, 38, 57
Crowner		1
DEATHS. Registration of		117
Definitions in Coroners Act, 1887		243
Demise of the Crown		5
Denbigh. County of		79
Deodands		14, 150
,, abolished		169
De Officio Coronatoris		89
Depositions to be sent to Central Criminal Court		176
,, ,, ,, the Public Prosecutor		209
,, ,, supplied to prisoners		178
Deputy Coroner. Appointment of		227
,, ,, for County and Borough. Appointment and powers of		270 *et seq.*
Detached parts of Counties		149, 242
Disqualifications of Jurors		189
Drunkards Act. Habitual		208
Durham. Coroners of the county of		127–8
ELECTION of County Coroners		102, 119, 226, 228

INDEX.

	PAGE
Ely. Jurisdiction of	119
,, Coroner for	119
Essex. Coroners for	98, 99, 118
Evidence. Criminating	222
,, The Laws of	153
,, Register when not	201
Exeter. Statutes of	50
Explosives Act	203
FACTORY and Workshop Act, 1891	267
,, ,, ,, 1901	276
,, ,, Inquest in case of death by accident in	276
Falmouth Court of Quarter Sessions	186
Fees	68, 69, 92, 95
Fees and disbursements. Schedule of	285
Felo de se. Interment of	105, 218
Felony. Appeals of	10
Felons. Pursuit of	35
Fine on Coroner for neglect	226
Fire. Inquests on	225
Fish. Royal	8
Flintshire. County of	79
Form of declaration of office	247
Franchise Coroners	70, 78, 238
HALTON FEE. Lord of Manor of	147
Hand. Swearing with uplifted	263
Household. King's	74
,, Coroner of King's	84
,, Appointment of Coroner of King's	78, 237
INFANT Life Protection Act, 1872	189
,, ,, 1894	274
Inquests. Expenses of holding	129–132
,, Place of holding	269
,, necessary. A second	223–4
,, When to hold	220
Inquisition and Rolls	18, 96, 97
,, to be amended, not quashed, for defects	232
,, Form of	248 *et seq.*
,, etc. to be sent to Public Prosecutor	209
,, Quashing of	151, 221
,, Sealing of	21, 51
JURISDICTION	40, 224
Jurisdictions of coroners. Abolition of certain	244
Jurors. Attendance of	231

U

INDEX.

	PAGE
Jurors fined for non-attendance	109
Jury in early times	5, 60
,, Exemptions from serving on	106, 188, 284
,, of the King's Household	75
,, Qualification of	61-2, 109
KENT. Coroners of	100, 113
Knights of the shire	4, 31, 65
LANCASTER. County of	241
Langbaurgh. Wapentake of	194
Licensed premises. Inquests shall not be held in	284
Licensing Act, 1902	284
Lincolnshire Coroners Act, 1899	275
Local Authority. Definition of	242
London. City of	38, 289
Lunacy Act, 1890	264
MARSHALSEA	75
Medical witnesses. Attendance of	120
,, ,, Payment of	120, 123, 130
Military prisons	210
Mines. Inquests on deaths from accidents in	170, 184, 191, 192, 218
Mortuary. Early meaning of	204
Mortuaries	186, 265, 269
,, Power of Local Authorities to provide	204
Mortuary. Power of Justices to remove body to	268
,, for unidentified bodies	265, 269
Municipal Corporations Act, 1882	214
,, ,, ,, 1883	216
Murder	72, 75, 76, 78
,, or Manslaughter. Inquisition for	184
,, ,, Proceedings upon inquisition of	222
Murderers. Trial of	88
Murders. An Act against	64
OATH of Jury. Form of	248
Oaths Act, 1888	262
,, Validity of certain	132
Office. Duration of	5
PALACE. Precincts of the	27, 78
Payment of Coroners	68, 69, 90, 92, 95, 179
Pleas of the Crown	1, 33, 57
Post-mortem examinations	233
,, ,, Place for making	187, 205, 268
,, ,, Removal of body for	285

Prisoners. Inquest on bodies of	186, 207
,, to give evidence at inquest. Warrant to bring up	178
Proceedings at inquests	221, 229
Public Health Act, 1874	204
,, (London) Act, 1891	267
QUALIFICATION. Oath of	104
Qualifications of Coroner	31, 59, 227
,, Jurors	109
RAILWAY Accidents. Returns after	193
,, Meaning of the word	148
Rape. Appeals of	18
Recognizance. Fees on	229
Recognizances forfeited to be sent to clerk of peace	179
,, etc. to be sent to Public Prosecutor	209
Refuses to hold inquest. If Coroner	181, 228
Register when not evidence	201
Registration of burials	197
,, ,, deaths	197
Removal of body for post-mortem examination	235
,, ,, Coroner	182, 225, 240
Rolls. Coroners'	18, 49
,, Sealing of Coroners'	21, 51
SALARIES. Coroners'	244
Sanctuary	10, 47, 72, 84
Schedule of persons exempt from jury service	284
Schedules in Coroners Act, 1887	244–255
Sea. Reward for picking up dead bodies at	145
Seal of 14th century	(*frontispiece*)
,, ,, Description of	20
Sheriff. Coroner acting for	228
Soldiers. Exemption of	211
Stillborn. Burial of the	198
Surrey. Coroners in	114
TREASURE-TROVE	7, 55, 240
Twelve years of age. Attendance of those	85, 86
UNIDENTIFIED bodies. Mortuaries for	265, 269
VERGE. The	24, 25, 55, 56, 57, 58, 75
View of body. Inquest void without	221
WALES. Statutes of and coroners for	42–49, 71, 79
,, Election of Coroners for	46

Westminster. Good Government of	83
" Regulating proceedings at	85
Witnesses. Attendance of	231
" Not attending. Penalty on	235
" Binding	82
" Fees to	234
" " Medical	233
Workshop and Factory Act, 1891	267
Writ for choosing a coroner. The Form of	46
Wreck	8, 36, 88
YORK. Coroner for	119
" Jurisdiction of	119
Yorkshire Coroners Act, 1897	273

LONDON: PRINTED BY WILLIAM CLOWES AND SONS, LIMITED,
DUKE STREET, STAMFORD STREET, S.E., AND GREAT WINDMILL STREET, W.